CONSCIOUSNESS AND CIVILIZATION IN THE AQUARIAN AGE

Theosophy Trust Books

Consciousness and Civilization in the Aquarian Age

BY

Raghavan N. Iyer

———

Theosophy Trust Books

Norfolk, VA

Consciousness and Civilization
in the Aquarian Age

Copyright © June 19, 2021 by Theosophy Trust
Library of Congress Control Number: 2021901812
ISBN-13: 978-1-955958-00-4

Publisher's Cataloging-In-Publication Data
(Prepared by The Donohue Group, Inc.)

Names: Iyer, Raghavan, 1930-1995, author. | Blavatsky, H. P. (Helena Petrovna), 1831-1891, contributor. | Judge, William Quan, 1851-1896, contributor. | Iyer, Raghavan, 1930-1995. Gupta Vidya.
Title: Consciousness and civilization in the Aquarian Age / by Raghavan N. Iyer.
Description: Norfolk, VA : Theosophy Trust Books, [2021] | Includes index.
Identifiers: ISBN 9781733465083 (paperback, white stock) | ISBN 9781955958004 (paperback, cream stock) | ISBN 9781733465090 (ebook)
Subjects: LCSH: Theosophy. | Aquarius (Astrology) | New Age movement. | Consciousness. | Civilization. | LCGFT: Essays.
Classification: LCC BP565.I97 C66 2021 (print) | LCC BP565.I97 (ebook) | DDC 299.934--dc23

Theosophy Trust books may be ordered through Amazon.com, CreateSpace.com, and other retail outlets, or by visiting:

http://www.theosophytrust.org/online_books.php

Articles herein may be found at https://www.theosophytrust.org/

Printed in the United States of America

CONTENTS

INTRODUCTION i

ABOUT THE AUTHOR.. xv

EDITOR'S NOTE.. xxi

THE GUPTA VIDYA ESSAYS 1

  THE AQUARIAN TIDE..3

  AQUARIAN CIVILIZATION 15

  AQUARIAN HARMONY 30

  AQUARIAN THERAPY 41

  AQUARIAN SPIRITUALITY 56

  THE AQUARIAN ELIXIR 72

APPENDIX I: AQUARIAN ONTOLOGY 87

  WHO, WHERE, AND WHAT IS GOD? 89

  "WHO AM I?" "THAT THOU ART." 91

  THE DIMENSIONLESS CAUSE OF UNCONDITIONED
  REALITY 93

  THE ETERNAL BALANCE OF THE MANIFEST AND THE
  UNMANIFEST 95

  THE ZERO PRINCIPLE..97

  THE TAO IS EVERYWHERE 99

  THE FIRE OF THE ONE LIFE....................................101

  LAW OF KARMA ORDAINS A DIVINE DESTINY 103

  THE FOUR YUGAS..106

  THE KEYNOTE OF THE EPOCH 108

  THE AVATARIC IMPULSE IN THE PRESENT CYCLE 110

APPENDIX II: AQUARIAN PSYCHOLOGY 111

  THE DESCENT OF ATMAN 113

  SPIRITUAL LIFE IS IN THE MIND 115

  DEVELOPMENT OF THE REASONABLE PART OF THE SOUL .117

  COOPERATING WITH THE EVOLUTIONARY SCHEME.......119

THE FUSION OF BUDDHI AND MANAS.................................. 121

NOTHING IS UNNECESSARY 123

CONTINUITY OF CONSCIOUSNESS 126

THE RELEASE OF SOUL-MEMORY 128

LIVING SEEDS OF CREATIVE THOUGHT............................ 130

MOVING BETWEEN STATES OF CONSCIOUSNESS............. 132

COME OUT OF THE OLD AND DECAYING ORDER 135

THE TWO REQUIREMENTS....................................... 137

CHERISH THE DISCOVERY WITHIN 139

APPENDIX III: THE AQUARIAN PATH 141

THE AVATAR... 143

THE HEALING OF CORRUPTION OF CONSCIOUSNESS..... 145

THE HOUR HAS STRUCK....................................... 147

THE CHOICE 150

SPIRITUAL MOUNTAIN CLIMBING............................ 152

KRISHNA'S MEDICINAL METHOD............................ 154

THE FIRES OF PURIFICATION, PURGATION AND RESOLVE. 156

CONSTANT LEARNING 158

THE GOSPEL OF GRATITUDE................................. 160

MAKE EVERY NEW BEGINNING COUNT 162

USING OUR SKILLS AND SPIRITUAL RESOURCES............. 164

THE HERITAGE OF HUMANITY 166

A DEEPER SENSE OF BEING................................... 168

ENJOY FELLOWSHIP WITH THE ENTIRE SOLAR SYSTEM. 171

APPENDIX IV: OTHER SOURCES 173

AQUARIAN AXIOMS.. 175

THE THEORY OF CYCLES 176

THE CHRONOLOGY OF THE BRAHMINS 184

CYCLES 196

CYCLES AND CYCLIC LAW 209

GLOSSARY 217

INDEX... 225

INTRODUCTION

Readers of a certain age will recall the universal response to "The Age of Aquarius," the joyous song released by The 5th Dimension in 1969. While the words might not have impressed studious astrologers—after all, the moon is in the seventh house monthly, and Jupiter aligns with Mars periodically—the deeper sense of the song touched something profound in human beings. "This is the dawning of the age of Aquarius," was quite true then, and humanity on earth is now in the second degree of the Aquarian Age, still the dawn of a period that will last over two millennia. As the song intuited,

> Harmony and understanding
>
> Sympathy and trust abounding
>
> No more falsehoods or derisions
>
> Golden living dreams of visions
>
> Mystic crystal revelation
>
> And the mind's true liberation

are fundamental themes of this dawning age. While popular songs and fashionable media come and go, thereby testifying to their transient and illusory nature, songs, literature and the other arts often reflect the deeper evolutionary pilgrimage of humanity. The essays and texts in this volume explore the Aquarian Age and its profound meanings for humanity and its ongoing development from what has long been known in the East as the Eternal Doctrine and in the West as Theosophy, the knowledge and wisdom that underlie the Universe. This is the Gupta Vidya, the Secret Science, the truth behind all appearances, illusion and partial understanding.

Theosophy is rooted in and built upon what Helena Petrovna Blavatsky called the "three fundamental propositions." A proposition is a statement to be proven, and her vast, wonderous and revelatory treatise, *The Secret Doctrine*, sets out the proofs that can be given, the conditions necessary for understanding those proofs, and work required of individuals who would understand them. Anyone who has attempted to train in higher mathematics, quantum physics, or microbiology well knows that to master and understand the theories developed in those areas requires intense study, concentration, reflection and critical analyses. The study of the profound ancient wisdom is no different. It would be odd to think that grasping the nature of reality, humanity's role in it, and one's place in that larger picture could be achieved by reading a few simple tracts or listening to a lecture or two. One must muster all one's mental resources in the effort to understand the complex cycles of evolution of the universe and the human being. And yet, as William Quan Judge made clear, anyone can start with simple steps and then proceed as far as one chooses. In this effort, no one is tested, coerced or compelled to go farther than he or she chooses, for all relevant tests are exercises in self-examination, because the question "Who and what am I?" can only be answered by the individual. The whole of the Gupta Vidya (the Secret Science) serves as an aid to the sacred project of answering that question. The articles in this volume on Aquarian consciousness and civilization are drawn from the three-volume work of Raghavan N. Iyer entitled *The Gupta Vidya*, and they focus on selected aspects of the effort to answer the most fundamental question a human being can ask – Who am I? – and on what is supremely relevant to the individual and to humanity at this moment in human history.

The first of those three fundamental propositions noted above is that there is a boundless, inconceivable principle or source of all past, current and potential existence, the fundamental ground of all reality. That Absolute reality, sometimes referred to as Be-ness, or THAT, is beyond all thought and activity, hence beyond all categories and definitions. Being no-thing, nothing can be said of it. It is not being, nor is it non-being, neither something nor nothing, often referred to in the ancient texts as *Tat*. In Sanskrit, *Tat* is the demonstrative pronoun 'that,' and as such is a pointer with no inherent content or meaning.[1] One might say THAT is the *sine qua non* of all that is, being everywhere and nowhere. In Helena Blavatsky's monumental work, *The Secret Doctrine*, it is symbolized as absolute abstract space, THAT which cannot be conceived by itself and yet without which nothing can be conceived. It is also symbolized as absolute abstract motion, which represents unconditioned consciousness, that is, consciousness without any limit and without any object of consciousness. Motion represents change and change is essential for consciousness.

A more easily understood symbol of THAT and the process of its unfoldment is "The Great Breath," combining the idea of outbreathing, suggesting manifestation and differentiation, where even the most abstract thought and ideation has its manifest beginnings, and the idea of inbreathing, implying withdrawal into pure potential. Thus everything that unfolds, the universe, is motion in space and conscious in some degree.

The second fundamental proposition is intimated in what has been said. It is the idea that there are numberless universes that manifest in time and ultimately dissolve, though in timespans that boggle the imagination. Hence this symbolic "breathing" is cyclic in nature, which is profoundly relevant to any discussion of the Age of Aquarius.

The third fundamental proposition is that all individuals in their real natures (sometimes called their souls) are identical with a "universal soul," the One Life, traceable to that bare subjectivity of

---

[1] Demonstrative pronouns like 'this' and 'that' have no meaning but only point. A noun like 'apple' or a verb like 'to run' do have meanings. This is why we cannot hold up an orange and say it's an 'apple,' because the meaning does not apply to oranges. Nor can one sit down and say "I'm running," because the meaning of the verb 'run' is an activity that sitting does not match. Demonstratives like 'that' can apply to anything that can be pointed to, from an apple to the universe as a whole. Here, THAT (*Tat*) points to what is beyond all conception.

unconditioned consciousness. This identity implies that all human beings – immortal souls or spiritual monads – are on a pilgrimage through the evolutionary process governed by the cycles of the outbreathing and inbreathing of the Great Breath. Hence, Theosophy logically teaches both reincarnation and karma, the latter because of the ceaseless motion of rebalancing all activities in light of *rta*, cosmic harmony, the dynamic homeostasis of the evolving universe, and the former because the true nature of each individual is as eternal as existence itself and so periodically incarnates in transient bodies, evolving with the whole.

Albert Einstein, whose tremendous scientific insight developed relativity theory and contributed importantly to quantum mechanics, now both at the heart of scientific cosmology and the search for the ultimate structure of matter, forever altered our conceptions of space, matter and perception. He warned that the discoveries we make about nature depend on the questions we ask. His "thought experiments" developed theories that led to innovative experiments confirming his thinking. His insights involved radical changes in perspective and perception. To achieve these remarkable advances required thinking about and looking at nature in new ways. The ancient doctrines of Theosophy teach the same. If we are to understand ourselves, our present existence and our future, we must transform our thinking and our perceiving to be in accord with the realities of the cosmos if we are to grow spiritually and participate in the stream of evolution to be in accord with the realities of the Cosmos. The essays in this volume point to the means by which we may do just that.

As noted, the Great Breath implies a cyclic nature to all motion, and this applies to every level of existence. On the purely physical level, imagine a person standing somewhere on planet Earth. We stand still and seem to be motionless. But we know that we are rotating with the Earth at a rate that varies with the latitude, but making one full revolution in a day. At the equator, that is about 1000 miles per hour. But the Earth travels around the sun, completing one orbit in a year, moving at around 67,000 miles per hour. The sun, orbiting our Milky Way galaxy at about 515,000 miles per hour, takes a quarter of a millennium to make one complete circuit. Our galaxy is part of what is called the Local Group of galaxies, and they move in respect to one another. Further, it seems that the Local Group moves as a whole in the greater cosmos. While we seem to "stand still" on the Earth, we are hardly still. Motion is the basic fact of existence.

Coming back to Earth, there is a further motion to be discerned. The Earth tilts on its axis in respect to its orbit around the sun. This tilt is now a little over 23 degrees, so earth rotates like a spinning top, and its axis describes a circle in the heavens, taking over 25,000 years to do so. This is why Polaris is presently our north star but has not always been so, and will not be so in the future. This so-called "wobble" is called the "precession of the equinoxes", for it slowly alters the time of the equinoxes and solstices in the calendar. It is this endless change that produces what are called the "astrological ages".

Traditionally, the sun travels through the twelve signs of the zodiac annually. The earth's equinoctial precession means that the sun seems to travel backward through the zodiac over the precession cycle, appearing slightly earlier in the zodiac each spring equinox. So the sun is in a zodiacal sign for about 2160[2] years, and in 1902 it backed out of the astrological sign of Pisces (the fish) into Aquarius (the water-bearer). Hence the Age of Aquarius began in 1902.

Astrologers have various views on what this means, tying this change of the sun on the spring equinox to the meanings attributed to the zodiacal signs. Much Western astrology does not take the equinoctial precession into account, which is why the typical horoscope still places the sun at zero degrees of Aries on March 21. But the astronomers of ancient India did take the precession into

---

[2] As each sign of the zodiac is composed of 30 degrees, each astrological age is roughly equal to about 72 (years) × 30 (degrees) = or about 2160 years.

account, and the Age of Aquarius recognizes the fact of equinoctial precession.[3]

As the Three Fundamental Propositions of Theosophy imply, everything is interconnected with everything else, and so what transpires in the heavens is connected with and affects events on earth. Rather than thinking in narrow reductionist and deterministic terms, these interconnections suggest profound resonances that reflect the human evolutionary process. As an analogy, think of striking middle C on a piano and observing that the C strings in lower and higher octaves will vibrate as well. This resonance is something that provides additional richness to the sounds produced by the piano. In looking to the heavens, one finds resonances on earth, and one might expect that moving from the Age of Pisces to the Age of Aquarius suggests fundamental endings and beginnings on Earth and for human beings. The materials in this volume address those opportunities to cast off social structures and modes of thinking and acting that are outworn and a hindrance to the Humanity and societies of the future. The present age is a time of disintegration of those elements of human life that cannot continue into the future, and this disintegration is painful, especially if one is overly attached to what is dying, but it is a joyous time for growth, anticipating new directions for the future life of every individual. The 5th Dimension's song suggests as much by the sudden change of the beat with the refrain "Let the sunshine in."

The unfolding of the universe and all existence is called – in the ancient Indian sacred texts – a *manvantara*, and when it withdraws into the latent potential of THAT, it is called *pralaya*. The manvantaric

---

[3] Astrology is both theoretical and empirical, as any science is. Empirically, much that is attributed to the zodiacal signs remains relevant because astrological observation bears out meanings attributed to the signs. The theoretical dimensions can adjust to observation, and so the two mesh. But from a deeper point of view, the precession is very relevant to the development of humanity. Theosophy has much to teach astrology.

unfoldment of existence, the differentiation of the One into the Many, is a complex process quite beyond everyday understanding, but we can gain a general picture of the process and its meaning, which can be further deepened by thought, reflection and meditation. What follows is a very high-level view of the process.

The awakening of existence begins with the One. Because all that can be is already in the One in potential form, it is sometimes called the One Life, from which spirit, matter and consciousness emerge. Analogous to pure white light passing through a prism and differentiating into the seven colors of the rainbow, each with its distinctive wave length, so the One Life differentiates into seven principles that are the fundamental features of existence. These seven principles constitute all that exists, both at the cosmic and the individual levels. They can be characterized in the individual as: (1) the physical body, which being the grossest differentiation is more an effect of everything else than a cause of anything; (2) the astral body, drawn from the universal astral light (*akasha*), the plan and structure on which the physical body is built; and (3) *prana*, the universal life force pervading all forms. *Prana* literally means 'breath,' and it is a reflection of the highest and most universal principle, *Atma*. Just as our breathing is absolutely necessary to staying alive, so *prana* sustains all life in every form. (4) *Kama*, meaning 'desire' (and sometimes 'love') is the principle that drives beings in various directions, depending on how they understand themselves (as we will see). (5) *Manas*, mind, is the thinking principle that can ideate and reflect on many levels, including the level of (6) *buddhi*, spiritual knowledge, which is fundamentally universal and can only reflect what is universal, not personal. *Buddhi* is also called the "spiritual soul", the basis in the individual for the light of (7) *Atma*, which is not a principle in the sense of the others because it radiates universally and equally on everything in manifestation, from the highest beings to the lowest. In this conception, the three higher principles form an immortal Triad, *Atma-Buddhi-Manas*, the Monad and the true individuality of each person. The first four – and lower – principles constitute the personal vehicles which allow a person to live and move in the world, to experience and to learn.

Three aspects of this rich conception of manifestation and existence command attention. The first is that the One Life remains one even as it is differentiated through levels of seven-fold manifestation from the highest unity to the maximally differentiated physical realm. The second is that the same principles necessarily constitute the whole universe as well as each thing and being within it. The third aspect is that these "principles" should not be thought of as separated like layers in a layer cake or, in Helena Blavatsky's favorite metaphor, like layers in an onion. They mutually interpenetrate, and their linguistic separation is for convenience of thought and understanding, just as the light passing through a prism is differentiated from our perspective yet constitutes one white light that contains the differentiations. Even the distinction between spirit and matter is ultimately illusory, matter being crystallized spirit, so to speak, and spirit the most ethereal matter. All manifestation is material from the standpoint of THAT, but matter is of many levels of homogeneity and differentiation, of which the matter of daily experience is the grossest.

Now one can better sense the meaning of cyclic evolution. The lower principles must evolve into bodies that can provide a basis for the experience of each individual Monad, so that manasic consciousness, which is self-consciousness, can come to learn what it is and is not. *Manas* – the rational, thinking principle – casts a ray of itself into *kama* – the principle of desire – so that consciousness can engage the world, and so learn what both are. As the human mind – *manas* – turns toward its spiritual parent – *buddhi*, reflecting the light of the *Atman* – it universalizes its understanding, self-consciously becoming universally aware, that is, understanding itself as identical with the One Life. Such an awakening requires lifetimes of work, since evolution does not move by leaps and starts but step by step, forming bodies for souls and then enlightening souls, to put it simply.

This vast conception of cosmic and human evolution again implies two fundamental features of existence. The first is that all of existence is intimately interconnected; hence there is a radical spiritual unity in the One Reality, and the same is necessarily true of individual human beings. It naturally follows that compassion and love – the recognition of our identity with all other beings – are the primary energies of the heart that alone can be supported by the cosmos. The second is that all of manifestation is, to some degree alive and even conscious though we are aware of only a small swath of such life and consciousness. We can recognize that animals are conscious and may even sense that plants are, but what about minerals, atomic particles and their subatomic components? It seems almost beyond our ordinary capacity to even imagine them as being alive and conscious. Even with obviously conscious animals, we find it very difficult to get a clear sense of just what that consciousness is. The philosopher Thomas Nagel wrote a famous essay on what it is like to be a bat, showing that our attempts to imagine what a bat's consciousness is like fail. We cannot grasp using echolocation to navigate rather than using eyes, and the thinking of a bat is beyond us. The best we can do is imagine what it would be like to be a human being in a bat body, and that is not at all what a bat is. If this is true of those orders below the human stage, it is similarly true in relation to those beings beyond our typically understood human stage. Theosophy holds that there are human beings so advanced in consciousness because of their efforts in the past, that we cannot really conceive what it is like to be a Buddha, Christ, Bodhisattva or Mahatma. Yet it is these beings who compassionately aid and teach us, sometimes openly and often in ways invisible to us. This is why people sometimes feel like they were given invisible help in troubled times through a thought appearing in their minds or in the words of others. One can readily conceive of hosts of spiritual beings being involved in the process and aiding it at every level.

Man, then, is more than a human being biologically conceived. Man is a thinking, self-conscious, reflecting being that looks "below" to the more material aspects of existence and "above" to more spiritual elements. None of this has to do with gender, ethnicity, or physical form. Whatever in the universe that has this dual capacity is Man. In fact, the road to universal self-consciousness, that is, consciousness of oneself as indivisibly one with the One Life, necessarily passes through Man. The evolution required to realize all this is cyclic. Both worlds in which human beings can dwell, and the sevenfold constitution of human beings, pass through rounds and races (not as the term is used today, but as stages in evolving Humanity). There is for each round and race a circle consisting of a descending arc of involution, in which the Monads become involved in increasingly differentiated matter, followed by a corresponding ascending arc of evolution in which they return to their more ethereal state, but now with the consciousness of that process. In the course of the *manvantara*, the process occurs seven times around the circle for each world and, within each round, seven times for each race. Theosophy teaches that present Humanity is the fifth sub-race of the fifth root race in the fourth round. Thus the Earth in its evolution is as material as it can be and is already beginning its arc toward pure spirituality. In a slightly amusing way, Darwin was right to speak of the descent of Man, and now the ascent is beginning. The Age of Aquarius anticipates and is a preliminary initiation in this ascent.

The cyclic nature of evolution, involving the descent of spirit into matter for the sake of gaining self-consciousness, and the refinement of matter into vestures that can accommodate the spiritual being called Man, is vast and complex, involving numerous overlapping and simultaneous cycles of vastly different lengths. The whole of what is called a *mahamanvantara* is over 311,000,000,000,000 years, and includes numerous *manvantaras* and *pralayas* within it, as an article by Helena Blavatsky explains in the "Other Sources" Appendix. On the human plane, we see that there is a cycle of ages, often called golden, silver, bronze and iron ages, and as we begin a new ascent, we are just over 5,000 years into the iron age (or *kali yuga*), which lasts 432,000 years. This is a dark time (*kali yuga* literally means "black age") because it is a time of great differentiation, comparison and contrast, hence competition and dissension, but it is also a time of great opportunity.

While the world passes through these cyclic ages, it also passes through the astrological ages, of which the Aquarian Age is now most relevant. And while all embodied individuals currently live in the iron age, individual consciousness does not have to do so. Buddhas and Mahatmas are here among us in this age, but in consciousness are in a universal golden age. Hence they are not caught up in the limitations of this time but can dispassionately and compassionately help those who are – ourselves. And we can rise in consciousness and taste more golden, universal strains of consciousness through our identification with what we really are, which is one with the One Life. We do this by ceasing to identify with the ever-changing physical body, then with our highly limited and often conflicted and fearful personality, then with deeper tendencies and dispositions of the past, including judging others, and with weaknesses such as wanting praise and trying to avoid blame. That is, we can grow in our capacity to think at a higher level, one that includes all other beings, and act from that basis, which means acting with compassion for all, recognizing that we are all pilgrim souls. If consciousness identifies with the physical form, it will use the physical senses to encounter a physical world. But this world of effects is the least real of all planes right up to the One Life. If in thought and meditation, one's consciousness can be raised up to the universal thinking of *manas*, the real Man, the mental organs of perception will encounter that world and grasp it as real. The old phrase, "as a man thinketh, so he is" is profoundly true.

All of this means that one can live in the golden age in consciousness even while participating in the world's iron age. The Aquarian Age is, therefore, deeply relevant here. As the ascending arc of the fourth round progresses, fifth sub-race Humanity is moving toward the distant sixth sub-race in anticipation of the even more distant sixth race. Theosophy teaches that the humans of the sixth race will be more spiritual than we can readily imagine at present and form a harmonious humanity quite beyond ordinary conceptions. But just as one can, in consciousness, enter and participate in the golden age now, so we can anticipate in consciousness the sixth race, which, of course, is our present fifth-race Humanity in the far future. But only those who can think, act and live as sixth race individuals will be part of that race. This means that in the far future every human being will face a fundamental choice: Is one living for oneself or for all others? Those who live for others will pass into that glorious future, into the currently almost inconceivable sixth round and beyond. Those who cannot will fall behind the vast numbers of those who have kept pace with the demands of the evolutionary cycles. They will have to wait for future *manvantaras* to make further efforts at spiritual growth, or, if truly selfish in the personal sense, to spiral down into self-destruction. The Aquarian Age is an anticipation of that distant and unavoidable choice. What we do now will affect our choice in that future, just as how we live and think affects the moment of death. The Aquarian Age offers the opportunity to transform ourselves into the beings of the future, where service is a joy, sacrifice a privilege, and personal wants and wishes are rightly prioritized as of far less importance than one's spiritual obligations to the whole of Humanity.

Professor Raghavan Iyer's valuable essays and excerpts and other Theosophical sources provided in this volume lay out the opportunities and challenges of the Aquarian Age for us. Each essay begins with the broadest possible view of human life seen as a sacrificial pilgrimage, sets out the nature and dynamics of various dimensions of this time in human history, and provides practical steps for spiritual and moral self-regeneration and transformation. Anyone can make good use of this deeply spiritual and practical advice. Here is a handbook for our individual destiny, what it is and how to prepare for it by using the opportunities the Aquarian Age offers.

In summary, the full sweep of the challenges and possibilities of this time in human evolution is captured in these words by Raghavan Iyer:[4]

> This is the timeless teaching of divine wisdom, and it has always had urgency for the individual, as in the days of Jesus, when he asked, "Whom choose ye this day?" A critical, ultimate, irreversible choice is involved. Now, when the opportunities are great for the whole of the human race, something has begun which will become in time a mighty stream that will nourish the earth. It will reflect the hidden fire of the Mysteries, known to those who have travelled far on the secret Path that leads to the invisible summits of enlightenment. At the first portal of the Path, there is the fateful inscription: "Abandon hope all who enter here." Abandon hope for the petty personality, abandon hope for ambition, pride and selfish desire. Abandon hope, above all, for one's own salvation if one would enter the Path, which leads to a galaxy of Gurus, mighty men of meditation and lovers of all humanity who are wholly dedicated to the sacred goal of universal enlightenment. They have said: "If you wish to know us, study our philosophy. If you wish to serve us, serve our humanity. If you take one step in our direction, we will take one step in yours."

Prof. Elton Hall
Ithaca, NY January 2021

---

[4] "The Joy of Devotion," *The Gupta Vidya*, II, p. 172.

About the Author

Shri Raghavan N. lyer was a man of immense magnanimity and deep spiritual and intellectual genius. Born in Madras, India in 1930, he matriculated at the University of Bombay at the precocious age of fourteen and received his bachelor's degree in economics at age eighteen. Two years later he received the Chancellor's Gold Medal, earned his master's degree in Advanced Economics, and was selected as the Rhodes Scholar from India to Oxford University. At Oxford, he excelled in his academic studies and avidly participated in Oxford's rich social, political, and cultural life. During his undergraduate years, he eagerly joined a number of Oxford University clubs and societies. He was apparently so well liked and respected that, in time, he was elected president of several prominent student organizations: the Oxford Social Studies Association, the Voltaire Society, and the Plotinus Society (which he also founded). His broader social sympathies and para-political concerns were served by joining and eventually becoming president of the Oxford University Peace Association and the Oxford Majlis Society (a debating society of Oxford students from South Asia that took up political issues). In 1954, he became president of the prestigious Oxford Union – perhaps the premiere debating society of his time. (Debates were usually spontaneous, witty, and packed full of appropriate references to recognizable historical figures in literature, politics, and society.) At year's end, he earned first-class honors in Philosophy, Politics, and Economics and later was awarded his master and doctorate degrees in Political Theory.

Shri Raghavan was an outstanding teacher of philosophy and politics throughout his public life. He assumed the mantle of teaching at the age of eighteen when he was appointed Fellow and Lecturer in Economics at Elphinstone College, University of Bombay. In 1956, he was appointed an Oxford don, giving tutorials in moral and political philosophy. In addition to teaching at Oxford, he lectured throughout Europe, America, and Africa, e.g., the

University of Oslo in Norway (1958), the College of Europe in Belgium (1962), Erasmus Seminar in the Netherlands (1962), the University of Chicago in America (1963), and the University of Ghana in Legon (1964). His profound insights, sparkling intellectual clarity, mastery of different conceptual languages, and his infectious enthusiasm inspired thousands of students on different continents and earned him the deep respect of his contemporaries.

After accepting a professorship at the University of California (Santa Barbara) in 1965, he taught classes and seminars in political philosophy until his retirement at the age of fifty-six. His introductory classes and graduate seminars were legendary for their philosophical depth, theoretical openness, and visionary richness. His class topics were innovative and they attracted the curious, the committed, the idealist, the political realist, and the culturally disenfranchised. The most inspiring (and exacting) undergraduate courses were always enrolled to the maximum and lectures frequently ended with spontaneous, standing ovations from the students. Those classes included: "Parapolitics and the City of Man", "Anarchist Thought", "Plato and the Polis", "The Dialectic from Plato to Marx", "Politics and Literature", "American Radicalism", and "The American Dream and the City of Man". His lectures were full of wit as well as wisdom, and they unfailingly inspired students to cultivate an abiding confidence in themselves as learners and to become viable contributors to the emerging City of Man. His formal lectures and innumerable informal gatherings affected generations of students who later contributed to diverse fields of work, worship, and humanitarian service.

In addition to his vast and varied gifts as a teacher, Shri Raghavan Iyer was a devoted consultant and lecturer to various world organizations committed to some form of universal human betterment. While an Oxford don, he became a member of the Executive Committee for the World Association of World Federalists (The Hague) and likewise became a consultant and lecturer for the Friends International Centre (Kranj, Yugoslavia). In a similar spirit of rendering service, he became a consultant to OXFAM and accepted the temporary post of Director of Studies, UNESCO Conference on "Mutual Understanding Between the Orient and the Occident". He was also a member of The Club of Rome, The Reform Club, and The World Futures Studies Federation. In later years he became a contributing member of the Task Force appointed by U.S. President Jimmy Carter to develop "The Global 2000 Report for the President" – a call for Promethean initiatives to meet the most compelling needs of an emerging global civilization.

Over the arc of his extraordinary life, Shri Raghavan wrote numerous articles in diverse fields of thought as well as authored and edited many works that point toward an emerging global consciousness – replete with multiple challenges and stirring prospects. In 1965, he edited *The Glass Curtain between Asia and Europe*. This compilation of essays by internationally reputed historians contained a fascinating dialogue between Shri Raghavan and the world's most eminent historian at the time, Arnold Toynbee. They mutually explored Shri Raghavan's thesis that there exists an obscuring "glass curtain" between Asia and Europe that needs to be recognized and dealt with before there can be true intellectual and cultural understanding between East and West.

His most well-known and prominent books are *The Moral and Political Thought of Mahatma Gandhi* (1973) and *Parapolitics — Toward the City of Man* (1977). Each of these remarkable pioneering works is accessible to both the profound thinker and the serious inquirer, the erudite scholar and the dedicated student, the earnest seeker and the committed practitioner. Later, in 1983, he edited an extraordinary collection of spiritually inspiring readings entitled *The Jewel in the Lotus* – aptly characterized by Professor K. Swaminathan, a noted compiler of Gandhi's collected writings, as "a Universal Bible." In addition, Shri Raghavan edited and wrote luminous introductions for numerous sacred texts, including Hindu, Buddhist, Jain, Jewish, Christian, and Sufi teachings.

The deeper replenishing current of Shri Raghavan's life, however, flowed from the empyrean springs of *Theosophia*. He became a

Theosophist at age ten when his father first took him to the United Lodge of Theosophists in Bombay. In time, he was introduced to the profound writings of H.P. Blavatsky and W.Q. Judge. Not long after entering the orbit of the Theosophical Movement, he made a sacred resolve to serve the Lodge of Mahatmas and increasingly assumed responsibility for forwarding the impulse of the worldwide Theosophical Cause of promoting universal brotherhood. For the rest of his life, all his efforts in the academic, social, political, and religious arenas were infused by his wholehearted devotion to the service of the Brotherhood of Bodhisattvas and to the enlightenment of the human race. This profound, ever-present golden thread of meaning that wove together all his worldly activities became more apparent when he emigrated to America.

In 1965, Shri Raghavan moved with his wife and son to Santa Barbara, California. (His wife, Nandini, a brilliant Oxford don who received a First in Philosophy, Politics, and Economics at Oxford, went on to teach in both the Philosophy and Religious Studies departments at the University of California, Santa Barbara until her retirement. Pico, their only child, was born in Oxford in 1957. He later graduated from Oxford University and became a contributing writer to Time magazine and is now a noted author of international standing.) Once settled in California, Shri Raghavan and Nandini founded the United Lodge of Theosophists, Santa Barbara. Beginning informally in October of 1966, the Lodge grew from fourteen initial students to over a hundred active associates. Soon after its inaugural meeting on February 18, 1969 (the death anniversary of Shri Krishna), Lodge members were invited to give talks and, in time, to co-lead Theosophy School classes for the young. In addition to evolving various modalities of giving and receiving Theosophical instruction, Shri Raghavan and Nandini founded several ancillary institutions that further served the global aims of the worldwide Theosophical Movement.

One such ancillary institution is the Institute of World Culture in Santa Barbara. On July 4, 1976 – the bicentennial of the American Declaration of Independence – Shri Raghavan and Nandini coinitiated this educational non-profit organization. Its "Declaration of Interdependence" elucidates ten aims that are the visionary basis of all its intellectually and culturally enlightening programs and activities. The Institute of World Culture regularly hosts engaging seminars, forums, lectures, study circles, and film series. There is a wholesome blending of spiritual, intellectual, ethical, and cultural themes for focused thought and extensive discussion. The Institute has proved to be a culturally "consciousness expanding" experience for many and has, in its own way, contributed to a deeper appreciation of the often unsuspected power of classical and renaissance cultures to provide illuminating perspectives on a host of contemporary national and global issues.

As a forward-looking extension of his sacred obligation to serve the Theosophical Movement, Shri Raghavan founded, edited, and wrote for the golden journal *Hermes* (1975–1989). This wide-ranging spiritual journal was dedicated to the pristine sounding of Brahma Vach and to the spiritual regeneration of humanity. The profound articles found in *Hermes* span the spectrum of human thought from the metaphysical to the mystical, the ethical to the psychological, the spiritual to the material, the mythical to the historical. They convincingly reveal the subtle Theosophical foundations of all religions, philosophies, and sciences. They ingeniously address the chronic problems of the age and provide much needed "correctives to consciousness" in an age that tilts away from soul-saving and revitalizing ideals.

As repeatedly witnessed by close students, Shri Raghavan spoke at many different levels and freely interacted with each and all – regardless of race, creed, or condition. He exemplified – for the sake of the future – a multitude of Aquarian modalities and qualities. He was, in one sense, very Hindu: a true Brahmin – spiritual, cultured, brilliant, full of the graces that immediately remind one of ancient India and of golden ages long past. He was also very English: confident, highly educated, extremely literate, and at ease with statesmen, scientists, educators, and royalty. He was also very American: a true and fearless rebel, innovative, resourceful, visionary, and the eternal friend of the common man. But, beyond all this, he was in a much deeper sense the Universal Man, original, *sui generis* and timeless. His sympathies were always compassionately inclusive and his repeated emphasis – from first to last – was to "draw the larger circle" through universality of thought, the richness of imagination, the therapeutics of speech, and the magic of selfless action.

The wide-ranging arcane teachings in all three of the volumes of *The Gupta Vidya* were transcriptions of talks given between 1949 to 1989 in India, England, and the United States and were carefully edited by Shri Raghavan shortly before his death. When meditated upon and skillfully applied to the realm of self-chosen duties, they purify the mind, cleanse the heart, and give birth to men and women committed to creatively contributing to the universal civilization of tomorrow.

Editor's Note

All of the essays in the first chapter, The Gupta Vidya Essays, and the quotations in the first three appendices, were first published in Prof. Iyer's magnificent three-volume set entitled *The Gupta Vidya*, also published by Theosophy Trust Books. The six essays in this first chapter form the groundwork for Prof. Iyer's teachings on the Aquarian Age, and the three following appendices contain extensive quotations found elsewhere in the three volumes of *The Gupta Vidya* - "supporting documents" - that amplify and extend the ideas in that first chapter. To our knowledge, the quotations in Appendices I-II-III are exhaustive; i.e., all of the mentions of the Aquarian Age in other places of the three volumes have been included.

As the Introduction and the biographical essay make clear, Humanity has now entered upon a new era - The Aquarian Age – and with it come new requirements for staying abreast of the burgeoning forward impulse of that new cycle. This new cycle, lasting some 2,000+ years, has already begun to present challenges to Humanity that are quite different from those of the preceding Age. The essays in this work - replete with inspirational visions of the future, frank warnings about the pitfalls ahead, constant affirmations of the immortality of the human soul, and a supreme confidence in the ability of Humanity to face and overcome the karma of the past - are intended to help us recognize those challenges as they appear and to take steps to meet them with creativity, compassion and a commitment to maintaining solidarity with all of Humanity.

Theosophy Trust is deeply grateful to Prof. Elton A. Hall for his illuminating Introduction, and to Dr. James E. Tepfer for his wonderful biographical essay on the author of these writings.

All of the articles and readings in this work can be found in digital format on the Theosophy Trust website at:
https://www.theosophytrust.org/RNI-article.

Editor, Theosophy Trust

THE GUPTA VIDYA ESSAYS

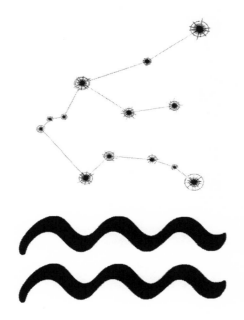

THE AQUARIAN TIDE

Let us prepare, and let us study Truth in all its aspects, trying not to ignore any of them, if we do not wish, when the hour will have struck, to fall into the abyss of the unknown. It is useless to rely on chance, and to await the approaching intellectual and psychic crisis with indifference if not with total incredulity, saying to oneself that if worse comes to worst, the tide will carry us quite naturally to the shore; for there is a strong likelihood of the tide stranding but a corpse! The battle will be fierce, in any case, between brutal materialism and blind fanaticism on the one hand, and on the other philosophy and mysticism – that more or less thick veil of the Eternal Truth.

It is not materialism that will have the upper hand.

H.P. BLAVATSKY
La Revue Theosophique, March 1889

AccORDING to the ancient maxim of Protagoras, "Man is the measure of all things; of things that are, that they are; of things that are not, that they are not." However interpreted, this evidently implies that every individual and collective crisis is a crisis of self-concept, self-reference and identity. It further implies that every response to a crisis is shaped and prefigured by factors within human nature. At root, one's ontological estimate of humanity and one's cosmological calculation of the position of man relative to Nature will determine one's capacity to respond creatively in any situation. It should be common sense that the expression of wisdom in human life cannot exceed the sum-total allotted to man by Nature. Nonetheless, the measure of human wisdom postulated by any human being or culture may be seriously defective or needlessly self-constrained. As practical self-knowledge inevitably involves self-reference, the human being who gives short measure to humanity will not be able to draw upon the full potential of human nature. The individual who seeks to integrate the Logoic principle of cosmos with the essential being of man in Nature can remain inwardly open to the whole measure of wisdom attainable by man. It is a paradox of human self-consciousness that Nature will always negate vanity, though it cannot negate despair without human assistance.

This asymmetry in human consciousness, with its awesome implications for pessimism and optimism, arises out of the basic distinction between the evolutionary and involutionary arcs of manifestation. The upward progress of humanity along the evolutionary arc ascending towards self-conscious realization of Spirit depends decisively upon human initiative. It is part of the tragedy of the modern age that, offered the Promethean fire of wisdom, it has chosen instead to bind itself into servitude to Zeus with the gilded chains of kamamanasic desire. Offered the call of the Christos, capable of resurrecting Lazarus from the dead, the western world adopted instead the self-mutilating worship of the cross of matter. Like Procrustes caught in his own clumsy contrivance, for nearly two millennia the West has suffered spiritual deprivation through its self-imposed idolatry of psychic materialism. Since the fourteenth century, the Great Lodge of Mahatmas has sustained a cyclic effort to ameliorate this anguished condition. The culmination of this effort, adjusting the entire range of human principles, was planned to coincide with the Avataric impulse accompanying the Aquarian Age and profoundly affecting the future races of humanity.

Thirteen years before the beginning of the Aquarian Age, in an essay entitled "The New Cycle", addressed in French to a European audience, H.P. Blavatsky powerfully spelt out the choices open to the West. By the latter decades of the nineteenth century, certain divisions of society and thought had already become acute. Millions were caught up either in the spiritual materialism of orthodox religion, or the soulless materialism of mechanistic science. Throughout the seventies and eighties of the Victorian era, a tremendous debate had blown up around human evolution, with science and religion drawing up lines on opposite sides. Going beyond the closed terms of this dilettantish debate, H.P. Blavatsky drew attention to what had already been noticed by a variety of writers, especially in Russia; namely, what she called the death-struggle between brutal materialism and blind fanaticism on the one side, and philosophy and mysticism on the other. This fierce battle, she affirmed, would be the crucial issue of the twentieth century, and, she prophesied:

> Everyone fanatically clinging to an idea isolating him from the universal axiom – 'There is no Religion higher than Truth' – will find himself separated like a rotten plank from the new ark called Humanity. Tossed by the waves, chased by the winds, buffeted by this element so terrible because unknown, he will soon find himself swallowed up.
>
> *Ibid.*

H.P. Blavatsky was actually sounding a grave and compassionate warning that those souls unable to enter the current of the future would be discarded by Nature. In the 1890's, and increasingly throughout the twentieth century, the growing perception of this fateful choice has instilled a tremendous fear in a despairing element within the human race. Instead of discovering brave and powerful responses to the challenge of the future, that minuscule percentage of the human race which is terrified, for karmic reasons, that it has no future, has developed literature and thought, a full-blown psychology of doom. Through the power of the printed word, and later the electronic media, and with the aid of pathological art and pessimistic fiction, this vociferous minority managed to transfer its psychological ailments to vast numbers of human beings. Entire societies have become caught up in this pathology – in Vienna before the First World War, and even more acutely after the war; in France before the Second World War, and especially during the war and after; and in pre-Nazi Germany. The pathology converged in England during the late 1930's in a literature of bitter disenchantment. It appeared in Russia, particularly during the early days of the Stalinist era, in pessimistic poems and novels, to be somewhat eclipsed by a more heroic stance in the later 1940's and 1950's. It has reappeared in England in recent decades, and it has been a constant problem in post-war America. Like the deadly emanations of the *upas* tree, it spreads its contagion wherever hapless individuals are neither self-inoculated through spiritual resolve nor actually immune through the protection of vital ethical traditions.

Through many forms of scholarship and literature, and a system of semi-institutionalized opinions and manipulated media, a modern system of negative thought-control fosters and diffuses a sense of hopelessness and helplessness. This entire phenomenon in fact represents the death-throes of those elaborate structures of psychology and philosophy rooted in the ideas of ontological scarcity and bourgeois materialism. The present manifestation is a long shadow cast by the seventeenth century where the power of the Catholic Church, particularly on the Continent, cramped those philosophers who sought to celebrate the human spirit. In trying to comprehend human nature, thinkers of the seventeenth century were unable to remove themselves from an obsession with original sin. As this notion became secularized and disguised through sociology and psychology, it came to pervade the intellectual life of the nineteenth century. And as an unsolicited and unsuspected term of debate, it crept into the twentieth century in every field of thought affected by theories of behavioural conditioning. In every case, it shrinks the conception of Nature and of human nature. But, ultimately, all such stultifying and self-crippling conceptions of man are doomed. Parasitic and vampiric, their borrowed and vicarious life may continue for a while, but they will become increasingly irrelevant to the human condition.

Already, millions are tired of nihilists and misanthropes and are stimulated instead by the positive urges of their own sporadic intuitions of the Divine. This is especially true in America, where mass belief is rarely registered by the media, which bases its claims upon limited surveys and the pronouncements of self-appointed experts who speak gibberish while presuming to represent the American spirit. Indeed, throughout the world, human beings refuse to be trapped within negativism. H.P. Blavatsky spoke of the time "when the flame of modern materialism, artificial and cold, will be extinguished for lack of fuel." The evidence of this can be seen in the decaying heart of the cities which were once the centres of civilization. In Paris and London, New York and Los Angeles, materialistic entrepreneurs and purveyors of the doctrine of inescapable selfishness are finding it difficult to find living human fuel to sustain the structures of human confinement. Their children simply will not go along. They would rather do almost anything else. Like Ahab bound to the sounding whale, the materialist is fast becoming lonely and hopeless, though at times angry and desperate.

It is not easy for the human soul to shake off the yoke of materialism, for even with a strong conviction in the immortal soul, one may unknowingly retain mental habits that are materialistic. Any concern for spiritual progress for oneself must, therefore, be rooted out and dispelled as a pernicious form of a spiritual materialism. Any tendency to identify with the physical body, or act for the sake of oneself as a separative entity in order to gain spiritual gifts and advantages, is incompatible with conscious life in spirit, as opposed to matter. To conceive truly of the *Atman* and *Atma-Buddhi,* the light of the Universal Spirit and the Divine Self, one must shun all separative thinking. It is to this contrast of the living and the dead within human nature that H.P. Blavatsky referred when she wrote:

> The Spirit of Truth is at this moment moving upon the face of these black waters, and, separating them, forces them to yield their spiritual treasures. This spirit is a force that cannot be either checked or stopped. Those who recognize it and feel that this is the supreme moment of their salvation, will be carried by it beyond the illusions of the great astral serpent.

> *Ibid.*

Those who are vitalized by the vigorous current of spiritual energy can enjoy states of consciousness and peak experiences that transcend the personality. Freed from the thraldom and tension of self-concern, they will become happy that other human beings exist, thrilled that there are babies on earth, and convinced that where there is a larger view, there is always hope.

Owing to the relentless pressure of the age, it is more and more necessary to abjure separative thinking and join the larger perspective of the majority of mankind. The intensity of the struggle happily compels individuals to choose. Those who pretend to remain indifferent to the prospects of the future only doom themselves to the "arid wastes of matter . . . to vegetate there through a long series of lives, content henceforth with feverish hallucinations instead of spiritual perceptions, with passions instead of love, with the rind instead of the fruit." Unless they scorn selfish assumptions, they will come to resemble the squirrel on its ceaselessly revolving wheel, whirling round and round chewing the nut of nihilism. But once spiritual starvation and material satiety move them to forget self, they will recognize the necessity of an intellectual and moral reform. The privilege of beginning this fundamental reform within oneself, and working for its fulfilment on behalf of other human beings, is extended by the Brotherhood of Bodhisattvas to every true friend of the human race.

> This reform cannot be accomplished except through Theosophy and, let us say it, Occultism, or the wisdom of the East. Many are the paths leading to it, but Wisdom is forever one. Artists foresee it, those who suffer dream of it, the pure in spirit know it. Those who work for others cannot remain blind before its reality even though they do not always know it by name. It is only the light-headed and empty-minded, the selfish and vain drones deafened by the sound of their own buzzing, who can ignore this high ideal.

Ibid.

Whilst many have dreamt of ideal wisdom, some actually know it. They know it in their bones and in their blood; they have tested and tasted it; they have found that it works, and made it the basis of their thought and their lives. In the best cases, they have made it the basis of their unlimited devotion to the interests of others, and in the unselfishness of their service they have become invulnerable and indifferent towards the world and its evanescent opinions.

This is a very high state indeed. But in contemplating it, one should not fall prey to self-recrimination and recurring doubt. To do so would only reaffirm the contagious materialism that one wishes to leave behind. It does not matter at what level a human being approaches Divine Wisdom. Even if one can embody only one percent of the ideal, one must hold fast to the conviction that what is real in oneself and can be realized in practice is the only element that truly counts. This alone must be taken as the focus of one's concentration. Whilst it is always possible at any given time to say that one can only do so much, and no more, it is also always possible to enjoy and contemplate the ideal in meditation. The ideal can, and must, be separated from the limitations of incarnated existence. Thus, two different types of development emerge. First of all, one is intensifying through devotion to the ideal the architectonics of one's thought with regard to the ideal. This will be elaborated in *devachan* after death in the celestial condition of dreams of goodwill and creativity which can cut grooves in the *karana sharira,* the causal body, and affect lives to come. At the same time, one may recognize in other aspects of the vestures, particularly in the *linga sharira* or astral form, that one is unfortunately enslaved by many habits.

Under the karmic curve of the present life, one cannot enormously increase one's power of concentration however much one tries, because one lacks the strength to resist negative forces. Therefore, whilst maximizing development within the present lifetime, individuals must also recognize how little they can do and consequently how modest and honest they must be in the day to day walk of life. By understanding this dual process affecting both the present life and future lives, one can awaken a balanced courage and a spirit of unconditionality in one's commitment to an ideal.

> To take the first step on this ideal path requires a perfectly pure motive; no frivolous thought must be allowed to divert our eyes from the goal; no hesitation, no

doubt must fetter our feet. Yet, there are men and women
perfectly capable of all this, and whose only desire is to live
under the aegis of their Divine Nature. Let these, at least,
have the courage to live this life and not to hide it from the
sight of others! No one's opinion could ever be above the
rulings of our own conscience, so, let that conscience,
arrived at its highest development, be our guide in all our
common daily tasks. As to our inner life, let us concentrate
all our attention on our chosen Ideal, and let us ever look
beyond without ever casting a glance at the mud at our feet.

Ibid.

It may be natural enough and even nutritionally sound for
children to eat a little dirt, but it is unnatural and unhealthy for adults
to savour the mentally negative or psychically muddy. They must
rather train themselves always to look beyond, towards the stars and
towards the future. By gazing towards the radiant though distant
summit of enlightenment, they can keep their heads above the waters
of chaos. By learning to float, by learning to tread water, they can
begin to swim, and even to deal with the shifting tides of the psychic
nature. Under karma, these forces work differently for different
people. Some can concentrate on that which is universal and
impersonal for long periods of time; others find that they cannot do
so for more than a few minutes at a time. Again, the length of
meaningful meditation is less important than the authenticity of the
attempt. The more one can calmly accept the limits of one's abilities,
the more those limits will expand. Here as everywhere the greater
one's application the greater one's results. And like many physical
habits, these mental exercises must be established at an early age.
What is easy for the young is not so easy for the old. If one acquires
healthy mental habits whilst young one should be grateful for the
auspicious karma. If one does not recognize the need for a mental
reform until later in life, again, one should be grateful for the
recognition itself, as for the counsel required to carry out the reform.
One must desire reform, and having embarked upon it, persevere
with courage. One must become a true friend of oneself and strive

without guilt, enjoying progress, without falling into the anxious traps that began with 'original sin'. Like Job, one must learn that one's burden is neither greater nor less than one can bear, and thus become receptive to every form of good.

As Pythagoras taught, spiritual courage arises out of the conviction that the race of men is immortal. From the soil of its lunar beginnings to its ultimate dwelling-place beyond the stars, humanity follows the cyclic path of transformation wherein each element of human nature is transmuted into a self-conscious aspect of Divine Wisdom. The acquisition and unfoldment of knowledge of these elements in man and in Nature is an essential component of the collective spiritual progress of the race. The vivifying ideal of wisdom itself is inconceivable apart from the practical acquisition of knowledge, and the perfection of human nature is thus impossible where the mind-principle is either degraded or defamed. It is the peculiar demerit of materialism enforced through the dogma of original sin that it attempts to accomplish both these negative ends at once. Thus in the last century, H.P. Blavatsky had to oppose materialism in both religion and science. Owing to concretized conceptions of progress connected with a unilinear view of history and a shortsighted enthusiasm about technological change, it was very difficult in the latter part of the nineteenth century to challenge a prevailing blind faith in science. Nonetheless, H.P. Blavatsky prophetically anticipated the demise of this faith, which would take place in Europe because of the First World War. She also anticipated and stimulated a series of revolutionary scientific changes in the early decades of the Aquarian Age. Since then, even at a popular level, people have begun to assimilate something of quantum theory and theories of light, much that was implicit in the work of Einstein, Eddington and the early biologists. They have come to see that most of the nineteenth century categories of science are obsolete and irrelevant. This perception was already common in Europe in the 1920's and 1930's, but was considerably slower in coming to America, which is perhaps the last colonial country left on earth and usually moves about thirty years behind Europe in acknowledging significant shifts in thought.

After the Second World War, America tended to nurture an adolescent glorification of technology, but even this was challenged in the 1960's, and most thinking individuals discovered that they could not return to their earlier blind faith in technology. Unfortunately, this has produced an actual obstacle to understanding how the fruits of contemporary science and technology, for example micro-electronics, can be used to extend the effectiveness of human potential. Attitudes in America, unlike those in Sweden or Japan, are often polarized by mass society. Science and technology are met with a sluggish indifference or an incapacity to understand how they may be put to constructive use. Through the powerful blandishments of economics, however, there has recently been an enormous increase in the numbers of people seeking training in the use of computers, so much so that the facilities of educational institutions have been sorely taxed.

What is important and unusual in these developments is that people have set aside their former blind faith and begun to learn whatever skills are needed to put science and technology to use. Instead of reinforcing and reinvigorating outmoded conceptions of science, many have now learnt how to use the media to acquire information about cosmology and astronomy, about the earth and the oceans, about the body and the brain. Suddenly Americans, like Russians over the past thirty or forty years, have become more aware of the spiritual implications of science. They have begun to understand that the best science forces a rethinking of one's view of human nature, human potential, and the place of man in the cosmos. Once the spirituality of advanced science is recognized, there can be no return to a merely materialistic interest in technology. Men and women are now concerned with the creative noetic uses of scientific knowledge, and also with the raising of scientific questions that go to the heart of human existence. The largest questions in science always prompt honest disagreement and ultimately a ready recognition of ignorance.

Today, as was not true of the nineteenth century, enough is known in every field of science to recognize that what is known is a minute fragment of what is possible to know; leading scientists distinguish themselves in their fields only by admitting that they know next to nothing about fundamentals. Physiologists cannot penetrate all the miracles of the human brain. The finest physicists admit that almost nothing is known about the ultimate nature of matter. The best astronomers readily allow that they know little of the depths of outer space. The foremost biologists remain modestly silent before the mysteries of embryology. All of this is consonant with the vital keynote of the Aquarian Age, and extremely hopeful for the future of humanity. It is to this keynote that H.P. Blavatsky made reference when she declared:

> . . . you Occultists, Kabalists, and Theosophists, you know well that a word as old as the world, though new to you, has been sounded at the beginning of this cycle . . .you know that a note, never before heard by the men of the present era, has just been sounded, and that a new kind of thought has arisen, fostered by the evolutionary forces. This thought differs from all that has ever been produced in the 19th Century; yet it is identical with what was the keynote and the keystone of every century, especially the last one: 'Absolute Freedom of Human Thought.'
>
> *Ibid.*

As more and more people become aware of what the best minds of every age have always known – that they have hardly touched the threshold of the unknown – they will, paradoxically, be thrown back upon themselves. The willingness of people to become self-dependent is an important sign of the inception of the Aquarian Age. It is becoming progressively more difficult to convince people through statistical polls that what several million people think is necessarily true. Many individuals now prefer to think for themselves. As the antiquated machinery of thought-control breaks down, individuals are now discovering within themselves a willingness to exercise their own faculties. As they discover the challenge of true self-reliance, they become less blindly acquiescent to narrow scientific or religious dogmatism. With every increment of mental, moral and spiritual freedom gained, grand vistas of human possibility are opened before them. Even though the average human being uses much less than ten percent of the brain's potential, and even less of the heart's, the tide has begun to turn. Even though many still live like spiritual paupers, well below their potential means, they have begun to recognize their possibilities and the need for initiative in improving the human condition. Relinquishing the mummeries of the past, they have begun to understand that only through developing the natural powers of concentration and spiritual attention can they enrich their collective future. Through the joy and the beauty, the dignity and the self-respect, that come from self-discipline, they can alchemically quicken their creative faculties and thereby tap the potential energies of the higher mind and heart. Thus, following the small old path depicted in every religious tradition and intimated in every authentic myth, each good and true human soul may discern the spiritual possibilities of the Aquarian Age and stay abreast of the vanguard of humanity.

AQUARIAN CIVILIZATION

*Our races . . . have sprung from divine races, by whatever
name they are called . . . . Every nation has either the seven and
ten Rishis-Manus and Prajaptis . . . . One and all have been
derived from the primitive Dhyan-Chohans of the Esoteric
doctrine, or the 'Builders' of the Stanzas. From Manu, Thot-
Hermes, Oannes-Dagon, and Edris-Enoch, down to Plato and
Panadores, all tell us of seven divine Dynasties, of seven
Lemurian, and seven Atlantean divisions of the Earth; of the
seven primitive and dual gods who descend from their celestial
abode and reign on Earth, teaching mankind Astronomy,
Architecture, and all the other sciences that have come down to
us. These Beings appear first as 'gods' and Creators; then they
merge in nascent man, to finally emerge as 'divine-Kings and
Rulers' . . . . There were five Hermes – or rather one, who
appeared – as some Manus and Rishis did – in several different
characters . . . . But under whichever of these characters, he is
always credited with having transferred all the sciences from
latent to active potency, i.e., with having been the first to teach
magic to Egypt and to Greece, before the days of Magna Graecia,
and when the Greeks were not even Hellenes.*

The Secret Doctrine, ii 365-367

To take the entire subject of cosmic hierarchies at the human
level to its sublime heights, one must start with the
momentous recognition that many of the 'gods' of the ancient
theogonies belonged to the First Race of humanity. Human beings in
that First Race were gods or *devas*, and in the Second Race they were
demi-gods – celestial spirits still too ethereal to occupy the human
form that was being gestated by the lunar Pitris. Then, in the Third
Race, with the lighting-up of *Manas* and the incarnation of the
Manasaputras into human form, humanity underwent an evolution
which passed through several stages. Beginning with the
androgynous and bisexual, it proceeded through the protracted
dual-sexed epoch of the human race. There was the legendary era of

great heroes and giants. The seven divine dynasties were thereafter to be found in the Third Race and again in the Fourth Race, the Lemurian and Atlantean periods. Instructing humanity in diverse arts and sciences, they laid the primeval foundations of human culture and civilization around the globe.

Within this broad framework, the extraordinarily evocative power of the name and presence of Hermes is especially relevant to the 1975 Cycle and to the civilization of the future. Hermes is a generic name, associated with potent thought, and linked to Mercury-Buddha – a Dhyani – as well as with multiple incarnations in the history of humanity. As the god Hermes-Thot, he is the pristine archetype of Initiators in ancient Egypt, where he was reverenced as Hermes Trismegistus, a name applying to an entire lineage of Initiators. This solar line of spiritual Teachers can be traced back to Shiva as Dakshinamurti, the Initiator of Initiates. The hoary tradition which holds that Hermes taught all sciences to the nascent Mediterranean civilization suggests that he instructed those ready for divine theurgy. The arcane sciences transferred by Hermes from latent to active potency collectively constitute divine *gnosis*, a precise and comprehensive knowledge of the complex laws governing the seven kingdoms of Nature. These laws encompass the planes of matter, both visible and invisible, the planes from which noumenal prototypes become precipitated or projected into the phenomenal realm. Science in its essence is concerned with primary causes and is rooted in a mature apprehension of noetic consciousness. This is the true and noble meaning of science, *vidya* in the old sense, which was mysteriously intimated by the Mahatmas to European civilization in the seventeenth and eighteenth centuries to counteract the corruption of creedal religion.

Modern science is a recent flower, emerging sporadically after the Renaissance, and, in particular, after Giordano Bruno's activities in Germany and his historic visit to Oxford. The Royal Society was founded by heretical and courageous clergymen, men like the Warden of Wadham, who recognized that Aristotelian scholasticism was throttling the growth of human thought, that theology had become nothing more than a corrosive word-game. Together with bold patrons in the discreetly pagan aristocracy, these pioneering heretics founded a small club in London which they called the Royal Society. It was concerned from the beginning with the systematic support of all earnest experimental investigation into the natural world. In this, its purest sense, early modern science is one of the minor contributions of the Brotherhood of Bodhisattvas to the post-Renaissance world. Yet, in the context of the ancient meaning of science, it is a limited thing indeed, shadowy and modest. Originally, 'science' referred to a system of laws capable of application by human consciousness to what later came to be cherished by a few reticent brotherhoods as true magic or divine wisdom. Magic is an exact and definite knowledge of the noumenal laws of invisible Nature. Through the proper use of that carefully transmitted knowledge, one can affect the rates of growth and primary structures of energy on the Akashic and astral planes, and so affect conditions and combinations on the physical plane. Modern science, through its neglect of the primacy of consciousness, can hardly approach such a universal synthesis, fusing meta-geometry, meta-biology and meta-psychology.

In the ancient and archetypal view of noetic magic, there is a summoning from latency to active potency of arcane knowledge that was originally impressed in the imperishable soul-memory of all humanity. Going all the way back to the middle of the Third Root Race, when self-consciousness had been attained, human beings were in astral vestures that were capable of effortless and benevolent use of the spiritual senses. Human beings, therefore, through their intuitive knowledge of the correlations of sound, colour and number, were able to communicate effortlessly. In that Golden Age, shrouded in the myths and mists of antiquity, they showed spontaneous reverence to Magus-Teachers, Hierophant-Adepts moving openly among human beings, teaching in fabled "concord groves" all over the earth. Seated under banyan trees (varieties of *ficus religiosa*), they bestowed divine wisdom upon those who were ready to learn. In that idyllic time the vast human inheritance of spiritual wisdom and scientific magic was assimilated into the *karana sharira*, the permanent vesture of the monad. It is in that inmost vesture, which is the container of all soul-memories, that the original wisdom and theurgy of humanity lie latent to this day.

It is suggestive and significant that contemporary physicists, like Roger Jones, have come to see that a great deal of what is known in particle physics and quantum mechanics points to a necessary transcendence of conventional space and time. This is strikingly reminiscent of the recondite concept of the *karana sharira*. A few intuitive scientists find the idea of such a causal field or morphogenetic matrix intensely meaningful because it intimates modes of action that are independent of many of the restrictions that hold in ordinary space and time. Because it allows for what would appear from a physical standpoint to be simultaneous transmission, it suggests the operation of laws very different from those applicable to the objective-seeming world of disparate material entities. Hence, it may have application or relevance to some of the energy fields and the "broken symmetry" that pertain to fundamental particles. Considered in relation to noetic consciousness and benevolent magic, the significance of the *karana sharira* is that it is the ground of the latent knowledge called to active potency by Hermes.

Hermes is the paradigm of the oldest sacred tradition, going back a million years ago to India *(Bharata Dwipa)*. There, among the Initiates, the basis was laid in all the Mystery Schools for the manasic development of the seminal civilizations of the Fifth Race. When the most creative minds of the Aquarian Age gain a sufficient knowledge of Sanskrit, they will come to see that all latter-day sciences are but pale and poor fragments compared with the systematic ontology and epistemology of *Brahma Vidya, Theosophia* or *Dzyan*. With reference to astronomy, to physics, physiology and to chemistry, to the mathematical and geometrical sciences, even to mechanics, transmission devices and aerial transport, the lost knowledge of the ancients was overwhelming. Some of this knowledge, still accessible through scattered texts, is being slowly recovered today by remarkable young scholars like David Pingree, who has dedicated his life to the translation of available Sanskrit texts in astronomy. This is only one small field within a vast body of information, but by the end of the century many such texts should be accessible to those who can effectively use them.

The foreshortened view of the emergence and growth of civilization which has characterized the last two hundred years is rooted in a habit of mind extending back over a period of some two thousand years, but nonetheless a minor incident in human evolution. Historians tend to focus upon the material aspects of civilization and cultures, to become obsessed with power and violence; yet since a nation's spiritual decline accompanies its material ascent, such a truncated approach can only distort the truth and mislead the unwary. Any attempt to account for this messianic history of recent millennia must begin fundamentally with a recognition that many human souls were badly scarred in decadent Atlantis, and, having lost the Third Eye, were left merely with an external sense of power connected to a crude conception of energy which still mesmerizes them through awe of tangible bigness and gross strength.

This is reminiscent of Plato's memorable reference to the contest between the Gods and the Giants. Whilst such events go back far beyond even the declining period of Egyptian dynasties, it does not, after all, characterize the entire million-year history of the Fifth Root Race. Certainly, such a shrunken perspective does little or no justice to the more than eighteen million years of human existence on this globe, or to the immeasurable reservoir of soul-memories garnered in the earliest golden ages. Every major culture reflects, to some degree, these finest and persistent intuitions in human beings. That is what gives many people a kind of reverence, however confused, before the Native Americans and other so-called 'primitive' peoples. Even if many of these cultures have lost their spiritual knowledge, and so have fallen to the mercy of inferior races, these same Monads may yet recover and re-enact their wisdom in future civilizations.

This process has recurred again and again. It was played out before the days of Magna Graecia in events that were encapsulated by Herodotus in his brief work, *Euterpe.* Therein he acknowledged the debt of gratitude that the Greeks owed to the grand Egyptian civilization which preceded it. This is even more explicit in Plato, who made Socrates speak of Solon, and the great Egyptian teachers of Sais, next to whom the Greeks were as little children. Yet whilst the reverence of Herodotus for predecessors was genuine, and expressed with almost religious awe, he also wrote that more familiar kind of historical narrative through which he is known as the "Father of History". In an often overlooked passage, he commended the Persians for their exemplary bravery and sense of truth, which, he said, were lacking among the Greeks. The courage to tell the truth and stand by it, the sense of the sacredness of a man's word of honour – these, he thought, were virtues that the Greeks could learn from the ancient Persians.

At the same time, however, Herodotus, in dealing with the Persian legal system, began to generate some of the snobbery that long prevailed among Athenians when they contemplated their *polis* and its democratic institutions. Through dramatized contrasts with the corrupt despotism of Persian institutions, Herodotus managed to compress, and devalue, the scope and successive phases of Persian civilization. In virtually every subsequent account of the supposed history of ancient civilizations, this same compression is found compounded. It arises because of decadence and the disappearance from active human memory of the greatest epochs of antiquity. This has led to the extraordinary and confusing conclusion that all the collective knowledge of the human race can somehow be made readily available to the common man. Some even insist that the less one knows, the more one has a right to demand all and sundry information.

This puny standpoint is seriously threatened by the fact that the seminal periods of human evolution are hidden and secret, and yet span millions of years which are inaccessible except through initiation. The profoundest truths were never written about in popular chronicles. They were available only in glyphs and symbols, in monuments, in secret libraries in central Asia and elsewhere. They were not for the eyes of curious crowds. In any event, even ordinary people in more mature cultures have a natural reticence about spiritual wisdom. Just as, in old age, those beset by a sense of failure, a fear of death and a feeling of audience deprivation seek refuge in reminiscence, so too cultures grow infatuated with telling their inflated history only after they have begun to decay. They become compulsively autobiographical, repeatedly retelling their life story. The truly creative, mindful of the enormous potency of mathematical and spiritual knowledge, are careful to protect that knowledge. They will make it available to those who can use it constructively; but they will keep it away from those who may abuse it, delude others and harm themselves.

Seen from this perspective, one can begin to appreciate the sense in which much of modern science is based upon the half-baked occult secrets of the semi-esoteric groups that persisted from the days of the early Church Fathers to the Renaissance. Whilst it may come as a surprise to post-colonial Europeans, it is still held by the Ashanti elders that had they been more careful with their accumulated wisdom, modern science and medicine could have avoided their premature and amoral growth. What such wise elders knew, and what was intuited by Pauwels and Bergier – the authors of *The Morning of the Magicians* – is that what is presently extolled as modern science is significantly based upon the scattered and leaked secrets of medieval and ancient classical knowledge.

The disappearance of alchemy and the authentic occult arts is inseparable from the karmic record of those souls who were not capable of handling theurgic teaching and practical knowledge in relation to the various secret sciences. But something of that tradition remained in the Platonic Academy, which lasted for nine hundred years, among the early Muslims in Cordoba, and through them, among their pupils in Italy and France. At about the same time, out of small beginnings in a few houses the University of Oxford was born. All these communities struggled towards an understanding of the seven sciences, the *trivium* and *quadrivium*. Respect for these sciences is the origin of what were once sacred terms – bachelor of arts and master of arts. These were degrees going back to old initiations, carrying memories of earlier times. Then they became attached to universities which, since the twelfth century, have helped to bring knowledge to thousands of people who would otherwise have had no access to it. Until Wycliffe, for example, no one who was poor or ignorant of Latin could read the Bible.

This breaking down of the closed circle connected with knowledge in general, and sacred texts in particular, is not yet complete. It is thus a vital part of the present climactic Cycle: over the coming decades Sanskrit and Greek will be simplified and taught so that anyone may acquire them. Languages will be rescued from the grammarians. For so-called experts, who have never penetrated the inner meanings of ancient texts, nonetheless manage to discourage the spiritual enquirer from learning the language. At a certain level, this renaissance in ancient languages will be part of the Hermetic work of the 1975 Cycle.

To understand the work of Hermes at a more fundamental level in relation to civilization, one must begin to generate a conception of the cosmic hierarchies in Nature and in Man which unites the spiritual with the physical, and both of these with the moral and the political. This fundamental recognition of the relationship of the celestial and the terrestrial must be forged through a living link in the psychological realm. That link is Man. Only through the rediscovery within human nature of all orders of being from the gods to the elementals can there be a recovery of the continuity of the Great Chain of Being from the highest to the lowest. All hierarchies – from the Dhyanis through the *danavas* and *daityas*, to the *devas* or gods, the *devatas* and elementals – are represented within the individual human being. The five middle principles of human nature, leaving out of consideration the *Atman* and the physical body, are the direct gift and transmitted essence of the six-fold Dhyani Buddhas. That is why even *kama manas* is in essence sacred. It is lent to human beings to show them how to connect and how to discriminate.

If this is difficult to perceive, it is because all of these intermediate principles have been polluted, all have been abused on behalf of the shadowy self, of egotism and separatism. Human beings of the past, like little children in the present, showed an innate confidence that comes from knowing oneself as a ray of the Divine. They recognized themselves as immortal souls, centres of consciousness capable of expansion and contraction, of diffusion and concentration. Thus they could regard the body as an instrument, to be used by the soul as a horse by its rider. The mind is a necessary and useful tool of the soul, but it must be regularly cleansed. A person who senses this does not identify with his clothes in the spiritual and philosophical sense. Instead, he is always turned inward through meditation, and upward through aspiration; he is forever rising heavenward towards the invisible cosmos. It becomes natural for him to start with the cosmic and come down to the human, to descend from *Hiranyagarbha* – the luminous golden egg of Brahmā – to the recognition of one's own egg, from *Mahat*, or cosmic mind, to *Manas*, his small share in cosmic ideation. Descending from the universal to the particular is essential to the Hermetic method.

Modernity, by contrast, stands on its head, tries to move upward, and thus severs off the umbilical connection between man and cosmos. This approach, antithetical to the spiritual nature of man, had to be corrected by the Copernican revolution, which clarified the relation of the earth and the sun. But while the contemporaries of Copernicus thought they were discovering new truths, they were, in fact, only recovering the ancient laws of Pythagorean wisdom. If a sense of the right relationship of heaven and earth is to be restored, the sort of reorientation and recentering that has taken place in astronomy must take place psychologically and metaphysically. This can be attempted in many ways. Ordinary people could, for example, develop skill in consulting the *I-Ching*. They would not be able to use it for precise prediction, for that mysterious science requires a great deal of reverence. But by simply considering the *I-Ching*, they will be reminded that there are seasons, and continuous connections between heaven and earth.

A recognition of the correspondences between the celestial and terrestrial is the beginning of wisdom. The fear of God is not the beginning of wisdom. Wisdom is attainable only through love of the gods and recognition of their immanence within the human temple. The realization of human nature as a living psychological link between the celestial and the terrestrial will come about only through meditation and contemplation in the highest sense. Through the awakening of Buddhic feeling, one may feel close to the stars and to the galaxy. But one will also feel close to that which corresponds to *Akasha* within the astral brain and spiritual heart, and also within the *karana sharira*. Without this therapeutic and creative feeling, true learning and science can never progress. A few pioneers have recognized that for three centuries now science has been a mutilated victim of methodological dogmatism. This has led to a mechanistic reductionism, often trumpeted only because people are not good at mathematics. When they are lacking in mathematics in the highest sense, they become addicted to the habit of tinkering with jars and lamps. Owing to the delusion that has shadowed the diffusion of science, the tremendous integrity of the highest mathematical method has been inaccessible to the majority of practitioners, who have become like Shaw's barbarians. They resemble the civilized savage, who, upon switching on the light, thinks he knows about electricity.

Fortunately, this adolescent state of science is coming to an end. Yet, although many people now recognize that science must deal with consciousness, most scientists are still encumbered by a philosophically narrow view of sense-data, sense-experience and inductive logic. As a result, pioneering researchers who want to elevate consciousness have difficulty in doing so. They must meditate, consult maps of consciousness, employ philosophical criteria, if they are to make any genuine progress. In the Aquarian academies of the future, they will have to submit themselves to certain rigorous tests. They will have to prove that they have the powers, not just of concentration, but also of directing consciousness towards universally constructive connections and correlations. This will involve both analogy and correspondence, intuition and mathematics; it will draw upon meta-sciences as yet only dimly formulated. In general, what is required is a conception of mind correlated with a conception of matter, both of which exist on many levels. Different planes of matter corresponding to different states of mind are richly interconnected with each other in different sets and subsets, systems and subsystems, as well as supersystems. All of this has application to the arrangement of atoms and molecules, but also to what lies beyond what are presently called atomic and subatomic particles. These are but ghostly shadows of the invisible atoms in which inheres the eternal motion of the *Atman* and which may be spoken of as the *Atma-Buddhi-Manas* of the atom.

Science will not truly advance unless it goes beyond the mere analysis of physical matter, the mundane tricks which for a while bewitched hordes of ex-peasants coming out of villages. It was advantageous to have a little vulgar technology in the age of the automobile, the steam engine and the electric motor. It was comforting to share in a collective sense of automatic progress. But that time is over. The present aim must be to transcend the mere classification of matter which characterizes, for example, most of modern medicine, and instead to determine critical and relevant factors through theoretical and experiential knowledge of general and universal laws. This capacity must extend not only over the realm of physical phenomena, but also over psychological and moral life, and the social and political realms of human existence.

Ultimately, this capacity will derive from strong foundations in spiritual self-awareness that can only be laid through a fundamental inner change. One might say this decisive change will require not merely framing the Hippocratic Oath but directly experiencing a reverence for life and truth. Early in the century such a spirit blessed the scientific academies of Germany, Switzerland and England.

Since 1914, however, much of this has been lost in the tumultuous rush after more technology and mere techniques. That is why the shining example of Mahatma Gandhi is so important to everyone who is authentically concerned with the disinterested pursuit of pure truth, while secure in its indifference to worldly concerns. The celestial was joined to the terrestrial in the West in certain monastic and intellectual communities, but since that connection was lost, to recover it requires something far more fundamental – a discriminating knowledge of metaphysics strong enough to broaden all one's categories and to deepen one's insights.

The radical regeneration of civilization and the restoration of a golden age can ultimately only be understood in relation to the descent of the gods. The golden age is eternally associated with Shiva-Saturn and the hosts of the Kumaras, whilst its terrestrial incarnation is inseparable from the incarnation of divine dynasties and king-hierophants. Thus, Thot-Hermes was the secretary of King Saturn presiding over the pre-dynastic Golden Age. Plato, in *The Statesman,* speaks of the Golden Age as a time of universal well-being wherein all basic needs were fulfilled. This dream continually recurs in myth and literature, for example, in the vision of Gonzalo in *The Tempest.* But it is more than a dream. It is a recollection of reality. It refers not just to the Third Root Race, but also to certain recurring moments in human evolution. The time of Rama, a million years ago, was the last great Golden Age. It was possible then for Divine Instructors to move openly among ordinary human beings. As kingship was sacred, rulers in that age could exemplify benevolent magic, exercising a just and compassionate custodianship over their close-knit communities. In the age of Shiva-Saturn, the cooperative hierarchies of human relationships mirrored the cosmic hierarchies of invisible Nature.

However, as Plato recognized in *The Statesman*, once the Age of Zeus began, it was no longer possible for Divine Instructors to come openly into the world. Here Plato is referring to the beginning of Kali Yuga five thousand one hundred eight years ago. It is a familiar characteristic of the Iron Age that human beings must rely on rules to restrain their weaknesses and vices. But it is also well known that all rules can be manipulated and that in rule-governed systems oligarchy and inequality work continuously. The pervasive recognition that rule-governed societies are only dim reflections of some higher ideal is itself evidence that one cannot extinguish from the human heart an innate sense of devotion to true Teachers, Gurus and ethical leaders. One of the crucial contributions of the 1975 Cycle has been to awaken soul-memories in many peoples around the world. This had to be done before the beginning of the present Cycle, because no one can benefit from it until he or she has first been shown how to learn and to respect Teachers. Because all of this was significantly accomplished before 1975, many people are now more open and willing to function in environments that are precursors of the secular monasteries of the future, spiritual centres profoundly hospitable to learning and to oral instruction by true Teachers.

This was wisely anticipated by Damodar K. Mavalankar in the nineteenth century, who understood that the Theosophical Movement has essentially one object and no other. As a natural logician, Mavalankar knew that what he understood, others would also understand, namely, that if Mahatmas and Adepts can move freely among human beings, any one of them can solve myriads of persisting problems among myriads of responsive human beings. One need only open the door to the free movement of such enlightened beings. This could not have been attempted during the last Cycle; if anything it was retarded, first by ignorant misuse of the Teachings, and later by abject cowardice. The lifeless thought-forms, crippled images and paranoid vestiges of the past millennia must be bypassed through the progressive initiation of the Aquarian *sanghas*, the academies and the lodges of the future. As this Pythagorean fusion attains fruition during the next century, there will around the globe be widespread hospitality to the wisdom and necessity of acceptance of the Guruparampara chain. There will be a willingness to learn, which can draw upon the natural reciprocity and self-validating strength of the relationship between teacher and taught. Like a deep and loving relationship between a parent and a child, this cannot be manipulated by a third party. Its reciprocity arises within the unique context of a particular karmic field, and points to the timeless ideal of the Guru-chela relationship.

This universal Aquarian diffusion of the true ideal of spiritual science and lifelong learning will enable human beings to awaken a vibrant sense of universal justice, universal compassion and universal concord. It will enable people to learn anew how to think, how to speak and how to contribute fearlessly yet appropriately to the collective fund of human wisdom: how to evoke benevolent spirits. If one employs harsh words, or even gentle words in a harsh manner, one will attract negative elementals. These, over time, accumulate, blocking the capacity to question or to formulate truths. But, by purifying words, speech and the aura around words and by cleansing one's motivation, one's tone of voice and one's movements, one can reorient oneself and so draw finer elementals into one's sphere. Through this elevation of the orbit of one's consciousness, one may become more benevolent and more magnanimous, while at the same time learning to use potent knowledge with more deliberation, courage and compassion.

The regeneration of global civilization through such a tapping of the inward spiritual resources of humanity is the enigmatic Hermetic and Avataric function exemplified by Hermes-Thot. It is the sacred function central to every Mystery School in recorded and unrecorded history. It goes back directly to Dakshinamurti, the Initiator of Initiates, and it has never been absent from the earth. It has been self-evidently crucial when the beginnings of civilizations were laid in different parts of the world. To make it now a vital part of a universal outlook in the dawning Aquarian Age, where there is more freedom from competitiveness and more openness to universal truths, could lead to a new kind of soul-etiquette. Founded upon the principle of drawing the larger circle, there could be the elaboration of a new code of relationship between human beings which would be more hospitable to the profoundly paradigmatic teachings of the *Upanishad*, "Sit down near me and let me whisper in your ear." This is the ancient Platonic-Upanishadic method, born with the human race, perpetually nourishing it, and recognized by the noblest precursors of the Aquarian Age.

AQUARIAN HARMONY

'Our old writers said that Vach is of four kinds . . . para, pasyanti, madhyama, vaikhari (a statement found in the Rig-Veda and the Upanishads) . . . . Vaikhari-Vach is what we utter.' It is sound, speech, that again which becomes comprehensive and objective to one of our physical senses and may be brought under the laws of perception. Hence: 'Every kind of Vaikhari-Vach exists in its Madhyama . . . Pasyanti and ultimately in its Para form . . . . The reason why this Pranava is called Vach is this, that these four principles of the great Kosmos correspond to these four forms of Vach . . . . The whole Kosmos in its objective form is Vaikhari Vach; the light of the Logos is the madhyama form; and the Logos itself the pasyanti form; while Parabrahmam is the para (beyond the noumenon of all Noumena) aspect of that Vach.'

The Secret Doctrine, i 432

Harmony is the central idea in Aquarian thought. Compassionate sacrifice and intelligent suffering are the necessary means to an understanding of harmony; their eventual fruition is noetic self-knowledge. Spiritual growth is epitomized by the image of the silent, ceaseless construction of the Temple of Truth, precipitated in its crystalline splendour by meditative action out of the Akashic waters of life. True spiritual will, the conscious direction of energy by intelligent ideation and self-conscious volition, is the supreme criterion and sovereign talisman of Aquarian humanity. Opposed to this vision are the irrational and involuntary forces of blind desire, the persistent and obscuring veil cast over human perception and action through lives of thoughtless involvement with the grosser fields of material nature. Aquarians can readily grasp this problem, but they are few and far between. The therapeutic Aquarian standpoint depends upon a fundamental appreciation, through meditation, of the metaphysical structure of all reality and Nature, of God and Man.

The idea of cosmic harmony and human solidarity is as old as the Vedas and is vital to every authentic spiritual tradition. Long before the Christian era, at the time of Confucius and Buddha, when the basis for civilization was being laid in different parts of the world, Pythagoras required all his diligent pupils to study arithmetic, geometry, astronomy and music. Musical harmony was considered one of the four branches of mathematics, a reflection of the deeper nature of spiritual harmony. At some instinctive level, all human beings recognise the difference between harmonious and disharmonious movement. In one of the first human rites of initiation, learning to walk, it is necessary to learn, to assimilate and to embody some understanding of the relationship between harmony and self-direction. The art of physical movement is analogous to the mystical process of treading the spiritual Path. Pythagoras said that he could understand the inward nature of a human being by watching the way he or she walked, because he comprehended the continuous embodiment of universal harmony which extends from the highest to the lowest in Nature and Man.

> Pythagoras esteemed the Deity (the Logos) to be the *centre of unity* and 'Source of Harmony.' We say this Deity was the *Logos,* not the MONAD that dwelleth in Solitude and Silence, because Pythagoras taught that UNITY being indivisible is *no number* . . . . The Pythagoreans asserted that the doctrine of Numbers – the chief of all in Esotericism – had been revealed to man by the celestial deities; that the world had been called forth out of Chaos by Sound or Harmony, and constructed according to the principles of musical proportion; that the seven planets which rule the destiny of mortals have a harmonious motion 'and intervals corresponding to musical diastemes, rendering various sounds, so perfectly consonant, that they produce the sweetest melody, which is inaudible to us, only by reason of the greatness of the sound, which our ears are incapable of receiving.'

> *Ibid.,* i 433

To rise above a merely instinctual awareness of harmony and to become a more receptive agent and instrument of cosmic harmony, one must apprehend the idea in reference to the mind and the heart and understand too the rhythms of the invisible vestures. One must reflect upon what it means, first of all, to see oneself as a source of harmony, a Logoic being, capable of centering oneself in consciousness at that point in abstract space which is indivisible, unconnected with any form. This point is a focus of concentration, and also a point from which there can be diffused in every direction, as in a sphere, radii reaching out with deliberation and benevolence towards every life-atom. Whether putting on one's clothes, or eating food, or sitting down, one is always dealing with life-atoms. How grateful and gentle is one towards everything that one has the privilege of touching and using? To increase benevolence one must locate oneself correctly through meditation, heightening awareness from a central point of harmony. In the Bhagavad Gita, Krishna instructs Arjuna to take the point between the eyes as his starting-point in coming to see himself as a centre of harmony. A being is not his eyes, his ears, his mouth, his head, not any of his organs nor his entire body. But he can be the mystical point between the eyes.

This meditative exercise to see oneself as a monadic point should be complemented by an effort to see what is at the core of every relationship with other human beings. What gratitude does one owe one's father, who initiated one's physical incarnation by providing not only one's bone structure but also the seminal essence out of which the body was formed? What reverence does one owe to one's mother, who gave not only the flesh and soft tissue of the body, but also the egg itself from which was born the embryo that was gestated for seven months in the womb and then protected for two more months before being delivered? What does one owe one's spouse and children in the present lifetime and one's former spouses and children in all one's former lives? What is crucial in one's relationship to one's friends and neighbours and their families who constitute the community one lives in, and what is at the core of one's relationships in one's sphere of work?

All such questions highlight the crux of one's *dharma*, that which upholds a human being, linking him or her to the entire fabric of human life. If human beings would only begin to centre themselves through meditation, reflection and preparation, they would realize the great privilege of entering the world. One must prepare oneself inwardly before using one's eyes, if one would see other human beings reverentially as points of light. If one is going to speak compassionately, not compulsively, one must consider before speaking how one's words may be relevant or beneficial to another. "Please" or "Thank you" must be said sincerely, not automatically; favours must be asked kindly, not imperiously. By coming to see life in terms of the primary facts of birth and death, one may learn to act with deliberation and noetic discernment, like an orderly in a hospital who, though always very busy, does not mind being overlooked. By a smile, by a word or by silent exemplification alone, one may remain centered as a monadic point, giving off therapeutic vibrations to all.

Seen in this way, life can be extraordinarily beautiful and simple. Life seems difficult only because so much comes in the way of understanding oneself as a source of harmony. Human beings are continually concerned with the boundaries between themselves as individuals, yet those boundaries exist only in the realm of ephemeral forms, and therefore provide no stable basis for self-centering. Without deep meditation and fundamental metaphysics, it is impossible to learn anything significant about centering oneself in consciousness. Thus, thousands of people who use those terms loosely are looking for disciples and not finding any who will stay with them. That is because they never stayed with anything themselves; they have hence not centered themselves in their own consciousness. Like the dilettantes Plato warned against in his portrayal of democracy, they have no internal sense of priority or proportion, and hence no spiritual will. Yet there exists today an increasing number of Aquarian pioneers, like the scattered droplets presaging the monsoon, who have begun in earnest the difficult task of gradually centering themselves in the Verbum – *Brahma Vach*.

By removing what is excessive and by refining a sense of what is essential, they are learning to radiate benevolence and intelligence. They are learning the constructive use and dissemination of thought, feeling and will-energy. They have become self-consciously engaged in the transformation of the energy-field of the entire earth, that grand project which is the task of the Aquarian Age. The forces of harmony will be progressively strengthened, whilst disharmony will become nothing but a dialectical opportunity for growth. As the Aquarian Age unfolds, there will be a continuous increase in human awareness, a deepening of privacy. Each human being will become more of a solitary person of silence and meditation. In mature Aquarian culture, what is said and done will be meaningful and thoughtful, deliberate and discerning, but rendered with ease, sweetness and even beauty.

Clearly, the transformation from Piscean to Aquarian civilization poses an extraordinary challenge. Yet the resources available to any human being who wishes to assist this transformation are tremendous. The internal reservoirs of Akashic energy and ideation potentially available to the aspiring human soul are virtually infinite. To tap them self-consciously and thereby to contribute to the civilization of the future requires an understanding of metaphysics grounded in meditation as well as a moral self-discipline enlightened by at least some preliminary understanding of the arcane teachings about cosmic hierarchies. The greatest conceptual barrier to a practical increase in the sense of human solidarity is the mistaken notion that human beings must do something to unify the world. It is an ultimate and irreducible metaphysical fact that the world is already one. All beings are one, and all Being is One. Since all beings are one in a primordial invisible state, the true task is to mirror that unity on the lower, manifested planes of differentiated thought and action. This is impossible without first reaching towards that invisible unity, and hence Pythagoras taught his disciples to be extremely humble about That which is No Number. That is not zero, a place-holder in the number continuum. It is, rather, the source of dynamic harmony that lies behind all the spheres and circles of the metaphysical and physical universes. The key to the harmony and Akashic continuity of the One and the many lies concealed within the mystery of the zero and the point.

To convey this to the modern age, the great Rishi, masquerading as H.P. Blavatsky, set forth before the world the ancient *Stanzas of Dzyan*. During the nineteenth century, the Sixth Century Impulsion in the septenary series initiated by Tsong-Kha-Pa, the term *'Brahma Vidya'* was often used as an equivalent to *Theosophia*. Whilst *Brahma Vidya* refers to the sacred science, spiritual knowledge has not, over a hundred years, been put to intensive use by very many individuals. In that sense, the Theosophical Movement was once again a comparative failure. As it had failed over two thousand years ago in the time of Jesus, it failed again and again throughout the six impulsions of recent centuries. It failed especially, dramatically and poignantly, in the eighteenth century, despite an extremely powerful infusion. It gained a partial success on the secular, social and political planes, but the true import and teaching of the Enlightenment was subverted. "Liberty, equality and fraternity" did not come about in the true spiritual sense in which it was envisaged by the great Adepts of the eighteenth century.

In the 1975 Cycle, no quarter is given either to spiritual pretensions or to paranoid empiricism. The clutter and lumber of the past, whether pseudo-Theosophical, pseudo-religious, pseudo-scientific or pseudo-political, are being wiped out, so that human beings must endure severe testing before they can return to the timeless basics of living. They are being forced to ask themselves what it means to be a human being and how one uses sound and speech. Given the course of human evolution over the last five million years, a situation must be created in which the word 'human' cannot any more be applied in the future tense to someone who misuses sound and speech. Nothing can be done about the right use of speech on the plane of appearances without getting to the root of the problem on the plane of thought. There must be a restoration of the Mysteries and an elimination of the worldly worship of secondary and tertiary emanations through religious systems and mindless rituals. New rules must be created for speech, and new criteria must be created for silence, so that meditation can become more widespread and constructive. It must be brought home that *Dzyan* means self-reform through meditation, and that maturity is nothing more than mastery over the power of speech.

For these reasons, *Brahma Vidya* in the 1975 Cycle has been supplanted by the term *'Brahma Vach'*, as a synonym for *Theosophia*. The aim is to get to the root of that which is beyond even the pre-cosmic sidereal gods. Whether it is called the Logos or *Vach* or *Brahma Vach,* it is the primordial latent sound and light in *Parabrahm.* That latent sound and light in *Parabrahm* is *Para Vach,* and that *Para Vach* is beyond both manifestation and nonmanifestation. It is the Great Breath beyond the cosmos that vitalizes root matter, the eternally self-existent vibration of eternal motion. It transcends the distinction between *Mahamanvantara* and *Mahapralaya,* and even the creative vibratory light of the *sandhya* at the dawn of differentiation. In the dawn of manifestation that light exists in its most virginal, luminous and noumenal potential state. Its latency becomes meditated upon and thus draws upon the ideational energy of the Logos. This is *Pashyanti Vach,* coexistent with the Logos and inseparable from its own highest self-awareness. *Para Vach* is like a ray from the primordial ever-darkness of *Parabrahm,* flowing out of the precosmic sources of all as *Kalagni,* dark spiritual fire. It is misleading to think of it as actually emerging from *Parabrahm,* because it is always the ever-concealed potency in *Parabrahm.* There is a stirring within that eternal state from which arises the awareness of latent light and sound, which becomes *Pashyanti Vach,* yielding the Logos, Brahmā, Ishwara, Sanat – the Ancient of Ancients. Simultaneous with the emergence of the androgyne Logos is the emergence of its feminine counterpart, which is Vach.

Vach thus refers in its *para* form to that which is absolutely latent light and sound. Vach also refers to Brahmā, who, as the Logos, is Vach, whilst Vach as the consort of Brahmā is the light of the Logos – *Daiviprakriti* – which is Vach in its *madhyama* form. In other words, given latent light and sound, and given ideation upon that latent light and sound, that ideation is expressed in a most pristine form in the dawn of manifestation. It is like the dawn of Venus on the terrestrial plane; physically, there is darkness, but a most noumenal light is irradiated on earth. Cats have a psychic awareness of this and wish to be outside at that time; even the glow-worm enjoys the light before dawn. Human beings should understand the analogy between terrestrial dawn-light and the noumenal and causal light of the invisible Sun. On the plane of *Buddhi-Manas* intellectual light is consubstantial with the essential light-energy of *Suddhasattva*, the substance of the gods. In this sense, Vach, as the consort of Brahmā and the Light of the Logos, is also the mother of the gods. She is Sarasvati, the goddess of wisdom and beauty, and Aditi, out of whose noumenal form emanate the seven primordial rays, each of which carries a luminous vesture.

The substance of these vestures is not matter in any sense that can be understood by terrestrial criteria, but rather rays so luminous and radiant that they are called the sons of *Daiviprakriti*. These sons are preconditions to a cosmos, and it is from these primordial seven that there is a rapid multiplication in sevens and fourteens, in tens and twelves, producing *en masse* the array of the hierarchies. It is these in turn that produce the objective manifested universe, or *Vaikhari Vach*. Thus, H.P. Blavatsky speaks of Vach as

> the most mysterious of all the Brahmanical goddesses, she who is termed 'the *melodious* cow who milked forth sustenance and water' (the Earth with all her mystic powers); and again she 'who yields us nourishment and sustenance' (physical Earth). *Isis* is also mystic Nature and also Earth; and her cow's horns identify her with Vach. The latter, after having been recognised in her highest form as *para*, becomes at the lower or material end of creation – *Vaikhari*. Hence she is mystic, though physical, Nature, with all her magic ways and properties.
>
> *Ibid.*, i 434

The conception of Vach as mystic Nature points to the continuity of the entire field linking *Para* to *Vaikhari Vach*. The two opposite poles, the one beyond all manifestation and the other representing the maximum degree of differentiation, the most transcendental and the most immanent, are held together by *Akasha*. It is a supersensuous, fiery, fluidic ether surrounding the earth and the solar system, but also pervading the brain, the heart and the entire human body, which is largely composed of water and empty space.

> 'Waters' and 'water' stand as the symbol for Akasa, the 'primordial Ocean of Space,' on which Narayana, the self-born Spirit, moves; reclining on that *which is its progeny . . . *. 'Water is the body of Nara'; thus we have heard the name of water explained. Since Brahmā rests on the water, therefore he is termed *'Narayana'* . . . . 'Pure, Purusha created the waters pure . . .' at the same time Water is the third principle in material Kosmos, and the third in the realm of the Spiritual: *Spirit* of Fire, Flame, Akasa, Ether, Water, Air, Earth, are the cosmic, sidereal, psychic, spiritual and mystic principles, *pre-eminently occult*, in every *plane* of being. 'Gods, Demons, Pitris and men,' are the four orders of beings to whom the term Ambhamsi is applied (in the Vedas it is a synonym of gods): because they are all the product of WATERS (mystically), of the Akasic Ocean, and of the Third principle in nature.

> *Ibid.*, i 458

Akasha-Vach is mystic Nature pervading the entire cosmos. It is the celestial virgin and Alkahest of the alchemists, the 'Virgin Mother' of the magician. It is the mother of love, mercy and charity, as well as the waters of grace which can only be tapped by true meditation, total benevolence and selflessness. That is why it is only possible to gain self-knowledge through selfless love. A mother blessed with pure love can, just by a glance, avert impending danger to her child. Through the power of pure love, the mother and child become one, experiencing *Akasha*. This notion of two identities fusing is neither simple in itself nor vague. Although it may be readily observed in the animal kingdom, it cannot be understood through terms like 'instinct'. Crude notions such as 'mother instinct' are worse than useless. In seeking to understand *Akasha,* it is best not to speak. The less one analyses, the better. Too many people analyse too much instead of living and learning from the simplest aspects of life.

Mystic Nature is extremely close to everyone. It flows in and through the human form. This can be seen as soon as one investigates the pressure points in one's hands and feet, gently and lovingly, but also with firmness and courage. Suddenly one will discover that there are many knots throughout the body, causing people to fall ill. The same lesson may be learnt by treating objects gently, using *Brahma Vach* in daily life when washing dishes or walking, when putting on clothes, or touching any object. If one does not learn harmonious and gentle action in the sphere of daily duties, which are the *ABCs* of *Theosophia,* one will never become even remotely able to understand the Mysteries. Above all, one must learn harmony in speech, for sound is the leading attribute of *Akasha-Vach.* When an Adept sees the aura around a human being who has not yet entered the Mysteries, the Adept is interested only in whether that human being will learn before death the *ABCs* of life. Has the person learnt how to be humble, how to learn, how to apologize, how to mentally prostrate before elders and teachers? The degree to which a human being has learnt generosity and gratitude during life will infallibly determine his or her state of consciousness at the moment of death.

If the basics have been learnt in this lifetime, then karma will be kind in the next. The person will find birth in a family where the parents are not much moved by likes and dislikes, and raise their children accordingly. Such parents will give their children few options, and they will also probably be impoverished peasants. The child will have no option but to learn the only arts that its parents have to teach – farming, carpentry, housekeeping. For the fortunate soul, life does not consist of menus; there is only one thing to eat. In such an environment the soul can perfect the lesson of the *ABCs* and advance towards self-knowledge. Many people are terrified that they are not learning the *ABCs,* that they are merely repeating formulae and not really learning, and this is indeed a widespread and dangerous condition. But instead of exacerbating it through futile fears, they can begin letting go of the tight, knotting egotistical grip they have on themselves, can begin to renounce the psychic claustrophobia that imprisons them. Many lifetimes may pass before they can hear the Akashic sounds of the mystic heights or before they can feel the flow of the *Akasha* within the heart and brain.

Such persons can still look up at the sky and have their vision healed by it. They can still appreciate the light of the dawn and have their hearts renewed by it. They can still sit quietly in the twilight and sense in the sounds of Nature its uninterrupted harmony as day recedes into night. They can behold the midnight sky, thrilling to the sight of stars more numberless than human beings, and gain an inward sense of the spaciousness of the cosmos. Seeing the sky as the great purifier of consciousness, they may touch the veil of mystic Nature as the container of all things *in potentia*. Using the great Teachings in these ways, they may prepare themselves for preliminary exercises in meditation and lay the seeds for the discipline of silence, which is ultimately consummated in the full perception and self-conscious embodiment of universal harmony by the sovereign Adept. Every honest effort to follow this alchemical path is irrevocably a step towards the noonday Sun of Aquarian enlightenment.

AQUARIAN THERAPY

To suffer woes which Hope thinks infinite;
To forgive wrongs darker than death or night;
To defy Power, which seems omnipotent;
To love, and hear; to hope till Hope creates
From its own wreck the thing it contemplates;
Neither to change, nor falter, nor repent;
This, like thy glory, Titan, is to be
Good, great and joyous, beautiful and free;
This is alone Life, Joy, Empire, and Victory.

PERCY BYSSHE SHELLEY

In the Aquarian Age the mental fire of devotion and sacrifice means purgation, and no substitute will serve. Human beings may seek authentic confidence in their own divine destiny – out of pain through experience, by sifting, by meditation, by mistakes and learning from them. In time they can therapeutically release within themselves that mental breath and spiritual fire where they always feel benevolent towards all, but where that benevolence is backed by depth of thought directed by a precise, luminous intelligence. This great challenge is partly what W.Q. Judge meant when he prophesied that the time will come when powers will be needed and pretensions will go for naught. It is a strange advantage that now there are so many swamis, lamas and gurus of every kind, on almost every street corner, because once and for all people will have to go behind and beyond labels, externals, forms, names, claims and containers of all kinds. They will have to discover the life-giving stream of wisdom that becomes a self-sustaining current, fertilizing the soil of the mind, and giving birth to creative ideas and beneficent impulses. They will have to learn to direct the power to act in new ways, with willing cooperation in a context larger than themselves, and on behalf of a vision that is only dimly sensed. This is what Shelley suggested by pointing to the star,

The loftiest star of unascended heaven,

Pinnacled dim in the intense inane.

'Inane' in ordinary language means 'foolish', 'idiotic', 'chaotic', 'meaningless', and 'incoherent', but 'inane' in the archaic language of spiritual alchemy refers to something beyond primordial chaos. It is the original ground of creativity in the whole of nature, latent in the unmanifest realm. It is also specifically called a liquid fire, the word *aqua* being an alchemical term. Therefore, the idea of Aquarius the Water-Bringer, even at the simplest level – bringing water to a parched soil, to thirsty human beings, and connected with rain coming down from heaven – has timeless beauty to it. Everyone knows how sweet the earth smells after a generous shower of rain. Each can appreciate that it is universal and innate to feel a natural gratitude when one's thirst is slaked by a glass of water extended by a brother. But these are mere reflections on the physical plane of something metaphysically quintessential. The ancient Egyptians depicted Aquarius as a serpent coiled in a spiral around a jar containing liquid fire. This image has reference to those who can tap the highest sources of primordial energy in invisible Nature, and channel it, bring it down and apply it, as in the restoration of sap in a piece of desiccated wood by applying resin from a pine tree. They are able to do as much revitalizing as is allowed by forms that are, alas, nearly dead.

The sacred metaphor of fire is profound, whether applied to the fire of enthusiasm, the fire of devotion, the fire of intelligence, the fire of creativity, the fire that warms, the fire that glows, or to the fire that makes one see beyond to That – TAT. Anybody who has sat by a log fire and watched it for a long time has seen something extraordinary. Behind the leaping flames there is an invisible colour. What is seen on the outside is golden yellow but inside there is actually an electric blue. Through such analogies one begins to get more and more to the core of the hidden source of creativity in human beings. More significantly, the Great Teachers of Gupta Vidya hint that the noumenon of the Three-in-One – the inmost invisible Triad in every human being and the source of all thought, will and feeling – itself has an invisible central point in *Akasha,* the noumenon which is the very essence of spiritual fire.

If one is going to learn to kindle this fire, one has to make a beginning somewhere. Consider a person who is fortunate not to have much to unlearn and whose mind was not contaminated, either because the person did not take seriously pseudo-education, or sifted it all and started to think originally. Such a person does not need to make claims to know, but can get excited about a great idea, and can incarnate it by continually dwelling upon it. The idea of aspiration, the idea of harmony, the idea of solidarity in its deepest sense – any of the ideas that are the living germs of Aquarian therapeutics – can be put to use and made to light a fire. By intensely dwelling upon such an idea, a person can actually ignite a small spark which will be sustained by regular return to the thought, looking at it in different ways – from north, south, east and west, above and below, at least from six points of view – without becoming entranced by any false crystallization or rigid formulation. Through returning again and again to the main idea, a person can, in time, light up a radiant centre in the human constitution which may serve as a hooking point from which the person can go deeper and come closer to the noumenal. This can also be done in the realm of action. Sometimes one experiences an immense exhilaration from doing one thing crisply and cleanly, even if it be only taking a bath or sitting down to perform something very simple. To do it crisply, honestly and noetically brings about a perceptible release of silent self-respect.

Spiritual will has to do with true self-esteem, moral firmness and continuity of consciousness. If a person begins without self-esteem – because the person is mauled, extremely weak-willed, or is weighted down by the recurrent karma of incompletion and passively expects it to continue throughout life – the person will complete nothing. Everything seems fraught with failure. But suppose such a person is truly honest and still says, "There is some one thing on the basis of which I can respect myself. I can do it. It is the best I know." Such a person, as Kierkegaard suggested in *Purity of Heart,* can one-pointedly will the good. Through the very attempt – not the planning, the anticipation, the calculation, and the anxiety, but just in the simple release of the will in the single act – the person can also come in time to light up the spark of self-confidence by acting in the name of something greater than the shrunken self.

The ideal way and the greatest mode of doing this, going back to the Golden Age of infant humanity in the presence of Divine Teachers, is devotion. This is the Gem of *Bodhi*, the hidden flame in the heart. When the mind is polluted, when the will is perverted, there is still somewhere a small spark of decency in the human heart. If its inaudible vibration were totally destroyed, the person would perish. Months before a person dies this silent sound ceases, the constant pulsation of the spiritual heart known in Sanskrit as the *Anahata*, the indestructible centre. There is a deathless core to the heart of every human being. There is a ceaseless if unheeded hope. Therefore anyone can respond to Shelley's vision in *Prometheus Unbound*. Despite all the most negative evidence, one can still go on. This is why even a tormented person who is about to take his life one day can still get up and make another effort, even if it seems wholly futile.

Instead of merely showing devotion fitfully and fearfully, which is like running away from the divine temple, one must seek it positively, nurturing the finest, the truest, the most valid feelings in one's own heart. One must not make devotion conditional, saying, "I will only give where I can be sure that the other person is going to give back." One should not even think in this way. One must experience the thrill of giving so much that it is impossible to expect anyone else to give anything like the same in return. The outpouring of love and joy cannot be manifest on the external plane, for when it is real it is as constant as breathing. Such is the inaudible hum, the unspoken mantram of the indestructible heart. A person who constantly cherishes this with true humility can effortlessly adopt the mental posture of unostentatious prostration. One of the most beautiful postures that the human body can ever assume is bending low and prostrating on the floor. It is also extremely relaxing and regenerative, in the teaching of Raja Yoga. A person who can assume this as a mental posture in relation to a vast ideal that is relevant to the whole of humanity can begin to perfect mental devotion to what is at the heart of the human heritage – devotion to all the Mahatmas, Bodhisattvas, Krishnas, Buddhas and Christs that ever existed in millions of years, exceeding the possibility of reckoning or measure, beyond the shifting boundaries of recorded history.

If a person can light up that deep devotion and focus it in one direction, serving one's *Ishtaguru* or chosen Teacher, and can totally concentrate with undivided, unbroken, uninterrupted love, loyalty and obedience, there is then the absolute assurance of fanning the flame in the heart. However dark the world appears to be, however heavy one's suffering seems, however confusing the karma of the times, the secret flame ever strengthens itself. Ever reaching upward, it helps *Manas* to salute the *Atman* and to become one-pointed in seeking the *Atman* without expectation. Then as surely as there is a law of periodicity that cannot be confined to the trivial timetable of the ignorant personal self which does not know the vaster cycles or the previous lives of its indwelling monad or what is at the very core of its own being, invariably and infallibly the strength of that impulse will prepare one for that perfectly right moment when the *Atman* through *Buddhi* can initiate and instruct. The *Atma-Buddhi* is the Guru. It speaks to the soul as the inner voice of the *daimon*, the voice of the Master, who is the invisible escort. That is the sovereign experience of true initiation.

A constant flame, enabling one to come to ever-higher levels of purification, the ceaseless self-purgation that is a prelude to total self-transformation, can be lit from small beginnings. Such endeavours must be sifted, honed down to a fine authenticity, and not even whispered to a single living person. But at the same time the line of life's meditation must not be forgotten by oneself. That is difficult. Maintained steadily and with continuity of consciousness, sincere efforts will lead from what, at one level, is the spark of simple devotion to an unknown object, to that deeper fire of inward devotion of the whole of one's sense of being in a manifest form, and then to the invisible prototype that is the Guru. This is signified by the higher line in the symbol of Aquarius. It is the vibration of universal consciousness, *Mahabuddhi,* which is always capable of being mirrored in the fleeting moment. It is also capable of dissolving the inverted and perverted image of itself formed in the waters of astral chaos out of conflicting feelings, ideas and wills. These can all be displaced and transcended by the deathless vibration of supreme devotion in the indestructible heart.

There is always that in a human being which says, "If I can only find that one real thing, it can cut through a great deal of the froth and darkness in my life." Even though people say this, do they really mean it? Are they in earnest? Or do they merely say it at one moment and forget it the next? To mean it, to maintain it in the mind and to make it the driving purpose of one's entire life is, doubtless, a daunting task. Just as individuals begin by self-definition to know that they can create this fire and sustain it through the darkness of minor pralayas, all human beings will have to admit that they must themselves start again, admitting that they do not know, but can still learn humbly, how to put two sticks together and light a fire. No one need be driven mad by the jackal voices of the jungle which is the crematorium of the psychic corpses of the sad failures in human evolution.

To start again means one must cure the fundamental alienation of the self so pervasive in urban society. When the mind is misused and mutilated, the whole of one's being cannot cooperate with that treacherous mind, and devotion seems to be impossible. When the mind is further alienated by constant association with a crippling self-image, one's condition is terrible. One is trapped by a sense not only of past failure but of permanent failure; a sense not only of how one once erred, but also of how one is irredeemably unworthy of one's innate destiny. In this condition one never really knows whether one was not up to it because of not giving oneself a chance in that mathematics class when one was a child of ten, or because of troubles at home, or because of that gossip next door who was interfering so much. One really does not know. But the fear that one can never accomplish anything real is too tragic. People even fear that they could never for the rest of this life put their minds to concentrate on a simple primer of geometry. Human beings fall prey to these fears because of the pressing pace of change and inexorable karmic precipitation, because of the tremendous sorting out that is going on, involving the collective karma of those who have failed spiritually as well as the karma of those who have misused and perverted the mind in the name of great ideas. They have done it in the name of the Church with the horrors of the Inquisition. They have done it in the name of the State with wars involving the innocent and unborn. They have done it in the pursuit of knowledge. When the karma of misuse is so heavy that there is an ever-growing fear, many neither know what is the root-cause nor sense the possibility of any cure.

This alienation of the mind is very real. It is most poignant in industrial society at this time. But even now there are people in many other parts of the world who are grateful to have the opportunity to sit by an electric light and enjoy the use of a tattered pamphlet. They are thrilled, when living far out in the wilds, to borrow a book or to have somebody send one to them, and to read it, enjoy it, and use it. There are awakened masses all over the globe. In Russia and Japan today, there is a greater *per capita* enjoyment of books than ever before in recorded history. This is happening all over the world. If it is not the same story everywhere, it is because of the changing karmic balances of peoples. Wherever there is a terrible mutilation of the mind, and a consequent anger, a crippling sense of self-alienation, there is the rush of the lemmings, as well as the desperate desire for a simple solution, a fervent wish to cop out altogether from their responsibilities.

When the mind is stretched only by bribe and threat (and more by threat than by bribe), and merely on behalf of restrictive and narrow ideas, then all the most insecure and frustrated souls, all the preachers without pulpits, the self-tormented teachers from past lives and all parts of the globe, grasp every chance to show pretension and fake wisdom in Kali Yuga, as the ancient *Vishnu Purana* prophesied. Even when such pseudo-teachers get their pulpit and their opportunity, they do not really believe in anything or in themselves. As this gets worse, year by year, they are constrained to concede to themselves that they do not really have anything to teach or exemplify, though they perfect the art of outward pretense. Thus all the vicious circles of antagonistic counterclaims multiply between the different sects of those who do not believe in themselves. Shelley wrote with poignant and powerful imagery about what happens to the mind when it is so totally immobilized, so wholly corrupted, so vampirical, that it becomes poisonous unto itself as well as to others. Why is such self-destructive manipulation doomed to disappear? The reason is that one cannot take an immortal soul that has journeyed much longer than is dreamt of by the boldest genealogists of the age of man, and expect such a being to swallow the rubbish of reductionism of every sort.

Human beings need ideas large enough to accommodate their sense of readiness for the future. This means that the only way to overcome self-alienation is by attunement to the Universal Mind through the contemplation of universal ideas. Because the personal mind has become flaccid, especially when it considers noble ideas enshrined in the platitudes of the past, it is liable to cling to mere externals. It must penetrate behind the visible forms to the formless ideas. Then it is meaningful to say, "I do not know," because each idea presupposes a larger idea which in turn ontologically presupposes one which is still more profound. There is an expanding transcendence of existing conceptions of space, time, motion and identity. The more one realizes this, the more genuine is the recognition that one does not know and the greater the possibility of developing the desire to persist, to function freely within a realm of pure anti-entropic thought which is completely potential, for which contemporary languages do not have any words. Sometimes from a Sanskrit root, a Greek term, or even an English word, one can extract a deeper meaning that was lost in the course of time. This is true of the word 'devotion.' It is true of most terms when traced back to their origin. There is a beautiful core to the word 'devotion,' from *de votum*, 'to dedicate by a vow.' As with any important word that has been used for a very long time, it has acquired accretions of meaning and limitations of usage. One has to take a stand somewhere in reference to the inbred tendency to identify the meanings of words ostensively or by rigid definitions, to become fixated on the conventional trappings of language. To start using the mind constructively and freeing it from habitual grooves is going to be difficult and at times extremely painful. It requires at least the level of minimal attention needed for training the lower mind, but which one did not give because it was demanded at too high a price by institutional reward and penalty.

All of this points to the unavoidable suffering caused by persisting errors through repeated mis-identification. Imagine persons who misused the gift of walking by kicking other beings. They might well have several lives without the use of legs. The terrible need and desire to walk and move is there, but they are crippled and bewildered. They need to wear out the karmic causes of their condition through that suffering, which is incomprehensible to *kama-manas*. Understanding such causes in terms of possible past misuse can bring them to a point where they will, when they regain the power of locomotion, never misuse it again. They will not dream of using it to kick another human being. They will not use it carelessly and impulsively. What is true in reference to legs is also true in regard to the eyes and to every human organ. Above all, it is true in reference to the mind, which is an invisible organ corresponding to the tongue, to the divine prerogative of speech, and to the power of conceptualization. When imagination is polluted, the mind goes awry. When imagination becomes sterile, the mind becomes paralyzed, and all it can do is to adapt and be imitative. Reductionists, puzzled by any glimmerings of something more to the power of the mind, try to freeze the situation by stating a restrictive theory, holding that the mind can only be adaptive, thereby engendering imitativeness.

The human mind, however, is original. It is self-reproductive. Patanjali says it is capable of two lines of self-reproductive thought. One of these is bound up with memory images, associations, and with likes and dislikes. It is possible to halt this compulsive self-reproductive chain of mere reactive thinking and get to a condition of balance – *nirodha* – if one persists in trying always to bring the mind back to one idea, holding oneself steady, exactly as people would do if they had partially lost the use of their legs and had to re-educate their muscles in a therapeutic ward. This must be done with the brain and the thinking faculties. Then a stage can come where another kind of self-reproductive power begins to be exercised by the mind, where it can maintain in a self-sustaining manner a level of thinking that is more universal and constructive, which is capable of a great deal of diversification, fertilization and replication. Then, when this flow is itself brought to a smooth and controlled pace, it is possible to move to a further stage where one can see oneself from outside, and remain disengaged from the uninterrupted steady flow of higher mental awareness.

Even though it must eventually come to a halt and meanwhile be diagnosed correctly at this point of history, the misuse of the mind is very old. It goes back many lives, to the time when the mind was enormously powerful and was employed on behalf of personal status and power. Every time one hears some person say, "I want to do this because I want to be famous," it is a sign that he is burdened by a fear of failure from the past. If such a person comes into contact with Gupta Vidya and still thinks in these ways, the resultant condition is tragic. There is an incredible misplacement and displacement of human energy. What a price to pay when one is young to over-compensate for little hurts and petty slights to the personal self, which needs to be refined into an invulnerable if imperfect instrument for the immortal individuality. People nonetheless get into false and exaggerated attitudes when they want to use the mind, with its limited powers, for some ignoble purpose that involves the illusory security of the personal self. History has now come to a point where, with the abuse of print and the enormity of empty pontification, Nature is insisting that there be a halt to wastage and misuse. People can go on cutting trees to make paper. Society can go on mass-producing people who think they have something to teach, but the game of deception is speedily coming to an end. Frustrated and over-wrought teachers do not have credibility with themselves. They do not know how to win the trust of their students, even amongst captive audiences. They are exhausted by their mutual rivalry and they will feel increasingly alienated and miserable. This is the cumulative precipitation of a long process of religious and secular exploitation.

The mind is a glorious gift. In its true function as a means of reflective self-conscious thought, *svasamvedana*, it is the greatest gift of the human being. Plato warned his hearers never to be so naïve as to think that any pleasure can ever have any meaning to the heart if the mind and imagination are not involved. To recover the true power of self-consciousness requires a tougher discipline and a larger perspective than can be encompassed by the personal self. It requires *dianoia* based upon Aquarian axioms and involves, above all, a new posture of humility. It is crucial to train human beings in contemporary culture to say, and to enjoy saying, "I do not know." This had become easy for many people at other times and in other places. In a highly competitive society, however, people are encouraged to claim to know when they do not. To acknowledge ignorance is very painful, but that pain is necessary for the restoration of psychological health. It is one of the tasks of the present time to give people the release and strength of saying, "I do not know, but I wish to know." First they have to say, "I do not know," and then they have to learn to practise it, however painful it is, until they burst through the pseudo-image of false knowledge. Then they have to say, "I do not know, but I want to know. I really want to know." They have to hunger for knowledge. This is required for the readjustment of the *psyche* and the awakening of *nous*.

They have to want to know out of devotion to some great purpose for its own sake, which is very difficult to understand in the context of corrupt instrumentalism. They have to want to know for the sake of some larger good, and hence they must think of a larger good in the context of which they have no position of privileged access. This is the ultimate Aquarian paradox. One does not really know what the larger good is, yet one is asked to think about it. This is superb discipline for the human soul. Keep thinking about the good of others, the good of all. One may not know what it is, but keep thinking, practising *dianoia*. Above all, in the process of doing so, one must totally negate any concern for oneself in the future. Through this practice or *abhyasa*, the lower line of the Aquarian glyph, the serpent of self that has got coiled in the wrong way, is being stretched and brought back to a condition where it can be subdued. Paradoxically, when one has totally forgotten any concern for one's own future, then one's true purpose as a soul, one's deeper destiny, will speak as the voice of the spiritual heart. It is the destiny of the divine prototype of every human being who has become alienated, like the estranged face in *The Hound of Heaven* of Francis Thompson. Self-alienation is caused by the wearing of the false mask of which Shelley speaks – the loathsome mask of the personal self. The divine prototype will not reveal the hidden purpose of this incarnation until the loathsome mask is seen for what it is and stripped away, layer by layer.

The purgation of self-crucifixion is painful and protracted until one can fully prepare the ground and find the true self amidst the darkness and agony of not knowing whether one's life has any point. But each will know in time, in a way that is unique and inimitable, and through myriad intimations. Existentially, in the very act of doing something for others, one learns to say readily and simply, "I do not know what is going on in the world. I do not know the future course of history. Above all, I certainly do not know what is unfolding in the Aquarian Age. This means that whenever I hear otherwise, I will turn a deaf ear, without being rude to the individuals concerned." This is hard. Those who can go through such self-chosen mental asceticism will come to a point where they will be able to serve others in simple ways, sharing a vision that is grander than ever could be told to them. They could find themselves sufficiently to know at that beautiful moment when death comes as a deliverer and a friend, "My life had meaning and purpose. I have not lived in vain."

Those who sense the significance of being on the threshold of a New Age will cherish the practice of meditation, of self-study, of listening, learning, and preparing themselves cheerfully and ceaselessly. They must be willing to test themselves, out of self-respect, by prescribing their own daily discipline to follow for a week. Even reduced to this short period, it is very tough for too many. But if even a few persons can follow through for a week, there is a chance that they will do something worthwhile in their lives. Typically, given the widespread fragmentation of consciousness, most people are not going to be able to do this for seven days, much less for successive weeks and months between the solstices and the equinoxes. But they have to keep trying, week by week, testing themselves. "Can I take one thought and can I maintain it as a vibration in my mind and heart for a week?" This is a strain. It will not be immediately possible. The worst will be that one will not even know that one has forgotten. But, giving oneself a chance week after week, a point comes where one must succeed. There can be no respect for oneself if it cannot be cultivated when one's faculties are relatively healthy and when one has received so much from the teachings of the Mahatmas and the abundance of Nature. The very thing that is difficult has to be attempted. Where the entire educational system in a hedonistic culture is encouraging the weak to take what is easy and avoid what is hard, courageous souls should take the hardest test – to maintain one essential idea every day throughout the week.

If a person can really do this, then that person can carry something into the next week, can work with the cycles of the seasons, the solstices, the equinoxes. But, above all, that person will so significantly change the ratios in the astral vehicle that the result will show itself on the physical plane to those who know. Every true aspirant will be recognized and receive unseen help. Who are those who know? Simply those who have mastered this very practice. Anyone who does not even understand the nature of what has to be done is certainly hoping for something which is impossible – some sort of vicarious atonement, some kind of messianic salvation. The latest form of it is the collectivization of the whole of human consciousness, put in terms of evolutionary progress, which is automatically going to become enlightened. Human consciousness is going to do nothing automatically and never has done anything automatically or suddenly in millions of years. In this way the central problem is fudged. It is foolish to imagine that somehow automatically enlightenment will descend in a secular or spiritual garb. All of this is of the past, a ghost of the Piscean Age. Enlightenment can only be reached by thought and effort based upon a sense of individual and personal insignificance. It requires withholding judgment while cheerfully persisting, trying to get to the very core of meaning in every situation and thinking through one's sense of self until it really hurts. It is like squeezing an orange until the pips squeak. Think until the brain is ready to burst. Feel until the heart cries out. Do not stop short. Get to the root. Persist and come out of it a stronger person, regenerated through *tapas*. Then follow the great injunction of the Upanishad: "Awake, arise, seek the Great Ones, *and learn.*" The Rishis assumed that unless you did all of these you could not begin to understand the meaning of the Law.

Spiritual life is the paradigm of learning. Its reflections are all the other forms of learning, but these reflections no longer reflect. To recover the primordial sense of learning that is coeval with breathing requires a total break with existing thought-forms and habits of speech. They are the modes of the past. The one thing that many people rightly sense is that they may be left out of the current and the cycle of the future. But this cannot be safeguarded against by any external means. The only way to enter into that fast-moving and invisible stream, which will become a mighty river in the future, is by becoming capable, through voluntary self-training, of activating the unmanifest potency of the universe – the liquid fire that springs from deep devotion to universal good, and by reaching out to the whole of the human race, including the unborn who are always far more numerous than those who are presently incarnated.

This is a formidable task. But any person, by self-training in the art of using Aquarian axioms, can enter the evolutionary stream which will eventually produce minds as pellucid as crystal and hearts which are wisely benevolent. Luminous with the intelligence of the universe, they shall have done with the pseudo-dramas of the past. They will recognize the beauty and dignity of being like a grain of sand at birth and death, assigning no false valuation to the pseudo-entity called the personality, which is merely a logical construction. Recognizing links at all levels between the atomic and the infinite, they will dispense with the fairy story of name and form, which was born at a certain time, died at a certain time, and achieved this and did not achieve that. Completely wiping it out is a mark of maturity. The currency of thought and language will radically have to change. Individuals will have to stand apart from many of the patterns which have become raucously agitated precisely because they are obsolete. The personality becomes most active when it is threatened. Something like this has happened collectively. This is inescapable and irreversible, and wholly to be welcomed from the mature standpoint of soul-evolution.

The most significant hope for the future may well be that people have no authentic way of celebrating festivals, no credible thoughts about the destiny of the world, no clear ideas about what they are going to do this year or next year. The voiding of all shallow expectations is extremely therapeutic. When people practise this sufficiently, they will learn to flow with the current of the whole. What can be seen in terms of law or of many levels of consciousness can also be seen quite simply as flowing like a small stream that must of necessity empty itself into the ocean. One may flow with the vaster forces of history, of humanity, and of the cosmos. When individuals forget themselves, then, paradoxically, they discover themselves. When they consider themselves as irrelevant, they become relevant. When they see themselves as unimportant, they become important. This is the mode of self-definition and the pedigree of the twice-born on the threshold of the epoch of Universal Enlightenment, the Aquarian Age, which has entered its second degree and moves steadily towards its millennial culmination.

AQUARIAN SPIRITUALITY

It is argued that the Universal Evolution, otherwise, the gradual development of species in all the kingdoms of nature, works by uniform laws. This is admitted, and the law enforced far more strictly in Esoteric than in modern Science. But we are told also, that it is equally a law that 'development works from the less to the more perfect, and from the simpler to the more complicated, by incessant changes, small in themselves, but constantly accumulating in the required direction.' . . . Esoteric Science agrees with it but adds that this law applies only to what is known to it as the Primary Creation – *the evolution of worlds from primordial atoms, and the* pre-primordial ATOM, *at the first differentiation of the former; and that during the period of cyclic evolution in space and time, this law is limited and works only in the lower kingdoms . . . . As the Hindu philosophy very justly teaches, the* 'Aniyamsam Aniyasam,' *can be known only through false notions. It is the 'many' that proceed from the ONE – the living spiritual germs or* centres of forces – *each in a septenary form, which first generate, and then give the* PRIMARY IMPULSE *to the law of evolution and gradual slow development.*

The Secret Doctrine, ii 731-732

Viewed from the impersonal standpoint of collective Karma and cyclic evolution, Nature suffers fools not unkindly but with compassion. Nature will not indefinitely indulge or underwrite human folly, for as Cicero observed, time destroys the speculations of man whilst it confirms the judgement of Nature. Through cyclic opportunities, Nature actually affords individuals innumerable occasions for the clarification and purification of perception and intention. If human judgement and design are to have adequate leverage on Nature, they must have as their stable fulcrum an intuitive apprehension of law. At the most fundamental level, human judgement and natural law alike stand upon a common ground, a single transcendental source of Being. It is only by rejecting all dualisms, mediaeval or modern, and by refusing to absolutize polarities that the designs of men and the differentiations of Nature may be brought into self-conscious harmony. In Gupta Vidya, there is no cleavage between the aim of Self-knowledge (Atma Vidya) and the practical ideal of helping Nature and working on with her (Ahimsa Yagna). To the perfected will of the yogin of Time's circle (Kalachakra), Nature is the ally, pupil and servant. Fully comprehending that man is the key to the lock of Nature, the wise yogin finds no intrinsic tension been obeisance to the judgement of Nature in Time and obedience to Shiva, the good gardener of Nature in Eternity.

This philosophic fusion of science and religion, of *vidya* and *dharma,* is essential to the structure of the Aquarian civilization of the future and enshrined in the axiom that there is no religion higher than Truth. In accordance with this evolutionary programme and in tune with the Avataric vibration of the age, the Brotherhood of Bodhisattvas has actively sought to dispel the delusive dichotomy between science and religion. Krishna conveyed the beautiful synthesis of *jnana* and *bhakti* in his classic portrait of the Self-governed Sage in the *Bhagavad Gita.* Spiritual teachers have repeatedly warned against the degrading effects upon the mind-principle of ahankaric greed and atavistic fear working through materialism and superstition. From the therapeutic standpoint of the ancient Rishis, the murky ferment of the twentieth century is not to be viewed as a creative tension between two viable cultures, the one religious and traditional, the other modern and scientific. Rather, it is to be seen as the ignorant and schizophrenic clash of two largely moribund inversions of authentic culture. Neither secular religion, with its crude demonolatry and selfish salvationism, nor materialistic science, with its cowardly conformity and slavish hedonism, still less the mutual recriminations and denunciations of one by the other, can offer human beings an assured basis for fulfilment and growth. Just as two wrongs do not make a right, no compound of these costly inversions can rectify the malaise of modern civilization. Neither fight nor flight nor unholy alliance can correct the deficiencies of two waning schemes of thought that do little justice to Man or Nature.

In order to participate freely in the regenerative, not the destructive, tendencies of the Aquarian Age, one must recognize that true religion and science do not need to be rescued from contemporary chaos by messianic crusaders. On the contrary, creative individuals must learn to cultivate moral courage and cool magnanimity so that they may plumb the depths of pure science and true religion within themselves. This cannot be done without assuming some degree of responsibility for the intense karmic precipitations during the present period of rapid transition. Without self-confidence based upon inviolable integrity, the bewildered individual will regrettably fall prey to the contagion of despairing diagnoses, sanctimonious effusions and evasive rationalizations offered by self-appointed pundits and critics alike. No shallow conceit, cynical or complacent, can substitute for the mental discernment and spiritual strength required of pathfinders in the Aquarian Age. Rather than sitting in idle judgement upon contemporary history and humanity, wise individuals will seek to insert themselves into the tremendous rethinking initiated by scattered pioneers in regard to the essential core of Man and Nature and the vital relationship between them. If through earnestness, simplicity and *dianoia* one can radically revise one's conception of Nature and Man, then one may powerfully assist that silent revolution and subtle healing taking place today behind the clutter of competing slogans and chaotic events.

As individuals increasingly recognize that the faults which bedevil them lie in themselves and not in the stars, they will progressively discern the Aquarian design woven in the heavens. Through the religion of renunciation of the personal self and the science of Buddhic correlation, one can begin the difficult ascent in consciousness towards comprehension of the mysteries of heaven and earth.

As above, so below. Sidereal phenomena, and the behaviour of the celestial bodies in the heavens, were taken as a model, and the plan was carried out below, on earth. Thus, space, in its abstract sense, was called 'the realm of divine knowledge,' and by the *Chaldees* or Initiates *Ab Soo*, the habitat . . . of knowledge, because it is in space that dwell the intelligent Powers which *invisibly* rule the Universe.

The Secret Doctrine, ii 502

Conceptions of space have varied significantly over the centuries, depending largely upon cognate conceptions of time, matter and energy. The arcane conception of space as at once an infinite void and an invisible plenum, replete with intelligence, offers a profound challenge not only to post-Einsteinian science but also to post-Gandhian religion. It demands an entirely fresh view of causality and consciousness, of activity and time. From the standpoint of contemporary physics, any object, including the human form, is almost entirely empty space devoid of anything that might be considered matter. Even without studying particle physics, perceptive individuals are prepared to accept that if they could visualize what an X-ray would show, they would find that only about one quadrillionth of any object is constituted of a few particles and that all the rest is seemingly empty space. Similarly, if they could visualize what various detectors operating over the visible and invisible spectrum reveal, they would find that every point in space is the intersection of myriad vibrating fields of energy. Again, if one were prepared to penetrate beneath the surface of personal and collective habits and institutions, through the discerning power of the disciplined conscience and awakened intuition, one would find an array of Monadic individuals suspended like stars in the boundless void of the unmanifest. To the resonant heart, this immense void would reveal itself as alive at every point with the vibration of the Great Breath in its complex rhythmic differentiations. Through such reflection one may recognize that the seeming solidity of things is mayavic. Their surfaces and contours as they appear to the physical senses and the perception of the psyche are enormously deceptive and strangely confining. By using the mind's eye one can come to see that what is seemingly full is void and that what is seemingly void is extremely full of Atma-Buddhi-Manasic or noumenal aspects of invisible atoms.

The term 'atom' itself conveys a wide range of meanings in ancient philosophy, including that connotation which has indelibly impressed itself upon the consciousness of the twentieth century. The Greek root of the term 'atom' literally means 'uncuttable', 'indivisible' or 'individual' and corresponds to the Sanskrit term *anu*. In its most metaphysical sense *anu* is the *Aniyamsam Aniyasam*, the smallest of the small, which is also the greatest of the great, equivalent to SPACE and a pointer to *Parabrahm*. In another sense, *anu* is the absolute Motion or eternal vibration of the Great Breath differentiated in the primordial manifested ATOM, equivalent to Brahmā. Neither in the pregenetic or primogenetic states is *anu* subject to multiplication or division. The first plurality of atoms arose with the pristine differentiation of the sevenfold *Dhyani*-energies in the *Mahatattwa* creation, which was in turn followed by further hierarchies of atoms in the succeeding two creations. The meanings of the term 'atom' as applied to the first three creations refer to spiritual and formless realities, including the use of the term to designate Atma-Buddhic monads. Beginning with the fourth, or *mukhya*, creation, sometimes called the *primary creation* because it is the first of a series of four creations connected with material form, the term 'atom' has a new series of meanings pertaining to the germinal centres of the elemental, mineral, plant and animal kingdoms. The term 'atom' used in the customary physical sense applies to the extreme degree of differentiation in this series. Just as the infinite points of differentiated spaces are inseparable from the One Point that is the indivisible sum total of boundless Space, the living atoms of every plane are indivisible from *anu* – the ONE LIFE – and all resound to the fiery vibration of its eternal Motion.

To grasp the noetic significance of the existence of atoms, it is helpful to compare the atom with the molecule. The term 'molecule' literally means 'that which is ponderable or massive', and refers in chemistry to the smallest unit of a substance displaying fixed chemical properties. Typically, molecules are complex compound entities produced and altered through processes of action and reaction. From the standpoint of metachemistry, atomic energies derive from the indivisible unity of the One Life, whilst molecular actions stem from the interplay of vital though secondary emanations. The same facts viewed from the standpoint of meta-psychology lead to the distinction between the noetic action of *Buddhi-Manas*, which draws upon the light of the one indivisible *Atman*, and the psychic action of the lower *Manas*, which is inherently restricted by the polarities of the *kama* principle to residual effects upon the composite mortal vestures. In essence, the difference between atoms and molecules, between noetic and psychic action, is the difference between seeing from within without and seeing only from outside. Hence, people often come closest to the core of things when they shut their sense-organs, which is where concentration and meditation begin.

By withdrawing, closing the eyes, closing the mouth, shutting the ears, by turning off the tumult of the mayavic kaleidoscope of the phenomenal world, one can draw within and enter into what initially seems like chaotic darkness. By persisting, one becomes more familiar with what may be called the photosphere surrounding every human being, the field of light-energies that operates beneath the visible world of form. As one becomes more sensitive to these indwelling energies, one can begin to apprehend that there are vast arrays of intelligent powers which invisibly rule the universe. What people ordinarily call intelligence is only the most superficial and limited aspect of a single distributed intelligence, working through cosmic hierarchies, and originating in a common transcendental source.

Something of the sacred potency and designing power of divine intelligence was broadly familiar to people in the nineteenth century, though in a distorted form due to the inversions of sectarian religion. Given that the impersonal nature of that intelligence can only be comprehended through the noetic faculties consubstantial with that intelligence, it is scarcely surprising that H.P. Blavatsky took such care to provide accounts of cosmogenesis and anthropogenesis free from any taint of the notion of an anthropomorphic creator. It is also suggestive, given the transcendental and *arupa* nature of the intelligence within cyclic evolution, that she so firmly repudiated the materialist conception of a blind, chemically-driven evolution. What was perhaps not so clear in the nineteenth century was her profound reason for pointing to the essential distinction between the atomic and molecular character of noetic and psychic action.

Humanity now finds itself at a fortunate moment; much of what is happening in the sciences is reminiscent of what was once called Hermetic wisdom. If one reads any first-rate book on the frontiers of science, one is at times encountering the threshold of Gupta Vidya. As H.P. Blavatsky prophesied, physics and chemistry have begun to penetrate the realm of atomic vibrations underlying the gross physical design of objects, and have partially revealed the complex matrix of differentiations of the ATOM, as they apply to the lowest planes. Whilst these sciences have not yet moved closer towards the metaphysically indivisible ATOM, they have clearly demonstrated that all physical structure is the superficial derivative of more fundamental differentiations. Although much of the systematic elaboration of these scientific insights has taken place since the commencement of the Aquarian Age in 1902, the critical moves were already made between 1895 and 1902, when there was a crucial intersection of cycles involving the close of the first five thousand years of Kali Yuga and the six-hundred-year cycle inaugurated by Tsong-Kha-Pa, as well as the zodiacal transition.

Towards the close of the nineteenth century, chemistry and physics found themselves up against myriad dead ends. Drawing upon Dalton's hypothesis of units of chemical type distinguishable by weight called atoms (1803), and Avogadro's hypothesis that standard volumes of gases of different compounds contain equal numbers of molecules (1811), chemistry was engaged in filling in the periodic table of the elements proposed by Mendeleev (1869).

Having mastered the arts of ballistics and bridge-building, physics was winding down the practical elaboration of Oersted's discovery of the relation between electricity and magnetism (1819), and its elegant mathematical formulation in the electromagnetic field theory of light-waves developed by Maxwell (1861). Late in the century a noted lecturer even assured the British Association that physics was a closed and completed field, and that young men ought to go elsewhere to find challenging careers. All of this changed abruptly in 1895, when Roentgen discovered an entirely unaccountable type of radiant energy, the enigmatic X-rays. In 1896 Becquerel was able to localize this internal fire of matter to the substance uranium, which was then called 'radioactive'. Following some researches of Crookes, Thomson discovered the 'electron' in 1897, the unit charge of electricity, a genuine fohatic entity on the physical plane. In 1898, the same year that the Curies discovered the existence and radioactivity of radium, Rutherford was able to identify two of the fohatic messengers of radioactivity – alpha particles and beta particles – the latter turning out to be identical with Thomson's electrons. In 1899 the Curies made the fateful discovery that radioactivity could be artificially induced. Pursuing quite different lines of thought, Planck proposed in 1900 that all physical change takes place via discrete units or quanta of action. In 1902 Rutherford and Soddy developed the modern alchemical hypothesis that radioactivity was both the result and the cause of the transmutation of atoms from one chemical element to another.

Drawing upon these critical discoveries and insights, the entire face of the sciences has been transformed in the first decades of the Aquarian Age, and the new alchemists have had more than a little impact upon society. In 1905 an unknown Swiss patent clerk wrote a series of articles synthesizing the discoveries of the time with such remarkable breadth, clarity and force that his name has become virtually synonymous with the atomic age. Within twelve months Albert Einstein demonstrated several revolutionary propositions.

First of all, he showed that all electromagnetic radiations, including light, were composed of packets or quanta of energy, or 'photons', thus resolving the nineteenth century wave-particle debate about the nature of light. This proposal corresponds to the principle that *Buddhi*, the light of the *Atman*, is both indiscrete in relation to the eternal motion of the Great Breath and discrete in relation to the mayavic field of vibratory Monadic emanations.

Secondly, he showed that physical energy and mass are mutually equivalent and interconvertible through a parametric matrix defined by the velocity of physical light. This corresponds to the occult axiom that spirit and matter constitute a double stream starting from the neutral centre of Being as *Daiviprakriti*, the Light of the Logos.

Thirdly, he showed that all physical measurements of distance, speed and time undertaken by observers moving relative to each other are transformed through a parametric conversion matrix defined by the velocity of physical light when passing from the frame of reference of one observer to that of another. This proposal, which put to rest the search for a crude material aether by joining light to the metric foundations of all physical phenomena, has its occult correspondence in the triadic unity of pre-cosmic Space, Motion and Duration on the plane of *Aether-Akasha*, mirrored in all relations and phenomena on the lower planes.

Fourthly, he showed the equivalence of the long-observed Brownian motion of small particles with a set of statistical laws of motion of molecules and atoms he derived from thermodynamics, thus developing the basis of the first empirical confirmation of the physical existence of atoms and molecules. This proposal, ending the nineteenth century career of atoms and molecules as merely rationalistic entified abstractions, has occult correspondences to the principles of distributive and collective Karma.

Since 1905 there has been a virtual explosion in the sciences, as successive dimensions and orders of microcosmic and macrocosmic nature have been explored. In 1911 Rutherford discovered the nuclear structure of physical atoms, in 1913 Bohr proposed the quantum theory governing that structure, and in 1913 and 1914, respectively, Soddy and Moseley re-wrote the periodic table of the elements in terms of modern atomic theory, thus resuscitating the entire field of chemistry. In 1915 Einstein himself proposed an as yet controversial, and only partially elaborated or confirmed, theoretical synthesis of space, duration, motion and force. This line of enquiry, if perfected, would correspond to the occult correlation of the differentiations of Fohat as it "scatters the Atoms" on the plane of *Aether-Akasha*. In 1927 Heisenberg formulated the 'uncertainty principle' concerning the limits of observation of location and motion, a principle which is gradually compelling scientists to include consciousness in their theories of atomic and subatomic physical nature. By 1953 the labours of many biochemists culminated in the work of Crick and Watson, revealing the double helix of DNA, thus joining atomic and molecular theory to the design of living forms.

Whilst the dawn of the Aquarian Age is as yet far from witnessing the emergence of a complete scientific theory integrating the One Life and the primordial ATOM with myriad lives and atoms on seven planes, it has certainly relinquished the stolid, compartmentalized conceptions of the late Piscean Age. People have now become far more aware that the invisible universe is an extremely intelligent universe; someone well trained in contemporary science is much more aware of the spiritual than those caught up in sectarian religion. Sectarians are often weak in theory owing to their weak wills in practice, and often are merely in search of alibis. But those who deeply ponder upon the cosmos with the aid of physics, biology and chemistry, and who show some philosophical or metaphysical imagination, can readily accommodate the idea that behind the sloganistic term 'vibes' is an exact knowledge governed by precise laws. Given this holistic standpoint, what is the necessary connection between directing these forces and that true obedience to Nature envisaged by the Gupta Vidya? This question became ominous and acute for human society on January 22, 1939, because on that day the uranium atom was split by Hahn and Strassman. Significantly, on the same day in 1561 Francis Bacon, one of the forefathers of modern science, was born.

Bacon's vital insight that "Knowledge is power" echoed the ancient Eastern view that knowledge can liberate men. This perspective made possible the enormous adventure of modern science and the correlative spread of universal education. Before Bacon, despite Renaissance affirmations of the dignity of man, few people were able to read or write. Even the Bible was a closed book to human beings who lacked sufficient knowledge of the language to appreciate religious texts. In the Elizabethan Age, at the turn of the sixteenth century, people had to look to Nature for learning; hence the Shakespearean affirmation that there are "books in the running brooks, sermons in stones," and hence, too, his reference to "the book and volume of my brain." Like the Renaissance, Shakespeare recognized the old Pythagorean and Hermetic conception of man as a microcosm of the macrocosm. If one studies the Elizabethan world, especially in E.M. Tillyard's enthralling book, one finds an extraordinary collection of reincarnated Pythagoreans inhabiting and regenerating a society in which it was the most natural thing to draw from the many great metaphors of the Mahatmic Sage of Samos.

Troilus and Cressida, in one of the most inspired passages Shakespeare ever penned, portrays the Pythagorean conception of cosmic hierarchies and their continual relevance to human society. Speaking of the precise degree and placement of everything in Nature, Ulysses affirms that each thing has a function, which stands in relation to that which is above it, that which is beyond it, that which is below it, and that which is beside it.

> The heavens themselves, the planets, and this centre
> Observe degree, priority, and place,
> Insisture, course, proportion, season, form,
> Office, and custom, in all line of order;
> And therefore is the glorious planet Sol
> In noble eminence enthron'd and spher'd
> Amidst the other; whose med'cinable eye
> Corrects the ill aspects of planets evil,

And posts, like the commandment of a king,
Sans check to good and bad. But when the planets
In evil mixture to disorder wander,
What plagues and what portents, what mutiny!
What raging of the sea, shaking of earth!
Commotion in the winds! frights, changes, horrors,
Divert and crack, rend and deracinate
The unity and married calm of states
Quite from their fixture! O, when degree is shak'd,
Which is the ladder of all high designs,
The enterprise is sick. How could communities,
Degrees in schools, and brotherhoods in cities,
Peaceful commerce from dividable shores,
The primogenitive and due of birth,
Prerogative of age, crowns, sceptres, laurels,
But by degree, stand in authentic place?

Troilus and Cressida, Act I, Scene iii

This was also the time of the great seafaring adventurers of Europe, with rich memories of Marco Polo's fascinating stories about customs and cultures prevalent in different parts of the Eastern world. It was truly a period of considerable excitement and curiosity about the cultures of humanity and the vast unknown potential and mystery of Nature itself. By the seventeenth century the alchemical and Rosicrucian traditions of mysticism and magic had laid the basis for what is now called modern technology, with its manifold implications in the social, economic and political arenas. The leading scientists of the nineteenth century showed a keen interest in patterns in Nature, and in the connections between them. For it is only by making connections between otherwise isolated and disparate events, and by discerning patterns, that synthesized conceptions of natural order may be developed. Creative individuals tend to think in terms of wholes, in terms of integrated and patterned arrangements of parts. Such holistic thinking is important to painters and poets and spontaneous amongst little children. But it is also central to the acquisition of that knowledge of Nature which, Bacon declared, is equivalent to power. Because the capacity to discern the patterns of Nature is the prerequisite for enlisting the forces of Nature on behalf of human designs, there is an inevitable moral component in every acquisition and use of knowledge. Bacon, a mysterious man, acknowledged this when he said, "We cannot command Nature except by obeying her."

In effect he showed a concern that there was already a certain presumption towards Nature which would later turn out to be exceedingly costly. Men were seeing Nature in terms of the outmoded conceptions of the Christian church, going back to Augustine and Aquinas, as something dead, inert and wholly apart from the soul. By the eighteenth century, many associated Nature with the chaotic wilderness, and displayed a cultural preference for horticultural hybrids, hothouse growths and elaborate gardens designed by man. It is true that there can be a great beauty in gardens, particularly those of Chinese and Japanese design, wherein beauty and tranquillity are created by the simplest arrangement of stones and plants. Yet, this need not involve despising Nature. And if people in the eighteenth century came to dislike the wilderness because they were frightened by the ghosts and goblins they encountered on the Yorkshire moors, this can hardly excuse the terrible exploitation and desecration of Nature in the nineteenth and twentieth centuries in support of industrialism and technology. This is precisely the hubris of Thrasymachus, in *The Republic* of Plato, criticized by Socrates as showing an inferior intelligence and character, a missing sense of proportion, and an ultimately self-divisive and self-destructive vanity. This Atlantean obsession with the will to dominate completely inverts the principles of proportion, degree and design that govern the evolution of the organic vestures which human beings presently inhabit.

If human beings would prove themselves worthy of the divine apprehension and intelligence within themselves, they must learn to design not merely gardens, but societies and cultures which observe and obey divine proportion and degree. They must learn to awaken and apply the noetic intuitive faculty to the arrangement and rearrangement of communities considering the relationships of individuals not only with each other, but also with empty space. By synthesizing their awakening Buddhic intelligence with the universal intelligence of the One Life, they must learn to cherish the intimations of infinite possibilities contained within the minutest elements of space. Following the Pythagorean conception of the ether as some sort of fluidic substance involved in vortical motion and filled with whirling bubble-like spheres equivalent to atoms, they must come to see that the mathematical laws governing the arrangement of atoms in living forms are the expression of Divine Thought mirroring unmanifest Harmony or R*ta*.

It is not possible to perceive a seemingly opaque world of form as a transparent and luminous manifestation of the One Life without arousing the noetic faculty. Furthermore, it is not possible to awaken the noetic faculty without learning to command the elements of the kingdoms below the fourth plane and without gaining joyous obedience to the Divine Will. It is this combination of self-command and self-obedience which Socrates characterized as *sophrosyne,* the self-government of the soul by its superior element coupled with the consent of the inferior element. It is also the basis of preparation for discipleship and entry into the Path leading towards Initiation. It is also equivalent to the Gandhian conception of *swaraj* or self-rule based upon *swadeshi* or self-reliance, which is sought by the devotee of *satya* in his experiments with truth on behalf of universal welfare or *Lokasangraha.*

If only because human beings have now learnt that there is enough physical energy present in a toothpick to produce twenty-five million kilowatt-hours of electricity, they have reached a point in evolution where they must gain *swaraj* through experiments in the use of soul-force and moral power if they are not to forfeit the divine estate of being truly human. Gandhi's soul-force is equivalent to the atomic noetic force of *Buddhi,* and his idea of moral power is equivalent to the psychic or molecular force of *prana,* moral perception and vital energy. Gandhi demonstrated and taught the possibility of noetic force using psychic force on behalf of human brotherhood and universal welfare. As more and more people come to see that selfishness, invariably rooted in the dissociation of human vital energy from its origins in the Great Breath, is inevitably suicidal, they also begin to recognize that it is only through noetic self-command that there can be genuine self-respect. If they are perceptive, they will readily recognize that the perils and crises of the atomic age are a physical parable of a meta-psychological crisis. As the current of the Aquarian Age compels people to turn inward, the idea is spreading that it is not merely by changing the external environment, or by protesting what other people are doing, that a genuine improvement can be gained in collective human life. As Gandhi taught, the peril of our time arises from the abuse, misuse and neglect of soul-force. In Pythagorean terms, the evolutionary degree, and hence the authentic basis of self-respect, for each soul is to be found in the totality of its intentional relations with the entirety of Nature, both manifest and unmanifest.

The science of spirituality and the religion of responsibility are rooted in the metaphysics of the universe, and therefore have the complete support of cosmic will and design. Hence *The Voice of the Silence* instructs all those who would set themselves upon a secure foundation: "Give up thy life, if thou would'st live." Without a total renunciation of what one hitherto called living – which is really drifting in some sort of psychic daydream – one cannot cultivate the heightened spiritual attention and awareness needed for adequate participation in the Aquarian civilization of the future. The Gupta Vidya affirms that it is possible for human beings to cooperate with the invisible world self-consciously and to find meaning and dignity through obedience to the Law of Karma, obedience to the Will of the Spirit, obeisance to the Divine Order, obedience to the Logos in the cosmos and the God in man. The test of integrity in this inward search is effortless lightness and joyous control.

In the Aquarian communities and secular monastic ashrams of the future, it will be possible by design to have both free play and also continuous recognition of the evolving patterns and possibilities of Nature. Emancipation from the tyranny of habit and the conscious insertion of spiritual will into one's life will enable men and women to take full advantage of the invisible elements within space, within their own rooms, their brains, their hearts, but also throughout the entire plenum of Nature. As they gain a sense of themselves as trustees of a mysterious set of living vestures composed of visible and invisible atoms and nourished by Nature's generous gift of the life-giving waters of wisdom, then, through gratitude, individuals will become more humane, and more worthy of the Aquarian design of *Civitas Humanum*, the City of Man.

THE AQUARIAN ELIXIR

SOMA *is the moon astronomically; but in mystical phraseology, it is also the name of the sacred beverage drunk by the Brahmins and the Initiates during their mysteries and sacrificial rites. The 'Soma' plant is the* asclepias acida, *which yields a juice from which that mystic beverage, the* Soma *drink, is made. Alone the descendants of the Rishis, the* Agnihotri *(the fire priests) of the great mysteries knew all its powers. But the real property of the* true Soma *was (and is) to make a new* man *of the Initiate, after he is* reborn, *namely once that he begins to live in his* astral *body . . . for, his spiritual nature overcoming the physical, he would soon snap it off and part even from that etherealized form.*

The Secret Doctrine, ii 498-499

In order to tap the vast potential of soul-wisdom in any single epoch of human evolution, it is vital to retain a reverential standpoint towards the known and the unknown, as well as towards That which is inherently Unknowable. At all times human beings seem to be surrounded by clusters of familiar objects and inexplicable events. Yet, with a minimal degree of introspection, individuals may discern that their mundane experience is largely conditioned by habitual states of consciousness. If they remain sensitive to the ebb and flow of the tides of earthly existence, yet aware of the strange illusion of temporal succession, they may ardently seek to reach beyond conventional norms of logic and morality so as to establish a firm foundation for cognition and conduct. Within the limits of every epoch, individuals foster an ideal image of themselves and formulate diverse strategies for the attainment of goals in different sectors of human life. Depending upon the clarity and care with which the ideal of excellence is pursued, it can exercise a civilizing influence upon individuals, cultures and societies. Whilst much of human striving and motivation may be comprehended within the scope of dominant civilizations and their goals, a more fundamental perspective is needed to understand the rise and fall of long-lived cultures.

The intuitive seeker of Gupta Vidya turns to the cryptic teaching of cyclic evolution, suspended between the impenetrable mystery of *Parabrahm* and the pivotal laws of karma and reincarnation. Affirming the immeasurable ontological abundance of TAT in the infinitudes of space and the triple hypostases of the *Atman* as the universal basis of harmonious manifestation, Gupta Vidya portrays cyclic evolution as encompassing incremental degrees of self-knowledge and self-regeneration, and at the same time affording illimitable refinement in the noetic apprehension of cosmic order and justice. In practice this means that the elements of mystery and discipline – wisdom and method, symbolized by the Tibetan bell and *dorje* – are correlative components of human growth and experience. No single testament of wisdom can embrace the exhaustless potential of TAT. And yet, not even a glimmering of spiritual insight is without value in the pursuit of universal good. Each successive phase of manifest existence, whether of individual Monads or of the entire human race, is new and unprecedented in a Heraclitean sense. Yet, every unfolding moment epitomizes the vast sum-total of the past, is replete with the rich potential of the future, and evanescently bubbles upon the infinite ocean of eternity.

When probing the meaning and significance of the Aquarian Age or any of the major and minor cycles of human evolution, it is helpful to retain a sense of mystery as well as an undaunted resolve to sift essential insights gleaned through an alert Manasic intelligence, whilst shedding vested illusions. The potential mystery pervading the present epoch is archetypally represented by *soma,* and the formative forces of the emerging cosmopolis may be glimpsed through contemplating the zodiacal transition from the Piscean to the Aquarian Age. *Soma* is the arcane symbol of initiation. The zodiacal ages indicate the alchemical transmutation of the meta-psychological elements underlying formative change. If initiation is to be understood as individuation through the universalization of consciousness, it must also be retained intact with increasing continuity of consciousness through the etherealization and specialization of the vestures needed for effective incarnation.

The alchemical significance of these interrelated processes was suggested by H.P. Blavatsky in her gnostic interpretation of the cosmogonic myths of Chaldea, Egypt, Greece and, above all, India. Each points to the physico-chemical principle of primordial creation:

> The first revelation of the Supreme Cause in its triple manifestation of spirit, force, and matter; the divine *correlation,* at its starting-point of evolution, allegorized as the marriage of *fire* and water, products of electrifying spirit, union of the male active principle with the female passive element, which become the parents of their tellurian child, cosmic matter, the *prima materia,* whose spirit is ether, the ASTRAL LIGHT!
>
> *Isis Unveiled*, i 156

Shiva, as Dakshinamurti, the Hierophant of Hierophants, descends from the empyrean in a pillar of fire, and remains aloof and invulnerable like the world-mountain Meru, an allegorical representation of primal cosmogony.

> Within the mysterious recesses of the mountain – the matrix of the universe – the gods (powers) prepare the atomic germs of organic life, and at the same time the life-drink, which, when tasted, awakens in man-matter the man *spirit*. The *soma*, the sacrificial drink of the Hindus, is that sacred beverage. For, at the creation of the *prima materia*, while the grossest portions of it were used for the physical embryo-world, the more divine essence of it pervaded the universe, invisibly permeating and enclosing within its ethereal waves the newly-born infant, developing and stimulating it to activity as it slowly evolved out of the eternal chaos.
>
> *Isis Unveiled*, i 157

Like the swans who separate milk from water, seekers of Gupta Vidya must learn to distil the divine *Akashic* essence out of the matrix of organic elements. The process of distillation takes place within the alembic of noetic consciousness and the secret sanctuary in the temple of the human form, not in any terrestrial location.

A genuine understanding of the awakening of the "man spirit" could begin with a calm consideration of the extraordinary commencement of human activity on this globe over eighteen million years ago. At the time of the initial lighting up of Manasic self-consciousness, there was an awakening of the potent fires of self-knowledge in all human beings. This sacred heritage has enabled the immortal soul to maintain intact its sutratmic thread throughout myriads of lives upon earth. It is the continuity of this spiritual thread that enables individuals to learn and recollect in any lifetime. None of the facile theories of behavioural conditioning or social imitation can account for the elusive mystery inherent in the infant's learning of a language. Still less can they satisfactorily explain xenoglossy. Many little children spontaneously speak ancient and forgotten tongues, including those which are not even found in exhaustive glossaries of modern languages.

Dr. Ian Stevenson, in his fascinating study of xenoglossy, has investigated a number of such cases, including that of a child in New York who spoke a language which simply could not be readily identified, but which, on detailed investigation, was found to be a long unspoken tongue from Central Asia. Similarly, in other studies concerning what often seem to be the nonsensical sounds of babies, it has been shown that what looked like nonsense had a definite meaning. Not only are there significant patterns in the sounds made by infants all over the world, but there are also recurrent features in a wide variety of children's games, which often seem simple, but are often more complex than adult sports. The significance of all such evidence for a universal grammar independent of cultures is sharpened by consideration of the work of Noam Chomsky in philosophic linguistics. Chomsky has effectively shown that there is no sound evidence to suggest that in learning the alphabet children are actually being conditioned from the outside. Rather, it seems as if there is a kind of innate response to sounds on the part of infants.

The learning of language essentially provides a telling example of how children bring back memories from other lives. More broadly, all knowledge is recollection in a Socratic sense. In alchemical terms, the signature of language is found in the Soul, and the sigils are learnt in childhood.

The relationship between sutratmic continuity and present learning is likely to remain obscure unless one is ready to probe deeply into the simplest things of life. For example, whilst it may seem easy to learn to walk, anyone who has ever made the effort to teach a cat or dog to walk on two legs would soon discover that it is exceedingly difficult. Circus trainers are able to get four-legged animals to walk like two-legged human beings for short lengths of time. With proper stimuli they can produce predictable responses. But these patterned responses are quite different from the intrinsic Manasic ability of children to hold their heads and spines erect and to be able to function as self-moving beings. The Socratic conception of the *psuche* as a self-moving agent, together with the Platonic idea of *nous* as the matter-moving mind, points to the initiatory potential inherent within every human being. Whenever an individual makes a new beginning, initiating a considered line of activity during a day, a week, a month or a year, such a commencement could signify the start of a new phase of learning. Whether one takes as the starting-point of such an endeavour one's birthday or any other cyclic reference-point in life, one is recognizing the permanent possibility for all individuals of making fresh ventures into the unknown. Ordinarily, human beings are protected by not knowing too much about their previous lives or knowing too much even about the immediate future of this one. Since individuals learn to live in ignorance of the unknown, and at the same time venture on the basis of what they do know, clearly there is an indestructible element in every immortal soul which enables a human being again and again to make a fresh start. This permanent element is not simply the *Atma-Buddhi* or Divine Monad, but also the distilled and assimilated wisdom of past lives gathered in the *sutratman,* the repository of the fragrant aroma of past learning.

If every human being brings this precious inheritance of prior efforts towards individuation into the present life, and if all have passed through several initiations in distant lives, what relevance does this have to the onset of the Aquarian Age? Commencing on June 19, 1902, and having completed its first degree, the Aquarian Age has already brought about an unprecedented heightening of self-consciousness, and it holds a tremendous potential for the future. Something of the fundamental significance of the Aquarian Age can be glimpsed by recollecting that the year 1902 was not unconnected with the increasing concern to fly in the air. In the nineteenth century, on the other hand, the ocean was the common term of reference for many people in regard to travel, exploration and geopolitics. If people in the last century took many of their analogies and metaphors from the nautical world, this was because they had such an impressive collection of imposing sailing ships and modern steamships. In Greenwich and in Plymouth, from Cathay to Cape Horn, the romance and excitement of the pioneering exploration of the world's oceans fired the imagination of adults and children alike. Beginning in the sixteenth century, the rapid expansion of sea trade lay at the basis of the commercial and cultural growth of European civilization. By the close of the Victorian Age, the idea of a maritime civilization had become crystallized in the minds of such writers as Mahan and Fisher and consolidated the image of a globe governed by sea power. The construction of large ocean liners capable of sailing thousands of miles at considerable rates of speed provided ordinary people with basic metaphors concerning the conduct of life. The exacting skills needed in navigation received an attention reminiscent of older conceptions in literature and myth, viewing man as the captain of his soul. Yet now, in the twentieth century, with the vast elaboration upon what the Wright Brothers began, there is a fundamentally new outlook that has emerged with reference to the atmosphere surrounding the earth.

Even early in the century, artists and visionaries were stimulated by grand, if sometimes fanciful, conceptions of what the implications of flight could mean to human beings in general. By the time of the First World War, shrewd politicians like Winston Churchill perceived with almost prophetic clarity the significant change in the balance of power brought about by the airplane and the appalling dangers that this new capacity could unleash. For most people, despite pioneering efforts by individuals and businesses, it was not until after the Second World War that they were able on a large scale to travel by air. Then suddenly they experienced what otherwise could only have been done by climbing mountains – they gained some sense of what it is like at different elevations. In the past few decades this upward ascent has passed beyond the proximate atmosphere of the earth, reaching into the empyrean of space. Tapping the theoretical insights of a few and drawing upon the cooperative labours of specialized teams of scientists and engineers, a small coterie of intrepid individuals has travelled into space and brought back beautiful images of the earth as a shining gem suspended in the void. Spacecraft with intricate instruments have ventured towards Mercury, Venus, Mars, Jupiter and Saturn, linked to earth only by the finest etheric threads of electrical impulse, and returning copious information regarding long-recognized globes in our solar system.

Broadly, the Aquarian Age is typified by the concept of vertical ascent, whereas during the nineteenth century and before, the idea of horizontal movement was far more prevalent. This is not to minimize the importance of the great circumnavigations of the globe conducted in the maritime era, nor to discount the considerable knowledge gained by daring explorers and naturalists in regard to diverse forms of life. At their best, the nineteenth century naturalists discovered valuable principles of continuity in living form and developed significant intuitions into the geometry of dynamic growth. But now, in the twentieth century, principally because of air travel, people are much more conscious of the enormous relevance of factors such as altitude and atmosphere in relation to the elevation of consciousness. Through the beneficent invention of pressurized cabins, vast numbers of people have had the opportunity to observe that the earth does not seem the same when seen from an airplane as it does when seen on the plains.

All of this merely suggests that there has been a vital change taking place in human consciousness progressively over the last eighty years. From a merely empirical standpoint the entry of human beings into the airy regions is conclusive of nothing. From the standpoint of the Gupta Vidya, however, these outward changes are emblematic of the shift in the fundamental perspective of human experience. The nature and significance of this change cannot be comprehended through conventional and pseudo-rationalistic schemes of popular astrology. Caught up in erratic frameworks and outdated calculations, most astrologers are no more aware of the true meaning of the Aquarian Age than the average person. Few, if any, have deeply reflected upon the precession of the equinoxes, or upon the essential differences between the Taurean, Piscean and Aquarian Ages. Nonetheless, an increasingly large number of individuals have begun to sense a new awakening of human consciousness. Whether they interpret this from a purely personal standpoint, or connect it to some form of. secular or sectarian millennial thinking, they can discern that a fundamental change is taking place in the global atmosphere of human life. Some who are sensitive see this in terms of a subtle beauty and alteration in the atmosphere of the earth itself, whilst those who are more perceptive detect a similar change in the atmosphere that surrounds each human being. In general, there is a growing recognition and widespread acknowledgement of a fresh opportunity for human souls at the present time of metamorphosis. Such glimmerings provide an array of opportunities which bring with them fresh avenues for awakening and growth.

Philosophically, all awakening is self-awakening. Self-consciousness represents an extraordinary privilege as well as a burden. It is a privilege because it brings with it the ability to choose, and through choices to comprehend connections between causes and consequences. It is a burden because it also brings with it the obligation to act in harmony with one's most fundamental perceptions. It is not possible to prove oneself worthy of the privilege of self-awakening through fulfillment of obligations and commitments without strengthening a practical sense of self-transcendence through contemplation and meditation. Whilst the Aquarian Age has already seen a surfeit of schemes for meditation which appeal to the suggestibility and gullibility of people who think that they can get something for nothing, the authentic and therapeutic teaching with regard to the true nature of contemplation is now available to more human beings than ever before. In their essentials, meditation and contemplation are neither episodic nor dependent upon any technique. Rather, they require the unremitting watchfulness of the mind and heart for the sake of restoration of purity of consciousness.

It is only through purity of thought, word and deed that the inexpressible yearning of the inner man for the infinite can find the fulfillment of its aspiration. It is only through the perfected continuity of the will, incessantly striving towards the highest ideal of divine manhood, that spiritual awakening through meditation can take place. There can be no increment of individuation or continuity of consciousness through any form of passivity. To give focus to aspiration, as *The Voice of the Silence* teaches, the mind needs breadth and depth and points to draw it towards the Diamond Soul. For example, one could take the Four Golden Links – Universal Unity and Causation, Human Solidarity, Karma and Reincarnation – as axiomatic starting-points for meditation. Beginning with an intellectual comprehension of these universal axioms, and deriving deductive inferences regarding particulars, a preliminary grasp of the true aim of meditation must be gained. Then, having worked out some tentative conception of the scheme of causes and effects to be comprehended, it is possible to pass inductively and intuitively from a contemplation of the known phenomena of the world of effects to the as yet unknown causes in the noumenal and unmanifest realm. Thus constructing and using a Jacob's Ladder of ideation, an individual can insert himself or herself into the evolutionary programme and explore the opportunities that it offers to the entire globe. It is the prospect and promise of this inward ascent in consciousness that so many people dimly feel, and which makes them sense the privilege of being alive at a critical moment in human evolution.

This inward ascent towards self-awakening consciousness is inconceivable apart from the acquisition of freedom of movement in and through the vestures. To move the centre of one's consciousness from a plane of relatively gross effects to a relatively subtle plane of causes implies a gradual transfer from a more gross to a more ethereal body. To learn to live in the physical world, but not be of it, is in effect to begin to live in the purified astral body. This means that anyone who genuinely begins to participate in a life of meditation and contemplation becomes, in an anticipatory mode, a partaker of *soma*. As H.P. Blavatsky suggested:

> The partaker of *Soma* finds himself both linked to his external body, and yet away from it in his spiritual form. The latter, freed from the former, soars for the time being in the ethereal higher regions, becoming virtually 'as one of the gods,' and yet preserving in his physical brain the memory of what he sees and learns. Plainly speaking, *Soma* is the fruit of the Tree of Knowledge forbidden by the jealous Elohim to Adam and Eve or *Yah-ve*, 'lest Man should become as one of us'.

The Secret Doctrine, ii 499

All human beings sense at times that the physical body cannot be seen merely as something restricted to the familiar plane of sense-perceptions. Though many may not be much aware of what is going on within the body, and though they may not understand too much about the blood and the cells, about the empty chambers of the brain and the heart, most do recognize that by the simple act of breathing it is possible to direct the physical body. Anyone who has engaged in extreme physical exertion and discipline over a period of seven years, perhaps as a runner or a dancer, will have experienced a distinct alteration in the range and rhythms of consciousness. Though this may be intolerably arduous for most people, almost every person is somewhat aware of the tangible ways in which the use of the physical body impinges upon his or her perception of the world. Every point in the physical form, each life-atom, is shot through and through with reflected *Mahabuddhi,* the latent power of self-consciousness.

The entire cosmos is intensely alive and there is intelligence in every point of space. There is not a single speck of space which is not ensouled by the light of universal intelligence. In the kingdoms below man this intelligence works without the self-conscious direction associated with the human kingdom. Thus, in those kingdoms, intelligence works precisely because of the cosmic hierarchies which act collectively and not individually. The world below the mineral kingdom is therefore understood as a realm of elementals, of *devas* and *devatas,* wherein there are myriads upon myriads of entities, hosts of life-atoms which work in perfect concert. Just as when human beings attend a concert and hear a majestic symphony, and come together to participate in the music, in a similar manner there is a complex symphonic harmonizing of nature in all its kingdoms. Whether one considers fire, air, earth or water, there is a continual expression of the intricate intelligence of nature. Some people have a child-like interest in sea shells and pine-cones, in seeds and acorns, because they can recognize in them the complex and mysterious intelligence of living Nature, which fills every point in the cosmos with burgeoning life and creativity.

Universal intelligence has attained a high degree of self-awareness in human beings. It is indeed possible for the human mind through meditation to gain eventually that degree of development, intimated in *The Voice of the Silence,* where one can slay one's lunar form at will. It is possible to gain continuity of consciousness through the night and through the three states of consciousness – *jagrat, swapna* and *sushupti.* One can gain an inkling of the *turiya* state of spiritual freedom from captivity to the three *gunas* – *sattva, rajas* and *tamas.* It is thus possible to alter the polarity of the *linga sharira,* the astral form. This is done by breaking up the clusters of elementals impressed with grosser or weaker types of life-energies and given a particular colouring and a certain tonality over a lifetime of habits. In order to cease from drifting as a victim and creature of habit, and in order to be able to rearrange the life-atoms of the subtle vestures, one must engage in an intimate and practical study of the astral body. Because the astral form is sevenfold, it is helpful to do this in terms of the number 7. Over a week of seven days, over seven weeks, over seven months or seven years, one could attempt to make some discoveries about the relative proportions of *sattva, rajas* and *tamas* in the life-atoms of the vestures. And, because there are four elements, excluding the synthesizing ether, it is also pertinent to consider the four quarters of the day, the four phases of the moon, and the four seasons of the year.

When one really begins to undertake such a study, it gradually becomes possible to comprehend the extraordinary relevance of the injunction to gain the power to slay the lunar form at will. Many enigmatic statements in *The Voice of the Silence* are practical instructions to the Lanoo which also could be taken as guidance for ethical experiments in the laboratory of the human temple. By treating the body as a temple and also as a laboratory for the making of judicious experiments through the powers of ideation and imagination, much can be discovered in reference to the different principles. In this way one can, from small beginnings, venture towards the sort of exacting discipline which ultimately leads to the complete awakening of conscious immortality during incarnated existence.

Those who would master meditation and contemplation and enter into the Path that leads towards initiation must ponder the profound meaning of the War in Heaven, the relentless strife between the sons of God and the sons of the Shadow of the Fourth and Fifth Races. This war must not be viewed as some distant event in the earlier stages of human evolution, but rather should be seen as a karmic heirloom, a living memory, affecting the spiritual striving of every human being on earth. It is to the *asuras* that spiritual humanity owes its most fundamental allegiance. They were born from the breath – *Asu* – of Brahmā-Prajāpati. It is only through the perverse inversion perpetrated by the enemies of Divine Wisdom that they came to be called *a-suras* or no-gods. In the oldest portions of the *Rig Veda* the *asuras* are the spiritual and the divine ancestors of Manasic humanity.

> They are the sons of the primeval Creative Breath at the beginning of every new Maha Kalpa, or Manvantara; in the same rank as the Angels who had remained 'faithful'. These *were the allies of Soma* (the parent of the *Esoteric Wisdom)* as against *Brihaspati* (representing ritualistic or *ceremonial* worship). Evidently they have been degraded in Space and Time into opposing powers or demons by the ceremonialists, on account of their rebellion against hypocrisy, sham-worship, and the dead-letter form.
>
> *The Secret Doctrine*, ii 500-501

In the present age, though popular opinion may not readily credit the fact, the allies of Brihaspati persist as the enemies of the allies of *soma*. The proponents of superstition, ceremonialism, hypocrisy and sham await the unwary pilgrim who is too weak-willed, vain or sentimentally naïve to acknowledge his or her own complacent ignorance of the occult world. Wallowing in the mire of seemingly self-devised exoteric ritual, he or she who does not know what it is to live in the world, and yet not be of the world, is incapable of guarding Self against self. No matter what pill or potion, fad or fancy, trick or technique, is taken up to mimic the realities of spiritual wisdom, the result is inevitably unconscious enslavement and voluntary degradation. That is why those who have learnt the painful truth regarding the pertinacity of the exoteric or thaumaturgic tendency in human nature, and have begun in earnest the entirely inward work of theurgy, of purifying their motive and volition, remain reticent before such sacred conceptions as *soma,* initiation, the Third Eye and *Kriyashakti.*

Like humble apprentices in a spiritual environmental protection agency, they would rather work to purify their own emanations than risk polluting the astral atmosphere in which others must breathe.

With patience, they can learn to penetrate the external skin of the earth and the palpable skin that covers all objects, discovering how to make a vital difference to states of consciousness through noetic control over ideation and imagination. This is much harder and takes more time and thought than any simple scheme of social amelioration aimed at quick results. But, if one is not afraid of spiritual mountain climbing, even though one's dharma may keep one at a great distance from legendary mountains, then one is willing to get ready one's mental and moral equipment, and also to plant patiently the nourishing seed-ideas that are generously available in the abundant storehouse of Gupta Vidya. By making preliminary experiments with altruistic breathing and abstract meditation, one could begin to see how to work consciously not only with the seasons but also with the days of the week and the different times of the day.

This is the beginning of the path of selfless service and inward ascent towards the realm of Divine Wisdom open to all human beings in the Aquarian Age. It is also the small old path followed by every true ascetic of every age, and presided over by Shiva, the mighty Yogin, the paragon of all the Adepts and the foremost ruler of the divine dynasties, the patron of the Mysteries in the Fifth Root Race. It is the path of unconditional realization of the *Paramatman* and the elixir of *soma,* and the divine discipline taught by Krishna to a long lineage of hierophants and faithful devotees. The *soma* of the Vedas and the Brahmanas was aptly associated with thunder and electricity, purification and speed, brilliance and fertility. *Soma* fills heaven and earth with rays like the sun, dispels darkness, invigorates and impregnates thought and action, heals the sick, stimulates the voice, and exhilarates every limb. *Soma* is the maker of seers, the generator of hymns, the protector of prayer and the soul of sacrifice. Even in the dawn of the Aquarian Age, some forerunners may be entitled to exclaim: "We have drunk *Soma,* we have become immortal, we have entered into light, we have known the gods."

APPENDIX I:

Aquarian Ontology

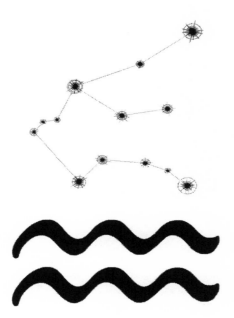

Who, Where, and What Is God?

The Dedication of *The Secret Doctrine* strikes the self-validating keynote of universality:

> This Work I dedicate to all True Theosophists, in every Country, and of every Race, for they called it forth, and for them it was recorded.

In the Preface, the same keynote of universality is strongly stressed. The teachings of Theosophy are not confined to the ancient tetrad comprised by the Hindu, the Zoroastrian, the Chaldean and the Egyptian religions. Nor is it the exclusive possession of the more recent Buddhist, Islamic, Judaic and Christian faiths. The Secret Doctrine is the essence of all these. "Sprung from it in their origins, the various religious schemes are now made to merge back into their original element, out of which every mystery and dogma has grown, developed, and become materialised."

Owing to the fall of all religions through false claims and creedal dogmas, true seekers everywhere today are longing to find the pristine source of Divine Wisdom, pure and unsullied. Naturally, even among such earnest seekers there is the ever-present danger of materialization. This can be minimized through close attention to the critical distinction made in the *Bhagavad Gita* between the external attributes and the immaterial essence of the Self-Governed Sage. Those who have eyes will always be able to see and will also be able to know how to come closer to the Trans-Himalayan Brotherhood, which is not to be found by external means. It has monasteries and schools and systems of initiation in secret sanctuaries which cannot be readily discovered by travel and exploration. Even the individual seeker who is able, by undertaking a pilgrimage, to come closer to the Brotherhood, is led on by the intuition of the heart, by inner guidance, and not by maps or any adventitious aids.

H.P. Blavatsky once stated that a single journey to the East undertaken in the proper spirit will do more than all the books in the world. She herself conducted such a journey but she was intensely concerned with fundamental questions: 'Who, where, and what is God?' 'How can man's spirit prove God's spirit?' These were the burning questions in her heart to which she devoted years of thought and enquiry. Having already had the vision of her Guru, asking these questions, she re-enacted for the sake of the entire human race the archetypal quest for enlightenment. This is part of the ever-renewed sacrifice of every Rishi or Mahatma, or great Teacher. Inquirers who have sought the Brotherhood of Bodhisattvas through external means are easily misled. In the Aquarian Age, especially, no encouragement can be given to people who want some kind of external and verifiable means of speeding their own growth. True spiritual growth is wholly internal, and only its efflorescence may illumine the external world through wisdom in thought, word and deed. This is the fruition of continuous meditation, and therefore one must realize, as many an ancient seeker knew, that the sacred places of pilgrimage correspond to secret centres in the human constitution. For example, Prayag, the meeting-place of rivers, corresponds to a spiritual centre in every human being. The symbolism of a sacred pilgrimage conveys clues to the inner meaning of the teaching, intimating the inward ascent through which a human being comes closer to planes of consciousness involving higher centres within the human vestures. It is possible, through deep meditation, to enter the inmost sanctuary within the tabernacle of Isis, Shekinah, Sarasvati, Kwan Yin, Brahma Vach. An indispensable pre-requisite is true devotion to the *Ishtaguru*.

The Life-Giving Stream, *The Gupta Vidya* II, 29-30

"Who Am I?" "THAT Thou Art."

In sober truth, . . . every 'Spirit' so-called is either a disembodied or a future man. As from the highest Archangel (Dhyan Chohan) down to the last conscious 'Builder' (the inferior class of Spiritual Entities), all such are men, having lived aeons ago, in other Manvantaras, on this or other Spheres; so the inferior, semi-intelligent and non-intelligent Elementals – are all future men. That fact alone – that a Spirit is endowed with intelligence – is a proof to the Occultist that that Being must have been a man, and acquired his knowledge and intelligence throughout the human cycle. There is but one indivisible and absolute Omniscience and Intelligence in the Universe, and this thrills throughout every atom and infinitesimal point of the whole finite Kosmos which hath no bounds, and which people call SPACE, considered independently of anything contained in it.

The Secret Doctrine I, 277

Self-consciousness is the Gordian knot of both philosophical psychology and arcane metaphysics. Its paradoxes can be unravelled only through a discipline that combines sacrificial action and meditation. As the aspirant proceeds along these parallel lines, recondite evolutionary mysteries will reveal themselves to the awakening spiritual sight. Beyond and beneath all of these, present both at the beginning and at the end of the quest, lies the riddle of Being and Non-Being, the crux of the process of infinite perfectibility within eternal divine harmony. Each stage along the way reveals fresh beginnings and tentative illuminations, all revolving around the talismanic question, "Who am I?" and its ever-enigmatic response from the depths of divine consciousness, "*THAT thou art.*" This timeless dialogue between the divine soul and its projected ray is repeated over myriad lives in countless diverse forms. It is the quintessential enquiry of enquiries, comprehending the divine and the mundane while serving as the archetype of every science and every symbolic system. Although this enquiry is perennially and universally relevant, it truly demands an ever-deepening sense of detachment and an ever-expanding feeling of compassion for all humanity. The restoration of the dual sense of individual dignity and human solidarity is a primary object of the Aquarian Age and a necessary prelude to participation in the succeeding age of Makara, of magical creativity.

The development of self-conscious humanity on earth began well over eighteen million years ago, following a much longer period of development during the first three-and-a-half Rounds of the earth chain. Throughout this vast period, successive ethereal hierarchies fashioned the sentient but non-intelligent vestures of future mankind. With each succeeding Round and globe, a different class of Builders evolved out of itself more and more dense shadowy projections. During the early portion of the present Fourth Round, the sixth group or hierarchy, counting downward from spirit, evolved out of itself the filmy astral vestures of the future physical man. The seventh, or lowest, hierarchy then gradually formed and condensed the physical body of animal man upon the ethereal frame. Neither the sixth hierarchy, which is connected with ethereal gods, nor the seventh hierarchy, which is connected with vast numbers of terrestrial spirits or elementals, was capable of completing self-conscious intelligent man. Thus, it became the task of the fifth hierarchy, the mysterious beings that preside over the constellation Makara, to inform the empty and ethereal animal form, creating out of it the rational man. This in itself is an awesome mystery which may be understood only through meditation and, ultimately, initiation.

The Scope of Self-Consciousness, *The Gupta Vidya* I, 274-275

The Dimensionless Cause of Unconditioned Reality

The *Diamond Sutra* teaches that any person can, in principle, see to the core of conditioned reality. He can do this through a clear-sighted recognition of the dimensionless cause of unconditioned reality within himself and everyone else. The jewel is within one's reach; one has to use it. When a person is ready to replace angular views with a rounded vision, he can activate the magnetic sphere of influence around him. At all times human beings, on all planes, either speed up or slow down. They exhibit either restlessness or inertia and cannot move equally in all directions at the same time. As one moves away from homogeneity into the realm of the differentiated, what one man cannot use, another man will appropriate. This applies not only to human beings but to all whirling centres of energy. Nature abhors a vacuum. There is nothing that is wholly unused except on the visible plane, and even this is mayavic. One's whole conception of the world of which one is a part can be profoundly altered. To the unfolding Buddhic perception of a person who is truly awake, the logic of relations in diverse realms of matter and consciousness has nothing to do with those eyes and ears which Heraclitus designated as false witnesses to the soul. If human beings had always trusted to the unreliable reports of their physical sense-organs, there would have been no real knowledge of any kind. It is thanks to the light of intelligence and self-reflection that there is knowledge. Souls that are fully awake radiate the inimitable lustre of the diamond through the magical fusion of wisdom and compassion. Buddha exemplified the sovereign human capacity of voiding the seeming full whilst also showing an unspoken, ever-present sympathy for everything that lives and breathes.

Whenever a person realizes the self-subsisting nature of truth, he enjoys the ineffable freedom which commands the power to see through the eyes of others, with and for them. He finds exhilaration in the expansion of consciousness that encompasses myriad perspectives. A point comes when one can do this not intermittently and by degrees, but ceaselessly by going to the very core, like the sage on a mountain who forgets there is a mountain, who sees no distinctions amidst the plains and between souls, but is replete with cosmic affirmation from what looks like bare negation in a limitless, azure expanse. These are imperfect representations of noumenal realities in the realm of consciousness. Every person has within him or her the possibility of coming closer to the Diamond Soul, the true Self of all. It is transcendent and need not be transfixed one-dimensionally or in as many dimensions as one may count, because it has a solidity and depth inseparable from the void. It is that which constantly rediscovers the voidness of the seeming full – the striking keynote of Buddha – and thereby prepares a person to do that which Krishna taught – to see the fullness of the seeming void. To bring these two archetypal modes together is the noble prospect and the divine destiny of the forerunners of the Aquarian Age. This is a time which spares no illusions or shadows, but which is spacious and fertile in opportunities for such expansion of awareness as may attract credible and sharable representations from the realm of *Akasha* into the free spaces among human beings.

Cognition and Freedom, *The Gupta Vidya* III, 234-235

The Eternal Balance of the
Manifest and the Unmanifest

The true teaching of cyclic causation implies neither a trivialization nor a mechanization of life in a vesture in terrestrial time. Instead, it intimates the mysterious power of harmony, the irresistible force of necessity, which resides in the eternal balance of the manifest and the unmanifest in every living form and phase of the One Life. The ceaseless vibratory motion of the unmanifest Logos is the stimulus of the complex sets and subsets of hierarchies of being constituting the universe; and of the intricate and interlocking cycles and subcycles of events that measure out its existence. The intimate relationship between temporal identity and cyclic existence is symbolized in the identification of the lifetime of Brahmā with the existence of the universe, a teaching which also conveys the true meaning of immortality in *Hiranyagarbha*.

From the standpoint of universal unity and causation, the universe is a virtual image of the eternal motion or vibration of the unmanifest Word, scintillating around a set of points of nodal resonance within that Word itself. From the standpoint of individual beings involved in action, the universe is an aggregation of interlocking periodic processes susceptible to reasoned explanation in terms of laws. Understanding the nature of cycles and what initiates them, together with apprehending the mystery of cyclic causation itself, requires a progressive fusion of these two standpoints. The exalted paradigm of the union of Eternity and Time is *Adhiyajna,* seated near the circle of infinite eternal light and radiating compassionate guidance to all beings who toil in the coils of Time. Established in Boundless Duration, all times past, present and future lie before his eye like an open book. He is Shiva, the Mahayogin, the leader of the hosts of Kumaras, and also Kronos-Saturn, the lord of sidereal time and the ruler of Aquarius. If humanity is the child of cyclic destiny, Shiva is the spur to the spiritual regeneration of humanity. And, if the

Mahatmas and Bodhisattvas, the supreme devotees of Shiva, live to regenerate the world, then it is the sacred privilege and responsibility of those who receive their Teachings to learn to live and breathe for the sake of service to all beings.

It is in this spirit that H.P. Blavatsky, in her essay entitled "The Theory of Cycles", suggested several keys to the interpretation of cyclical phenomena. We can readily discern the vast variety of periodic phenomena which has already been noticed in history, in geology, in meteorology and in virtually every other arena of human experience. We can also recognize the statistical recurrence of certain elements in reference to economics, to wars and peace, to the rise and fall of empires, to epidemics and revolutions, and also to natural cataclysms, periods of extraordinary cold and heat. H.P. Blavatsky's intent was not merely to persuade the reader of the pervasiveness of periodic phenomena through the multiplication of examples, but rather to convey the immanent influence of the power of number and of mathematics within all cyclic phenomena.

Integration and Recurrence, *The Gupta Vidya* III, 156-157

The Zero Principle

> The seven *Laya* centres are the seven Zero points, using the term Zero in the same sense that Chemists do, to indicate a point at which, in Esotericism, the scale of reckoning of differentiation begins. From the Centres – beyond which Esoteric philosophy allows us to perceive the dim metaphysical outlines of the 'Seven Sons' of Life and Light, the Seven Logoi of the Hermetic and all other philosophers – begins the differentiation of the elements which enter into the constitution of our Solar System.
>
> *The Secret Doctrine* I, 138-139

At this level the degrees of plenitude, self-sufficiency and self-regeneration connected with the *laya* principle are so profound that they have no comprehensible analogue within human life. This is the realm of Initiates. Nevertheless, every human being, as an immortal ray of the Central Spiritual Sun, has the opportunity and privilege of meditating upon the idea of Fohat, which is an emanation of the Seven Sons of Light. Whatever plane of self-consciousness a being inhabits, it is always helpful to a group of monads held together by an irresistible ideal and an overarching transcendental vision of the good to come together and strengthen their collective capacity to reduce themselves to zeros in the service of their common ideal. Training in this magical power of transmission is the essential meaning of the Sangha. When people come together, truly forgetting themselves and united by the magnetic attraction of the good, they emulate and serve in some small measure the Teachers of Humanity, the great galaxy of Buddhas and Bodhisattvas.

The highest beings learn to do this ceaselessly, invoking the Fohatic principle which is present potentially at every point in space. Even at the level of ordinary, unenlightened human beings, it is possible to take advantage of the zero principle at some elementary level. The integrity of human nature itself assures that every human being can mirror the transcendental beneficence of the highest beings. Ultimately, all the potentiality of the zero, of *shunyata* or the void, is present throughout the plenum. The void is the plenum. All of Nature stands as an open invitation to every group of human beings to take conscious advantage of the Fohatic potential that exists everywhere throughout the body of Nature, but which is most powerful in the realm of ideation, the realm of *Mahat,* universal mind or Aether-*Akasha.* This is an invaluable lesson for any group of pilgrim souls to learn if they would constitute themselves true helpers of the servants of humanity in the coming decades and in the dawn of the Aquarian Age. In all relationships – in one's household, at work and in the greater society – one may participate in the unfoldment of the ascending cycle that will stretch right into the next century.

The Zero Principle, *The Gupta Vidya* III, 363

The Tao Is Everywhere

All growth is invisible. No one can see or measure the growth of a baby or a little child from moment to moment. No one can mark by visible and external tokens the point of transition from childhood to youth. No one can put a date on the boundary between youth and manhood. These divisions are arbitrary and relative. When a person remains constant in his cool awareness of the utter relativity of all of these false and over-valued distinctions, he comes to understand that there is nothing dead and nothing alive. He is no less and no more than the Tao, and so is everyone else. The divisions and distinctions in consciousness arising from sense-objects, through words and by images, are a smoke-screen that obscures, limits and distorts reality. The supreme, carefree joy of non-striving that flows from the omnipresent light can no more be conveyed by one to another than the taste of water can be described to someone who has never drunk a drop. No truly meaningful experience can be communicated to another except in terms of his own modes of living.

The wisest disciples, teachers and sages learn from the Tao all the time. The Tao is not a book. The Tao is not a scripture. The Tao was not given by any one person for the first time to other people. It is everywhere and nowhere. It is what some call God, what others designate as the One Reality, and what still others salute merely by saying "I do not know." To the extent to which men do not understand the Tao, instead of their choosing the Tao, the Tao seems to use them. A great deal of what is often called choosing is an illusion. No one chooses except by the power of the Tao. No one chooses thoughts except by a self-conscious comprehension of what is behind the energy of the Tao. No one can be a knower of the Tao, a true Taoist, without becoming a skilled craftsman of *Akasha,* a silent magician of the Alkahest, a self-conscious channel for the universal divine flame which, in its boundless, colourless, intangible, soundless and inexhaustible energy, may be used only for the sake of all. Only these universal, deathless, eternal verities may become living germs in the emerging matrix of the awakening mind of the age of Aquarius, a current of consciousness that flows into the future.

Following the ever-young example of the Ancient of Days each and every person today may focus his mind upon the eternal relevance of the ever-flexible and never-caring Tao:

> Under heaven all can see beauty as beauty only because there is ugliness. All can know good as good only because there is evil.

Tao Te Ching, 2

How can one be flexible if one is fiercely attached to any external forms of good and of evil? There is the same mutual relation between existence and non-existence in respect to creation as there is between striving and spontaneity, effort and ease in respect to accomplishment. What is easy for one person is hard for another; what is easy for the same person at any time was hard once; and what is difficult now might become easy in the future. Fumbling with the strings of a musical instrument may be rather painful in the long period of apprenticeship, yet all can find supreme enjoyment in listening at any time to a great master of music who plays his enchanted instrument with lightness and versatile adeptship. The seeker who is patient and persistent, like the good gardener who plants the seed but does not examine it daily to gauge its growth, does no more than is needed, giving Nature time to do its own alchemical work.

Choosing the Tao, *The Gupta Vidya* II, 122

The Fire of the One Life

To honour this most precious Teaching is to be propelled forward in evolution and to receive immortal life-energy, or, if one receives it and does not use it, to be thrown backwards. In either case, the consequence is dependent upon the power of choice of *Manas*, the self-conscious freedom exercised by the individual, on behalf of what is strong or of what is weak. The strong must lift the weak, whilst the sick and the perverse must be let go. Every human being must choose between the baser, pathological and paranoid elements in the psyche, and the finer, purer and more selfless elements in his nature. The two are as incompatible as terrestrial fire and water. The cosmic fire of Agni is, however, correlated with the luminous waters of space called *Akasha*. All the physical elements are mere visible representations of the true spiritual essences existing on the higher noumenal planes.

None of the terrestrial elements is good or bad in itself, but each has its place in the formation, nourishment and disintegration of mortal forms. This much is owed to modern science; it has gone farther in the past ninety years than in the preceding three centuries in dispelling rigid and concretized conceptions of material nature and its elements. Such knowledge still lies beyond the mental capacity of many human beings, and even then, it remains worlds away from a full understanding of Spirit-Matter – the One Life. Life pervades the entire universe, whether slumbering in the atoms of dust or awakened to divine consciousness in a perfected Bodhisattva. Gradually, over the ensuing centuries and millennia, humanity will awaken to an Aquarian awareness of the fire of the One Life burning within its every unit. Meta-biology and meta-chemistry will flourish when particle physics is ensouled by unitary metaphysics and enriched by the ontological logic of integration and differentiation.

The perception and comprehension of mankind will be progressively transformed by the power of Buddhic intuition, vivifying and brightening the sight of the now dormant Eye of the Soul. This cannot take place without the deliberate use of the powers of thought and self-consciousness to create new matrices of ideation and to break up and discard the calcified accretions of past ignorance which blind the soul. As H.P. Blavatsky noted, Louis Pasteur was wise in his time to observe that microbic life can sustain itself by both aerobic and anaerobic processes, thus indicating the independence of the vital potency from external environments. Through each of its distributive units life builds and unbuilds, creates and destroys, every organic form from the most minute to the most macrocosmic. Integration and disintegration of form proceed hand-in-hand with the differentiation and synthesis of consciousness throughout all the octaves of manifestation from the formless worlds built up out of the divine elements to the shadowy realm of physical existence. All alike are impelled from within by the *Shabdabrahman,* the Divine Sound surrounded by the supernal light of the *Gayatri,* the immortal pulse in the secret heart – the Sound in the Light and the Light in the Sound.

Gestation and Growth, *The Gupta Vidya* I, 237-238

Karma Ordains a Divine Destiny

For the average person, whose highest vestures are veiled by the samskaric residues of past actions and present vacillation, the inner voice cannot be heard and the pre-birth vision of the soul is forgotten. Yet, they may be mirrored dimly in the muddled personal mind as vague and chaotic recollections, as feeble and faltering notions of some essential reform to be made in life, or some sacrificial act of goodness to be offered in the service of others. Through inconstant flickerings along the invisible spinal cord, there may be sporadic resolves to renew the most precious moment one can recall from early childhood or from fleeting contact with the benevolent current of past teachers. In a variety of ways, even if only fitfully and imperfectly, every person can receive help from internal conditions which can release the spiritual will. The greater the fidelity, the selflessness and self-assurance with which one cleaves to these inner promptings of the immortal soul, the more instantaneously they light up the immediate task at hand. Above all, the more they are heeded, the less the effort needed to sustain continuity. With the same certitude, the opposite consequences follow for those who foolishly ignore or flaunt this inner guidance for the sake of enhancing the delusive sense of personal self-importance. But even the most spiritually impoverished human beings are sheltered by the invisible protection of the Divine Prototype, and therefore even amidst the muddle and froth of psychic fantasy there is a concealed thread of truth. Wise and loving friends might be able to recognize and strengthen it. A true spiritual teacher could help to sift the wheat from the chaff, quicken the inward process of alchemical transmutation, and show the pathway to Divine Wisdom.

As the One Law of spiritual evolution, Karma is more generous to each and every human soul in need of help than the niggardly thinking of the nihilistic can envisage. It is neither a doctrine that is so abstruse and remote that it cannot be related to the present moment, nor is it nearly as inflexible and hostile as claimed by those who have gratuitously declared a vote of no-confidence in themselves and in the human race. Far from precluding the idea that each human being has a unique and inherently significant mission on this earth, the Law of Karma actually ordains that every single person has a divine destiny which he or she alone can and must fulfill. There is an authentic dignity and beauty, a profound meaning, to the uniqueness of the divine presence in and around every human soul. The sacredness of individual choice was affirmed as the basis of human solidarity by the inspired forerunners of the Aquarian Age, those luminaries who initiated the Renaissance and the Enlightenment in Europe. If the prospect has not yet smiled upon all, this is because too many have laboured under the dead weight of traditional theology or secular fatalism.

> Those who believe in *Karma* have to believe in *destiny* which, from birth to death, every man is weaving thread by thread around himself, as a spider does his cobweb; and this destiny is guided either by the heavenly voice of the invisible *prototype* outside of us, or by our more intimate *astral*, or inner man, who is but too often the evil genius of the embodied entity called man.
>
> *Ibid.*

The heavenly voice of the invisible Prototype is heard and felt, without any external tokens of empirical certitude. In the life of a good and simple person, who makes a mental image of Christ or Buddha, Shiva or Krishna, that voice may seem to come in a form engendered by the ecstatic devotion of the individual who has purity of heart. Many thousands of people all over the world belong to the invisible fraternity of fortunate souls who, having made a fearless and compassionate invocation on behalf of a friend or relative in distress, suddenly heard a vibrant voice of authoritative assurance and sensed an aureole of light soon after. This voice may appear to come from outside oneself, and, paradoxically, that other voice, the voice of the intimate astral, all too often the evil genius of man, seems to originate within. When it speaks, it aggravates the confusions of the compulsive persona, inducing the hapless listener to rush into mindless activity. When the heavenly voice speaks to the depths of one's soul, it has a calming influence and allays the anxieties of *kama manas*. There is a natural soul-reticence to tell others about the heavenly voice, and a grateful concern to treasure its words in silence. However well-intentioned, anything that is allowed to pass through the matrix of the psychic nature risks distortion and generates a smoky obscuration that acts as a barrier to further guidance and profounder help from the Divine Prototype. What begins as unthinking indiscretion soon becomes delusive, and unless promptly checked, culminates in abject servitude to the astral shadow. Then, deceived by this simulacrum, the shadow of oneself outside the path of dharma, one is drawn in a direction that may be contrary to one's true destiny. This abdication from the soul's self-chosen task in the course of evolution may initially be imperceptible but the choice of destinies remains as long as the two voices can be heard.

Karma and Destiny, *The Gupta Vidya* II, 226

The Four Yugas

The quickening of spiritual perception and the restoration of the primordial spirituality of the First Sub-Race of the Third Root Race by the end of the present Fifth Root Race are not nearly so distant as they may seem to human beings as yet unprepared in consciousness to slough off old skins. Indeed, they are the vital components of the Logoic impulse of the Aquarian Age. The incapacity of human beings in general to recognize the immanence of the restoration of archetypal spiritual humanity is bound up with their ostrich-like obsession with life in a physical form. The difficulty of extricating oneself from this mental obscuration is aggravated for many by the accelerated pace of karmic precipitation during the present Kali Yuga. This *yuga,* which has already passed away over five thousand of its four hundred and thirty-two thousand years, is a relatively short time when seen from the perspective of the Root Races and Sub-Races. It will indeed end before the completion of the present Fifth Root Race, and be followed by an ascent through the *yugas* towards the Satya Yuga, the whole process proceeding *pari passu* with the development of the final Sub-Races of the present Root Race.

The four *yugas* may be understood in terms of a descent from the most golden age to the most decadent, followed by a reascent to a golden age that represents a spiralling spiritual advance over the starting-point of the cycle. But these *yugas* do not mechanically and automatically apply to all human beings in the same way. Babies, for example, are not in Kali Yuga, but rather experience something like a Satya Yuga, albeit briefly. The *yugas* are relative to states of consciousness, and since all people even in a single city are on different planes of consciousness, their states of mind vary dramatically according to the dominant concerns of what may be called their line of life's meditation. So too they vary in their capacity to control the twenty-eight-day cycle of the moon and to master the cycles of the seasons of nature. Whether it be for a day, a week or an entire year, individuals must therefore train themselves to adapt their plastic mental potency to the prevailing conditions of periodic phenomena. Through the noumenal power of resolve they can always establish counterbalancing measures capable of producing successively higher levels of equilibrium.

For those capable of taking and adhering to vows, Kali Yuga affords a great opportunity. In other times one may postpone the results of one's actions; in Kali Yuga the results return very rapidly. Many people, experiencing this intensification of karma, have developed elaborate theories regarding the pace of change in the modern era, culture shock, future shock and the like; in truth, it is simply the result of an acceleration in the vortex of precipitation in Kali Yuga. When this factor is compounded by the embryonic forces of the Aquarian Age, everything happens much faster within a month, within a week, or even within a day, than was considered possible a century ago. Souls either lose their spiritual vibration more quickly, or hold a vibration and move much faster with it. They can more rapidly descend into a lower state of consciousness or more speedily ascend to a higher state of consciousness. As in mountain climbing, the higher one goes, the greater the danger of giddiness and falling, and the more precipitous the potential fall the higher and more rarefied the atmosphere in which it takes place. But if one maintains steadiness in the thin air of higher altitudes, one's perspective may suddenly expand. This is true both on the mental and physical planes; in Kali Yuga karmic causes may be rapidly exhausted, and illusions rapidly destroyed.

Involution, *The Gupta Vidya* I, 259-260

The Keynote of the Epoch

As the structures of the past atrophy and crumble, only that could replace them which would existentially reflect the inner truth of soul-evolution, the insights of monads that pierce the veil of forms. The inversions of the insecure, allowing moral pygmies to speculate upon spiritual giants, will have no sway in the civilization of the future. There will be a pervasive recognition of the logical impossibility for the lesser to judge the greater, and the sure sign of littleness is the tendency to convert beliefs into verdicts. The Aquarian Age will foster that openness in relation to the larger circle which will be a natural extension of the open texture of our primary relationships – with parents, teachers, siblings, so-called enemies and friends. There will be a more widespread acknowledgement that as veil upon veil may lift, there must remain veil upon veil behind. When the human race as a whole can afford to live with such mature awareness, it will be hospitable to the sort of spiritual and moral toughness that can cope fully with the accelerated pace of karmic precipitation. Many will readily grasp the elementary axiom of the mathematics of the soul that in order to comprehend an Adept or Mahatma, one must first devote a lifetime to true discipleship.

This is an immensely liberating prospect, when compared with the stifling spiritual limitations of the last century. H.P. Blavatsky had to undergo the pain of risking profanation in testifying to the existence of Mahatmas in the heyday of Victorian prejudice and conceit. The spoilt victims of centuries of sectarian stupidity, more skilled in image-crippling than in true devotion, were almost constitutionally incapable of understanding Mahatmas. Speaking of them was then a great sacrifice. This is fortunately no longer necessary, because those who need to participate in the clamour of pseudo-claims and shallow judgments are now confronted with an abundant supply of readily available gurus. This offers a considerable protection to the real work in the world of the Brotherhood of Bodhisattvas. During the 1975 cycle there is no more need to make any concessions to the weak in the West that were unknown in the East. This augurs well for the future of humanity. All over the globe, the paramount problem is one of renewing and maintaining the minimal standards of being truly human. Only those souls who already have a profound grasp of *sunyata* and *karuna,* the voidness of all and the fullness of compassion, will undergo the lifelong training of discipleship and awaken the *Bodhichitta,* the seed of the Bodhisattva. There is thus the immense gain that the mixing of incompatible vibrations may be mitigated in this century. At the widest level, universal good – *Agathon* – is the keynote of the epoch.

Drawing the Larger Circle, *The Gupta Vidya* III, 334-335

The Avataric Impulse in the Present Cycle

To do the right thing at the right time depends upon a lively awareness of the subtle phases and stable conditions of prevailing cycles. In the Aquarian Age it is helpful to acknowledge that human beings, having begun in the First Root Race as extremely ethereal and spiritual beings, have now completed their arc of descent into matter and are engaged in a progressive process of etherealization and spiritualization. In the Fifth Root Race, going from the Fifth Sub-Race to the Sixth Sub-Race, this process is giving birth to a profound spiritual sensitization of intelligence through the elevation of life-atoms. This is connected with the cosmic electricity of *Daiviprakriti,* the Light of the Logos. All the modes of physical and astral intelligence throughout the various kingdoms of Nature are nothing but masked manifestations of the synthesizing spiritual intelligence of *Mahat.* Along the upward involutionary arc of growth and spirituality, each human being, each individuated ray of *Mahat* in *Manas,* must self-consciously cultivate what Mahatma K.H. calls a "refined form of mentality commingled with spiritual intuitiveness". Refined mentality is *Manas-Taijasi,* and spiritual intuitiveness *Buddhi.* Thus, *Buddhi-Manas-Taijasi* is the colouring, the tonality and the number of the Avataric impulse in the present cycle. It is the spiritual essence of secular monasticism which, from its present *bija* or seed state, will flourish as a new mode of self-regenerating civilization in the maturing phases of the Aquarian Age. Like seeds that lie beneath the protection of mountain snows, every element of spiritual intuition, of mental refinement, and of the heart radiance that comes through compassion out of the mystic marriage *(hieros gamos)* of truth and love is being helped and nourished at this sacred moment and hour in the evolutionary history of mankind. Such seeds, sown in trust by courageous pioneers in the chill midnight of outward darkness, will bring forth a rich harvest for mankind in the warmer dawns of the foreseeable future.

Integration and Recurrence, *The Gupta Vidya* III, 163-164

APPENDIX II:

Aquarian Psychology

The Descent of Atman

The aftermath of two world wars and the slaughter of millions of people in this century have not brought humanity any closer to peace on earth and the reign of justice. Viewing humanity through the eyes of compassion and seeing the tragedy of human misery everywhere, one cannot help but notice the victims of injustice. To let them hear the Law, whilst at the same time the Law must take its course, would take something much stronger than was even imaginable in the time of Buddha and Christ. It would need something golden and generous and divine and free, such as in the time of Krishna or as sung by Shelley, but at the same time it would need the immense preparation that comes from the silent work of all the sages and rishis who know that human beings could only become truly human through meditation. Thus a time will come, though not in this century, when there will be men of meditation and exemplars of compassion in every part of the globe. In order to protect and promote the interests of the humanity of the future and to wipe out the humbug of the ages, the pristine avataric descent of the Aquarian cycle has been accompanied by a tremendous acceleration in the programme of evolution. The misuse of the human form had to be halted. All over the world this is sensed, and although there are those who, as Shakespeare put it, "squeak and gibber in the streets," there is a resonant feeling of joy amongst the greater portion of humanity which recognizes what has already begun to take root.

The meaning of the sounding of the keynote of the 1975 Cycle in relation to the great globe itself can only be understood in terms of the relation of the Logos, of Avalokitesvara, to the descent of Atman in the human race in its entirety. In the last century Mahatma M. gave a clue to the mystery when he said, "We have yet some Avatars left to us on earth." As it was in the past, it is now and it always shall be that the entire sacred tribe of Initiates serves Dakshinamurti, the Initiator of Initiates. For over eighteen million years they have been the faithful witnesses to the mysterious bond between the Ever-Living Human Banyan, the fiery Dragon of Light, Fire and Flame, and the seventh principle in the Cosmos which extends beyond all the manifested cycles of galaxies. Those who seek intimations of the meaning of the end of the old habits, modes and orders and of the auspicious birth of the new, which is the oldest of the old, should meditate deeply upon these words of Pymander:

> The Light is me, I am the Nous (the mind or Manu), I am thy God, and I am far older than the human principle which escapes from the shadow (*'Darkness'*, or the concealed Deity). I am the germ of thought, the resplendent *Word*, the *Son* of God. All that thus sees and hears in thee is the *Verbum* of the Master, it is the Thought *(Mahat)* which is God, the Father.
>
> *The Secret Doctrine* I, 74

Atma Vidya, *The Gupta Vidya* II, 69-70

Spiritual Life Is in the Mind

Words like 'telling,' 'knowing' and 'being silent' have to do with inner postures. As long as we seek *external* representations of the *inner* postures of the spiritual life, the spiritual life is not for us in this incarnation, and perhaps just as well. Maybe this is where humanity has grown up. There is now no need for mollycoddling. There is no need for giving in to the residual and tragic arrogance of those who are on the verge of annihilation, by pandering to them, yielding external tokens, or performing external signs. In this Aquarian age, spiritual life is in the mind, and people have got to be much more willing to assume full responsibility for all their choices. The reading of the signs requires a deeper knowledge, or a tougher kind of integrity. The only honest position for anyone is that, given whatever one thing he really knows in his life, in terms of that he is entitled, in E.M. Forster's phrase, "to connect" — to connect with what is told and what is not told. People are brought up in India, and indeed all over the East, to know from early on that what the eyes are saying is important, what the physical gestures are saying is important, and that ominous or peaceful silences bear meanings of many kinds. Brought up in the rich and complex poetry of silence, gesture and speech through all the seven apertures of the human face, there is no such problem as between knowing in one particular sense and telling in one particular sense.

A lot of the subtlety has gone out of our lives, probably all over the world, but nonetheless we must recognize that wisdom always implies an immense, incredible flexibility of method. Let us not play games, least of all adopt sick and self-destructive attitudes, where in the name of belittling ourselves we insidiously belittle our Teachers. What this really comes to is bargaining and even blackmail, and these never helped anyone. On the other hand, let us genuinely be grateful for whatever we receive at all levels. It is part of the meaning of the *Guruparampara* chain that if one were smart enough to be benefitted at some level and to be ever grateful to the person who first taught one the alphabet, then one is more likely to make good use of Teachers in higher realms. We are dealing with something archetypal in which our whole lives are involved, but in which each one will be unique in his or her response.

"By Their Fruits...," *The Gupta Vidya* II, 75

Development of the Reasonable Part of the Soul

Throughout the cyclic development of each soul, the proportional composition of the vestures out of the five elements is continually being adjusted. Through the attraction and repulsion of their coessence to the vestures, certain elements become the dominant ruling factors in one's life. Unless one engages in noetic mental asceticism, one will invariably remain passive to the psychic sway of these irrational forces. Without ratio, harmony and proportion, one cannot employ the vestures as channels for the benevolent transmutation of life-atoms: rather one will needlessly compound the karma of selfishness. The compassionate projection of the spiritual energies of the soul requires that the genii be made subordinate to the awakened Buddhi-Manasic reason. The genii

> permeate by the body two parts of the Soul, that it may receive from each the impress of his own energy. But the reasonable part of the Soul is not subject to the genii; it is designed for the reception of (the) God, who enlightens it with a sunny ray. Those who are thus illumined are few in number, and from them the genii abstain: for neither genii nor Gods have any power in the presence of a single ray of God.

> *Ibid.*, i 294-295

By the "few in number" is meant those Initiates and Adepts for whom there is no 'God' but the one universal and unconditioned Deity in boundless space and eternal duration.

The truly reasonable part of the soul is extremely important in the Aquarian Age. To think clearly, logically and incisively must be the true purpose of education. To unfold the immense powers of pure thought, the reasonable part of the soul must be given every opportunity to develop so that the irrational side is reduced. Its false coherence must be broken by seeing it causally. One must begin with a willingness to acknowledge it readily, and see that there is no gain in merely pushing it aside. The development of the reasonable part of the soul, which is not subject to the genii, culminates in the reception of the god who enlightens it with a sunny ray, the *Chitkala* that is attracted by contemplation. Clear, pure reason characterizes the immortal ray which is connected with the star that has its genii, good and evil by nature. The use of reason and clarity of perception in the spiritual and metaphysical sense involves the heart as well as the mind because they cooperate in seeing and thinking clearly. Once this is grasped, one can make a decisive difference to the amount of unnecessary karma involved in one's irrational emanations and wasteful emotions. One can begin to let go of all that and calmly cultivate the deepest feelings.

At a certain point it will become natural for the mind to move spontaneously to spiritual teachings and universal ideas whenever it has an opportunity. It would not have to be told, nor would one have to make rules, because that would be what it would enjoy. When it becomes more developed in the art of solitary contemplation, it will always see everything from the higher standpoint whilst performing duties in the lower realm, thus transforming one's whole way of living. This will make a profound difference to the conservation of energy and the clarification of one's karma. It will also strengthen the power of progressive detachment whereby one can understand what it means to say that the Sage, the *Jivanmukta,* the perfected *Yogin,* is characterized by the golden talisman of doing only what is truly necessary. He only thinks what is necessary. He only feels what is necessary. There is so powerful a sense of what is necessary in the small, but from the standpoint of the whole, that there is no other way of life that is conceivable or imaginable. This internal Buddhic logic can never be understood by reference to external rules and characteristics because one has to come to it from a high plane of meditation and total detachment from the realm of external expression.

Individuation and Initiation, *The Gupta Vidya* II, 177-178

Cooperating with the Evolutionary Scheme

If any sensitive person fully thought out what it means to be a self-conscious being, making meaningful connections in reference to all aspects of life and death, then one would verily become capable of cooperating with the evolutionary scheme by staying in line with those gods and sages who are the unthanked Teachers of Humanity. No such fundamental revolution in consciousness is possible without becoming intensely aware of both motive and method. Motive has to do with morality in the metaphysical sense, the rate of vibration of one's spiritual volition. Is the individual soul consciously seeking to help, heal and elevate every single life-atom? Or, owing to fear, ignorance, suspicion and doubt, is the fugitive soul trapped in a mechanical repetition of moribund hostilities inimical to those whom it irrationally and unintentionally injures? Through unremitting attention to such internal obstructions, one could rise above the lower or lunar planes of consciousness, seeing compulsive tendencies for what they are, and thus introduce by renewed acts of noetic will a strong current of spiritual benevolence. This would be the basis of Bodhisattvic ethics, a joyous mode of relaxed breathing. In pursuing this Aquarian life-style, one is certain to encounter various difficulties in the realm of the mind in regard to one's permeability to astral forces, one's personal vulnerability to reversals, perversion and pride, and also a strange susceptibility to distortions and awkwardnesses that come between what is spontaneously felt at the core of one's being and its deliberate enactment in the chaotic context of social intercourse.

One would have to become mathematically objective about the fluctuating patterns of mental deposits and tendencies that have cut deep grooves in the volatile vestures of personal existence. One would have to see all this in relation to human evolution as a whole, asking relevant questions about the uncouth Fourth Race as well as concerning what one really learnt in the first sub-race of the Fifth

Race of original thinkers and theophilanthropists who were effortlessly capable of creative ideation and concentrated endeavour. In asking such questions one has to lift ethical sensitivity beyond the level of the individual monad, through active concern with all humanity, to cosmic planes of cognition. In so doing one could gradually come to make fundamental readjustments in the elusive relationship between one's lower and higher centres of perception, volition and empathy.

Between Heaven and Earth, *The Gupta Vidya* III, 304

The Fusion of Buddhi and Manas

All this preparation encourages a balance between the centrifugal and centripetal forces which engage the incarnated ray more fully by the age of fourteen. The centrifugal power of spirit or *Buddhi* is capable of diffusing from a single point in every direction within a sphere. This omnidirectional diffusion mirrors the ceaseless motion of the *Atman*. In *Manas*, the capacity to hold, to focus and to concentrate these energies is associated with the centripetal energies. A helpful example in the balancing of these energies may be gleaned from those older cultures which never allowed people to speak when they were confused or excited until they had sat down. Adolescents must learn to collect themselves, to draw their energies together in calmness, if they are to avoid the rush, the tension and the anxiety endemic to the cycle between fourteen and twenty-one. Once they have developed some mature calmness, depth and strength, they can release the potential of the higher energies of *Atma-Buddhi-Manas*. In a sense, all humanity is presently engaged in this adolescent phase.

In the Aquarian Age a dynamic principle of balance is needed. Whilst this has its analogues on the physical plane, and even in the astral vesture, it must not be approached on this level, lest there be a degradation of the idea into Hatha Yoga. Instead, one must begin with the Buddhi-Manasic, with the emotional and mental nature, and find on the physical plane appropriate means of expressing that creative balance. Thus one can produce a rhythmic flow and a light ease in one's sphere of influence which reflects a life of deep meditation. The ultimate aim is a fusion of love and wisdom, which then becomes Wisdom-Compassion, the fusion of *Buddhi* and *Manas*. The fusion of *Buddhi* and *Manas* at the highest level is inseparable from the path of adeptship.

Because of the inherent pacing and cycle of soul-evolution, and because of the karmic encrustations human beings have produced in themselves through associations with secondary and tertiary hosts of daimons, no one can be expected to accomplish all of this in a single lifetime, or indeed in any immediate future series of lives. But each being can make a beginning, and, at some level, fuse *Buddhi* and *Manas*. Although overactive in *kama manas*, most human beings are mediumistic, yet in the *antaskarana* there are authentic longings for the higher. Such longings must first be purified and made manasic through universalization. This requires sifting finer thoughts and higher impulses from the dross of *kama manas*, then releasing them for the welfare of humanity as a whole. This means ignoring statistical portraits of humanity given by mass media and developing an inward sense of one's intimate relationship on the plane of ideation and aspiration with millions upon millions of immortal souls.

The more one can change the ratios of one's thought about oneself, one's thought about Bodhisattvas, and one's thought about humanity, the better. As these ratios change, the patterns of one's associations of daimons and elementals will shift, progressively transmuting one's vestures and refining one's capacity for benevolence. Gradually, as one thinks more and more in the direction of Bodhisattvas and of humanity, one will come to see oneself as someone who has the confidence and capacity to control elementals at home, at work and in the world. Thus, one can help oneself and so help others to recover the lost link with the Manasa Dhyanis. One may learn to become a being of true meditation and compassion, capable of serving as a self-conscious living link between heaven and earth.

The Inmost Sanctuary, *The Gupta Vidya* II, p. 372

Nothing Is Unnecessary

The universal process of adjustment of the external to the internal, which leads to involuntary reincarnation for human beings, must be understood in terms of karma. At the most primary level, whenever human beings entertain and succumb to emotional reactions, they establish mental deposits and astral grooves which require many lives for proper adjustment. That is why over eighteen million years so many people approach the Path again and again but stumble and lose their track just as often. They cannot make a fundamental breakthrough even when in the presence of great teaching. For those who have made the teaching an internal living power in their consciousness, this is comprehensible as essential, just as the world seems clear to a child when its eyes are directed to the light of the sun. Whilst this is true for all human souls, the philosophical recognition of how this works is important. Every emotion registers an appropriate record in the astral vesture. It is wear and tear on the *linga sharira* and is at the expense of something or someone else. Thus selfishness is increased. This is true even if the emotion is benevolent for emotion itself is a form of passivity. Emotion is quite different from deep feeling which is unmodified by cyclic change or external event and is totally independent of outward demonstration. Emotion is like cashing a check: whilst it makes money available, it depletes the account. It is a way of demanding proof. As a form of external indulgence it is a passive fantasy which weighs heavily upon the astral vesture. To that extent it obscures one's inmost feelings which are detached and compassionate. All the higher feelings are ontologically powerful and at the same time they constitute a pure negation psychologically. Though only an initial understanding of the problem, this is sufficient to explain why merely sitting down to postures and trying to control the external breath by *hatha yoga* exercises cannot make a significant difference to the inevitable adjustment of internal and external relations inherent in life itself. There is no substitute for facing oneself, asking what one is truly living for, how one is affected by likes and dislikes, and how one's temper — or *sophrosyne* — is unbalanced through various irritations.

In the ancient schools one would not be allowed to begin serious study of yoga until one had mastered one's temper. In the school of Pythagoras candidates were tested from the first day in regard to their personal vulnerability. That was the stringent standard of all schools preparing for the mysteries of initiation. The laws have not changed even though the external rules may seem to have been modified. It remains an inescapable fact of Nature and karma that if one loses one's temper even after a lifetime of spiritual development, one's progress is destroyed in a single mood. Like a city or a work of art, the time to construct is long, but destruction can be swift. One has to think out one's true internal and external state of being, even if one goes to the Tolstoyan extreme of seeing every kind of fault in oneself. Tolstoy did not do this out of pride but rather because he was so thoroughly honest that he simply could not think of a single fault in anyone else which he could not see present in himself. This sense of commonality, rooted in ethical self-awareness, leaves no room for judging anyone else or for running away from anyone because one sees that the whole army of human foibles is in oneself, and that every elemental is connected with internal propensities in one's astral form. To think this out Manasically is crucial in the Aquarian Age. The wise disciple will recognize that thoroughness, urgency and earnestness are quite different from fatuous haste and impulsiveness. Even if it takes months and years to think out and learn to apply the elementary axioms of the Science of Spirituality, it is necessary to be patient and persistent, rather than revel in fantasies that leave residues in successive lives. When something so obvious which one can test and comprehend is taught, this is an opportunity for growth which demands honesty in thought and intelligence in response. To receive the timeless teaching in this way enables the self to be the true friend of the Self. Not to do this is one of the myriad ways in which the self becomes the enemy of the Self because it is afraid of facing the facts and the laws of nature connected with relations and patterns in the vestures. Self-regeneration is a precise science and it is possible to test oneself in a manner that fosters *sophrosyne.*

This spiritual intelligence test is not a matter of making some sweeping moral judgement about oneself, because that will have no meaning for the immortal soul. It would simply not be commensurate with eighteen million years of self-conscious existence. It is really a waste of time to say "I'm no good, I'm this kind of person, I'm bound to do this." Such exclamations are absurd because they do not account for the internal complexity and psychological richness of sevenfold man, let alone the immensity of the human pilgrimage. It is more important to understand and recognize critical incipient causes, to see how the karmic process takes place, and to arrest the downward slide into fragmented consciousness. To do this firmly with compassion at the root, one has to meditate upon some fundamental idea. One might benefit from the golden example set by disciples who practise the precept: "All the time everything that comes to me I not only deserve but I desire." This form of mental asceticism is the reverse of psychic passivity and self-indulgent fatalism. It is a clear and crisp recognition that there is karmic meaning to every single event, that nothing is unnecessary even though one may not yet know what its meaning is. Ignorance of the process of adjustment of internal and external relations is merely a reflection of the limitation of one's own growth at the level of lower mind. To accept totally one's karma is like a swimmer recognizing the necessity of accepting the tidal currents of the ocean. A swimmer is not doing a favour to the ocean by accepting its sway. Deliberate and intelligent acceptance of oceanic currents is the difference between drowning and surviving.

Individuation and Initiation, *The Gupta Vidya* II, pp. 175-176

Continuity of Consciousness

The methodology of Gupta Vidya is linked to the process of self-regeneration. It focuses upon the purification and perfection of the vestures of the aspirant *pari passu* with the unfolding of perceptual mysteries. It is, therefore, inseparable from the actual course of human evolution itself. It is, in fact, evolution made self-conscious. In its conceptual framework, it mirrors the living matrix of both cosmos and man, and in practice it teaches the macrocosmic and microcosmic application of the different keys of interpretation to myths and symbols. These often offer hints about the vibrations connecting different parts of the universe and different parts of the human constitution. Anyone who begins to appreciate the richer classifications of the ancient world, especially in Sanskrit but also in Greek, will refuse to be bound by any simplistic cardboard categories such as 'mind' and 'body', 'irrational' and 'rational'. These are of little help in understanding the complex interaction between the cosmic and the atomic. Every human being has the same evolutionary task as every other human being who ever lived, lives now or will live in the future. In this pilgrimage there are ancient guidelines in cutting through the clutter of detail and getting to the core of noetic consciousness.

Owing to centuries of mutilation of the higher faculties by dogmatic religion and materialistic science, many people do not have metaphysical imagination. In mass society many find it difficult to generate abstract ideas or to sustain constructive thought. All too often persons get threatened if confronted by any idea that has no immediate concrete reference to their personal self-image. This sad condition demonstrates the inherited damage to consciousness which is transmitted, and even aggravated, by contemporary media. To correct this will require tremendous courage and compassion, and also great wisdom in altering the plasticity of the human mind. Eventually this subtle transformation will require that every human being make some effort to think metaphysically. After a point, what is initially difficult becomes easier, and suddenly a whole group of people who were once completely bewildered by metaphysical abstractions awaken a dormant aptitude for the exercise of creative imagination. The metaphysical must connect with the mystical.

Those who truly seek to prepare themselves for discipleship must choose a mode of life which can help to maintain an increasing continuity of consciousness. Using the method of analogy and correspondence, one will find that *The Secret Doctrine* is replete with instruction concerning meditation and self-study, about how to understand other human beings, and how to make a constructive difference to the collective karma of the human race. Each human being, every day and night, has microcosmic choices and opportunities which, if calmly understood from the perspective of the macrocosmic, enables an honest seeker to be truly helpful to the Brotherhood of Bodhisattvas. In the early stages this would be mostly unconscious to the lower mind, but entirely clear to the immortal soul. Even small differences wrought in the moral choices one makes by night and day can unlock doors for vast numbers of human beings and open pathways which will be relevant to the Races to come and the Aquarian civilization of the future. Aspiring disciples will find that sometimes just by taking a phrase or a sentence and writing it out, reflecting upon it and sincerely attempting to apply it to themselves, trying to use it at dawn, midday, the twilight hour or late at night, but always so that one may become the better able to help and serve the whole of the human race, they will tap the inexhaustible resources of *Akasha*.

Evolution and Consciousness, *The Gupta Vidya* I, 127-128

The Release of Soul-Memory

In order to release soul-memory and activate one's higher faculties, one must be fortunate enough to have come consciously and voluntarily to the spiritual life, not out of any compensatory motives but out of love and reverence for Divine Wisdom and with a deep longing to benefit humanity. Only those who live and breathe benevolently can avoid the awful consequences of misappropriating the higher energies in the service of the lower, thereby forfeiting the great opportunity gained under karma of coming closer to the immemorial Teachings and to authentic spiritual Teachers. For such seekers who are suffused with a profound humility and a deep desire for learning for the sake of others, there will be a natural protection. True *shravakas* or learners will be able to use the archetypal method from the first, proceeding from above below and from within without and emphasizing at each stage the steady assimilation of mental and spiritual food through moral practice. There need be no partiality and imbalance, no one-sidedness or bias, in the apprehension and application of Gupta Vidya. As Mahatma M. pointed out,

> In our doctrine you will find necessary the synthetic method; you will have to embrace the whole – that is to say to blend the *macrocosm* and microcosm together – before you are enabled to study the parts separately or analyze them with profit to your understanding. Cosmology is the physiology of the universe spiritualized, for there is but one Law.

In order to embrace the whole, one must grasp the fundamental continuity of cosmic and human evolution, establishing one's consciousness in a current of Buddhic compassion and unconditional love for all that lives. One must learn to move back and forth continuously between the macrocosmic and the microcosmic. One must strive to see the relevance of universal ideation to specific contexts. One must ever seek to bridge the universal and the particular in waking consciousness, maximizing the good even in highly imperfect situations. Tremendous aid can come through the Buddhic stream of Hermetic wisdom pouring forth from the Brotherhood of Bodhisattvas. With a mind moistened by wisdom and compassion, one may return again and again in meditation and self-study to seek appropriate connections and correspondences between the macrocosm and the microcosm. Drawing upon the rich resources of Gupta Vidya, one must grasp its universal synthesis before attempting to study the parts separately or analytically. This means that one must engage in daily *tapas* or mental asceticism. In the Aquarian Age we need to relinquish the entrenched modes of the inductive and analytic mind, replacing them by cultivated skill in deep concentration, creative imagination and calm receptivity towards universal ideation. In this way one will come to comprehend the connections between the most primordial and abstract and the most dense and differentiated levels of manifestation of consciousness and matter. The continuity of consciousness which one seeks is, in fact, a mode of mirroring the metaphysical integrity of cosmic unity.

Spiritual Perception, *The Gupta Vidya* III, 147-148

Living Seeds of Creative Thought

Solzhenitsyn states in *The First Circle* that when prisoners find that everything has been taken away from them, they suddenly experience freedom, the sheer joy of thinking. Many people would rather not think but merely emote, cerebrate and react passively. Once one develops a taste for such mindless activity, deep thinking becomes painful. It is like having one's teeth ground, since it will break down the incrustations of half-chewed and half-dead ideas that have settled down like a crust. Thinking forces these to be broken up because they have got to be eliminated. How much this will have to be done will depend upon the degree of damage already done by the crust. The mind can be always revivified by turning to seminal ideas which, like the rain on parched soil, will quicken germs of living seeds of regenerative truths. The plant of *Manas* will begin to take root. Long before it becomes a tree, it will release the fire of creative thought, making it a thrill to create by the power of ideation. Those who begin to do this are going to find that they are also tapping a subtler realm of matter. One cannot separate thought from matter, subject from object. To really think is to tap subtler life-atoms in one's vestures, and that means also to become more receptive and attentive to subtler life-atoms in visible forms, prepared to design new structures. This is necessary for *Manas* to incarnate further.

H.P. Blavatsky said in the nineteenth century that the Aquarian Age will bring about a lot of psychological disturbances. These arise in the vestures because of the unwillingness to let go of what is dead or dying. Many human beings have a morbid love of decay and are threatened by the Ray, terrified of living seeds. They are so fond of the husk that they have forgotten what the germ is like. The husk of indigestible, decaying ideas prevents the living wheat germ of spiritual ideas from giving birth to new thought-forms. Individuals who cannot do this now will have to do it by the end of the Fourth Round, because the great moment of choice must come finally in the

Fifth. This is far in the future, but even the highest two elements, the sixth and the seventh, which are now far beyond the range of human perception, will be sensed during the Sixth and Seventh Races of this Round, though they will not become known to all until the Sixth and Seventh Rounds. They will be aroused partially and by anticipation in the Sixth and Seventh Sub-Races of the Fifth Root Race. Those of the Fifth Sub-Race who are touched by the current of the Sixth Sub-Race with the help of Teachers using the seventh principle, the *Atman,* will be able to germinate living seeds of creative thought. This will enable them to serve in future civilizations in those arenas where the seed-bearers, the vanguard of human growth, will be vitally active. Those who cannot keep pace will incarnate in those portions of the earth where slower moving structures carry on the work of evolution. Evolution takes care of everyone. There is a joy and a thrill in activating *Manas,* the power of abstract ideation, with the help of seminal spiritual ideas and laying down fertile seeds of self-regenerating modes of thought and patterns of living.

The Dawning of Wisdom, *The Gupta Vidya* II, 58-59

Moving Between States of Consciousness

H.P. Blavatsky knew that the time was fast approaching when more and more people would emerge who have the courage both to examine ancient wisdom and to correlate it with the discoveries of science. It was for those who would ask questions, and make their own investigations by looking at the heavens and looking within themselves through meditation, that she partially unveiled the teachings of Gupta Vidya. Those who use these teachings – and daily consult *The Voice of the Silence* – in order to understand the profounder visions and longings of their hearts will progressively gain confidence in charting the seas of the psychic unconscious. With steadiness and persistence, they will become more skilled in handling the take-off and landing, the vertical ascent and descent in consciousness, so critical to the Aquarian Age. The ability to sustain oneself in any state of consciousness or meditation and the related ability to move deliberately from one plane or state of consciousness to another with relaxed control depend upon one's access to a fixed point of reference or vibration within consciousness. If the sevenfold human constitution were likened to a miniature solar system, the centre of consciousness would reside on one of the planets of that system.

Despite all the variations and fluctuations of cyclic existence affecting states of consciousness, all points of view within the system revolve in complex orbits around the central sun of the *Atman.* The motions of attention from one point to another are regulated by that central sun in accordance with its breath and heartbeat. As in the macrocosm of the universe, so too in the microcosm of human nature – all the oscillating motions and emanations of the MONAD and the Monad are comprised in an original fundamental vibration.

> All are contained within the *Maha-Yug,* the 'Great Age'
> or Cycle of the Manu calculation, which itself revolves
> between two eternities – the 'Pralayas' or *Nights of Brahma.*

> As, in the objective world of matter, or the system of effects, the minor constellations and planets gravitate each and all around the sun, so in the world of the subjective, or the system of causes, these innumerable cycles all gravitate between that which the finite intellect of the ordinary mortal regards as eternity, and the still finite, but more profound, intuition of the sage and philosopher views as but an eternity within THE ETERNITY. 'As above, so it is below', runs the old Hermetic maxim.

Ibid.

In so far as individuals can assimilate this radical perspective within themselves, they will not be so dependent upon transient fashion and fickle opinion, nor will they be so susceptible to volatile psychic influences. In a society where many have scarcely any conception of self-magnetization and magnetic purity, they perpetually throw off negative emanations through speech and the eyes and thought. Through the natural rhythms of daily life – the cycle of waking and sleeping, of going to work and returning home, of interacting with family and friends – strong focal points are established for the aggregation of psychic impressions. If one has not prepared oneself through proper meditation to use these focal points for the strengthening of positive vibrations, then they will by default turn into rats' nests of negativity. Through identification with the personal nature, one may tend to take every one of these disturbances literally and personally, and thereby make it the hooking-point for further infestation of the psyche. If, instead, one strengthens a meditative awareness of the manvantaric vibration of the Avatar, then these inevitable collecting-points in terrestrial consciousness can become powerful regenerative agents enabling one to meet one's own karmic responsibility and to lighten the burden of others.

Meditation upon the cosmos as a complex hierarchy of interacting cycles radiating from a common source may be aided by simple, yet suggestive, diagrams. One *yantra* represents a spiral seashell with a lotus at the centre, the outside of which is like the head of a coiling serpent. The diagram is in ceaseless motion. At the same time, because of the harmonizing of different strata – which resemble the skins of the earthy layers of language and concept, and even the different hierarchies of reality – the *yin-yang* alternation within the different strata harmonizes with the lotus-like sun in the centre. Thus, lines of emanation radiate out from the centre and return to it. Through meditation upon such a *yantra* one can break the fixity of the static geometry and the limited algebra governing one's responses to the world, and move on to a more dynamic and topological post-Newtonian conception of space, a more fluidic and flexible post-Euclidian geometry, and a more interactive conception of a post-Cartesian algebra founded upon matrices and groups. As one gains a sense of Aquarian meta-mathematics and meta-geometry, founded upon the triadic meta-logic of Gupta Vidya, one will prepare oneself to participate self-consciously in the dialectical calculus of the cosmos. Daily meditation can provide the basis for dynamic integration of distilled perceptions.

Integration and Recurrence, *The Gupta Vidya* III, 160-162

Come Out of the Old and Decaying Order

As H.P. Blavatsky noted in the last century, wherever spiritual truth is dishonoured and elementary discrimination is lacking, the mysteries of nature cannot be divulged. One must begin by honouring the humblest truths by honest application and through some philosophical comprehension before one may raise one's hand to the latch which guards the gate of the Greater Mysteries. Initially, one must be willing to honour the Delphic injunction "Know thyself" on the planes of relative learning, and thereby restore the power of inner perception before one may apprehend any absolute truth.

> Absolute truth is *the symbol of Eternity,* and no *finite* mind can ever grasp the eternal, hence, no truth in its fulness can ever dawn upon it. To reach the state during which man sees and senses it, we have to paralyze the senses of the external man of clay. This is a difficult task, we may be told, and most people will, at this rate, prefer to remain satisfied with relative truths, no doubt. But to approach even terrestrial truths requires, first of all, *love of truth for its own sake,* for otherwise no recognition of it will follow.
>
> H.P. BLAVATSKY

The Victorian age, with all its cant and hypocrisy as well as its latent sense of human dignity and integrity preserved through the recollection of the Enlightenment, is gone. It is now obvious to many that there was neither irony nor polemic, but only compassion, in the stern warnings that H.P. Blavatsky delivered on behalf of the Mahatmas to Theosophists and non-Theosophists alike. The collapse of the acquisitive and parochial civilizations of the past two millennia is approaching completion, and on behalf of the Aquarian dawn of the global civilization of the future, it was essential since 1963 to encourage rebels and victims alike to come out of the old and decaying order. This anarchic rebellion entailed the risk that the weak would become like Trishanku in the Indian myth, who was suspended between heaven and earth, neither able to land on his feet in the world nor capable of scaling celestial heights. This was a great but well-calculated risk, because large numbers of pilgrim-souls have awakened to a sense of their common humanity, both in the old world and the new.

Whilst the wisest statesmen and most perceptive peoples of the globe did not think that the Second World War had drained all the sources of discord on the earth, they were nonetheless willing to move towards the establishment of a juridical basis of enduring peace. What they did not foresee was that their endeavours on behalf of a new era of security and welfare for the whole of humanity would be flouted by the flagrant jingoists of the so-called American century, backed by sectarian bigotry and pervasive racism. Like Lisa in Dostoevsky's *Notes From The Underground,* they may not have comprehended the details of what America claimed to know, but they soon understood that their smug benefactor was so self-deluded as to be incapable of offering timely help. Perhaps now a growing core of Americans has realized that the decent peoples of the world dislike self-righteous bullies. They do not like the bombing of defenseless people, nor do they wish to see what happened to Dresden recur *ad nauseam* after the war. Rather, they expect true courage and ethical sensitivity from the proud champions of freedom and human solidarity. No one capable of resonating to the authentic meaning behind the American experiment could be but saddened to see it turning into a vulgar display of chauvinistic rhetoric and moral cowardice, an unholy alliance of Mammon, Moloch and Beelzebub.

The Healing of Souls, *The Gupta Vidya* III, 80-81

The Two Requirements

Put simply, two distinct requirements must be fulfilled: *first,* one has to get beyond oneself, going in consciousness to the core of what is common, cosmic and transcendent until one can come down and be wide awake in the world of particularities and contrasts, the arena of illusion, ignorance and delusion; *secondly,* one must also acknowledge in detail, at least unto oneself, one's persisting delusions, because if one looks for commonality at the expense of fruitful diversity, one evades one's ethical responsibility. If one is unduly caught up in the world, one is running away from the One Light, but if one vainly tries to grab instantly the light of spiritual will, one is running away from past karma. Therefore one has to recognize frankly that every moment is a precious opportunity to learn, that everything which comes in life is really one's guru in disguise. At every moment of each day, the stream of life is rushing in to teach the soul if it is willing to learn. If one takes proper advantage of these golden opportunities, one can clean and polish the lenses of the vestures. By working upon one's different vestures in deep meditation several times a day, and also by going beyond them during deep sleep, a point will come at which one is refining them deftly from both ends rather like a person who is both visualizing a plan for a new arrangement in a room and also cleaning out objects as they are. The one activity need not preclude the other. One can have some time each day to think out a new way of arranging everything, and new ways of thinking. Meanwhile, one can also dust each object as it is, keeping things as neatly as possible within the existing arrangement.

Applying the analogy to the vestures, one can simultaneously increase slowly the porosity of the grosser vestures to the light while also working through the subtlest vestures to invite the beatific descent of the Divine Light. As the grosser vestures are continually renovated and cleaned, and as the subtlest vestures experience through meditation the infusion of noumenal light, a point comes at which the two processes can be brought together, realigning all the vestures from a fresh standpoint. This process must be renewed and repeated again and again. The search for the spiritual is really hard work, and while it is good that so many people have rebelled against a social structure which was using labour as a means of confinement to a narrow bourgeois conception of the world, the deeper purpose of this widespread and anomic rebellion was not to encourage indolence and indiscipline. Work and discipline can be done in an Aquarian mode, as a form of silent worship and spontaneous sacrifice, flowing forth from a selfless motive to be of true service to humanity and to elevate human and global consciousness, thus furthering the noble impulse of monadic evolution.

Self-Emancipation, *The Gupta Vidya* III, 179

Cherish the Discovery Within

Let a man be without external show such as the Pharisees favoured, without inscriptions such as the Scribes specialized in, and without arrogant and ignorant self-destructive denial such as that of the Sadducees. Such a man, whether he be of any religion or none, of whatever race or nation or creed, once he recognizes the existence of a Fraternity of Divine Beings, a Brotherhood of Buddhas, Bodhisattvas and Christs, an Invisible Church (in St. Augustine's phrase) of living human beings ever ready to help any honest and sincere seeker, he will thereafter cherish the discovery within himself. He will guard it with great reticence and grateful reverence, scarcely speaking of his feeling to strangers or even to friends. When he can do this and maintain it, and above all, as John says in the Gospel, be true to it and live by it, then he may make it for himself, as Jesus taught, the way, the truth and the light. While he may not be self-manifested as the Logos came to be through Jesus — the Son of God become the Son of Man — he could still sustain and protect himself in times of trial. No man dare ask for more. No man could do with less.

Jesus knew that his own time of trial had come — the time for the consummation of his vision — on the Day of Passover. Philo Judaeus, who was an Aquarian in the Age of Pisces, gave an intellectual interpretation to what other men saw literally, pointing out that the spiritual passover had to do with passing over earthly passions. Jesus, when he knew the hour had come for the completion of his work and the glorification of his father to whom he ever clung, withdrew with the few into the Garden of Gethsemane. He did not choose them, he said. They chose him. He withdrew with them and there they all used the time for true prayer to the God within. Jesus had taught, *Go into thy closet and pray to thy father who is in secret,* and that *The Kingdom of God is within you.* This was the mode of prayer which he revealed and exemplified to those who were ready for initiation into the Mysteries. Many tried but only few stayed with it. Even among those few there was a Peter, who would thrice deny Jesus. There was the traitor, Judas, who had already left the last supper that evening, having been told, *That thou doest, do quickly.* Some among the faithful spent their time in purification. Were they, at that point, engaged in self-purification for their own benefit? What had Jesus taught them? Could one man separate himself from any other? He had told those who wanted to stone the adulteress, *Let him who is without sin cast the first stone.* He had told them not to judge anyone else, but to wait for true judgment. Because they had received a sublime privilege, about which other men subsequently argued for centuries and produced myriad heresies and sects, in their case the judgment involved their compassionate concern to do the sacred Work of the Father for the sake of all. The Garden of Gethsemane is always here. It is a place very different from the Wailing Wall where people gnash their teeth and weep for themselves or their tribal ancestors. The Garden of Gethsemane is wherever on earth men and women want to cleanse themselves for the sake of being more humane in their relations with others.

The Gospel According to St. John, *The Gupta Vidya* II, 153-154

APPENDIX III:

The Aquarian Path

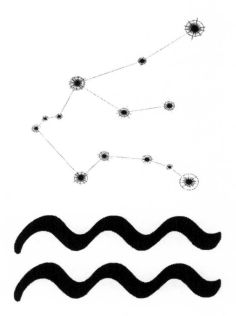

The Avatar

There are myriad avenues for the Logos to incarnate in the world. Indeed, every pure act of sacrifice releases and spreads the Avatar-light. Each pain endured in the probationary effort to transcend oneself for the sake of others cleanses a channel through which higher energy may flow, and A.E.'s humanized and incomplete notion of the Avatar draws upon this deeper esoteric truth. *The Avatars* portrays them not as the angelic beings or accredited Paracletes celebrated in canonical texts, but rather as a highly evolved and enchantingly magnetic pair of human beings who show a serene self-validating assurance of their ineffable divinity and a supreme sense of fullness of truth, love and beauty. This is undoubtedly a restrictive rather than a revelatory use of the term 'Avatar', but it does serve to highlight the universal possibilities for human growth. Above all, A.E.'s Avatars seem to be apostles of a silent, subtle and non-violent revolution, who come to inspire folk wisdom in new directions, to establish fresh patterns of communion and celebration, and to serve as microcosmic models for the future:

> The purpose of an Avatar is to reveal the spiritual character of a race to itself.
>
> *The Avatars*

An Avatar always transmits some fundamental and forgotten truths to an entire epoch and initiates a new cycle of inner growth and human fellowship. The resounding vibration disseminated by the Avatar provides the essential keynote for the epoch he inaugurates. Thus Lord Krishna came to teach a philosophy of joyous and unbounded love to a humanity about to descend into the darkness of the Iron Age or Kali Yuga. A.E.'s Aodh and Aoife similarly seek to propagate the Golden Age vibration of Krishna amidst the impotence and desperation spawned by the soulless materialism of the modern State. They transmit the glad tidings of an emergent humanity conscious of its divine kinship with all of

Nature. They transmute the everyday relationships between estranged human beings, kindling the sparks of magnanimous altruism, cheerful civility and thoughtful compassion to arise spontaneously as the basis of a spiritual culture, rooted in a shared reverence for the divine, foreshadowing the fecund promise of the global civilization of the dawning Aquarian age.

Myth and Redemption, *The Gupta Vidya* III, 406

The Healing of Corruption of Consciousness

The pervasive sense of the sacred and universal respect for freedom of thought and choice have become obscured in many victims of modernity owing to a hypnotic fascination with corruption and evil, forgetfulness of the divine mission of the immortal Soul, alienation from others and oneself, especially through fear of failure, estrangement through loneliness, distrust of oneself, and possible misuse in former lives due to cowardice and false ideas connected with evasion of the laws of Nature. Corruption of consciousness must be healed, and what is natural must be restored through the Golden Rule of reciprocity. Already, since 1963, many souls have taken birth in diverse cultures who have a recognition of the need to restore the ethical foundation of human society. This transcends the claims of all cultures to pre-eminence. Such souls will increase in number until a time comes when there will be so many for whom this is so natural that any encouragement given them will help the regeneration of the human race. This will be a distinctly different class of souls from those who came mauled and tormented by the degradation of two world wars, which helped to make popular the works of the corrupt. The attempt to make normal what was abnormal has failed, so far. It was tried in every way, but once the alternatives are known, then what is abnormal had to become more and more desperate and self-destructive because it could not any more pretend to be normal.

The twilight hour of sadists and masochists has now struck, and myriads of pilgrim-souls seek the Midnight Sun and the sacred constellation of the Aquarian Age, which began soon after the *fin de siècle*. The invisible dawn of the cosmopolis is summoned by the flute of the divine cowherd, beckoning home the matured innocents that dared to dream of a Golden Age. Meanwhile, Nataraja of Kailaś and Kala-Hamsa enacts the Tandava Dance over the heads of epicurean giants, stoical dwarfs and cynical eunuchs. The age of sectarian religions, technocratic politics and cultural envy is dead. *Kama manas* has been dethroned by *Buddhi-Taijasi,* the Light of the Logos. The age of humanistic science, authentic spirituality and mini-communes has just begun, foreshadowing the end of the twentieth century and the emergence of the City of Man. The inevitable return of initiative to the scattered supporters of what is innate, universal and spiritual, merely suggests that no special pleading is needed for true gratitude and an authentic sense of the sacred. Despite the failures of so many, the philosophy of perfectibility, the religion of responsibility and the science of spirituality will spread far and wide, like the myriad branches of the Ashwatha tree, with its roots in heaven.

Between Heaven and Earth, *The Gupta Vidya* III, 312

The Hour Has Struck

None but Mahatmas, perfect embodiments of the truth, are really capable of understanding the full meaning of the divine enactment of the Mysteries or the mysterious avataric descent of the Logos into the world. They alone are permitted to record the archives of the Teachings of Hamsa, and will permit no pseudoesoteric packagings of the truth to persist. Every sincere and devoted individual who is willing to become an apprentice in the arduous art of transcendent concentration and selfless meditation upon universal good is invited to enter the orbit of the Mahatmas. If one reads the *Bhagavad Gita* carefully, one will discover that Krishna always is surrounded by Mahatmas. It is only the consciousness corrupted by materialization and externalization which would mistake the allegorical scenes of the Mahabharata War for events constrained by the limits of physical space. The true locus of events is a matrix of divine Logoic ideation surrounded by the fathomless waters of invisible space, wherein Mahatmas, in their *vamanas* or aerial cars of inconceivably refined subtle substance, surround the Logos. They alone can see the invisible form of Krishna, and therefore they alone can tell the tale. The geographical space and colourful scene surrounding Krishna on earth is a form of *maya* hiding the "invisible garment of God". Within the invisible form of the Avatar there resides a galaxy of Mahatmas. Seated in ceaseless meditation and constant adoration within the matrix of the body of the Logos, they constitute the constellations, indeed the entire universe of enlightenment. Nothing of this can be known by going from without within, but something of it may be gathered by the intuition through contemplating Buddhist *tankas* showing myriads of Bodhisattvas surrounding a central figure of the Buddha like an aura of wisdom-light.

Once this central fact of human evolution is widely grasped, it marks the end of recorded history with all its pretentious pseudo-esoteric and secular accounts of the meaning of human existence.

When the glyph of man thinking is realized within to be identical with the matrix of the Logos surrounded by the galaxies of Bodhisattvas, it is no more possible to be taken in by the trumped up stories and packaged accounts of spiritual life promoted by the failures in human evolution. Stripped of illusions, nothing remains but to insert oneself by the power of one's own mystic meditation into the universal vision of Shamballa. This is the vision of the One Flame and its innumerable rays streaming forth, each of which is like a jewel in the Logoic form of Shiva-Krishna or Nataraja-Narayana. Every diamond-souled Mahatma is an eternal witness to this sacred truth, and no concession can be made to any lesser vision. It has long been known in Shamballa that the time would come when there could be no further accommodation either to the ill-intentioned or to the passive which would obstruct the inward spiritual growth of humanity. It has always been inevitable that at some point the fiery divine dragon of wisdom – the living Word of Truth – should burn away the obscuring dross of past error. This is a necessary preparation for the entry of the good gardeners of Nature, who will prepare the soil for the future Garden of Eden. Those who are so fortunate to earn under karma, through decades of striving, the golden privilege of thinking the right thoughts at the moment of death, may also be so fortunate as to reincarnate again in a human form at some point in time when they may hear of the actual presence on earth of a new humanity. To be worthy of the rare good karma of returning to the earth at this distant time, one must begin now to nurture the seed of the Buddha-nature through *Buddhi Yoga,* through gratitude and renunciation. Then one may hope to experience the immense thrill of being alive in those far-flung aeons when Men of Meditation, masters of the mathematics of service to humanity, will walk the earth openly and all human beings alike understand that the only purpose for being in a human form is to be a true servant to humanity.

Through understanding the real purpose of meditation upon sacred glyphs and symbols, which has to do with the inward invocation of the fires of self-purification and illumination through self-transcendence, one may come to appreciate the truth of what Hegel once said about history, that the dialectic must have its joke. In a sense, at this point in history the joke of the divine dialectic is the only significant fact in history. The dialectic is smiling the smile of the Buddha. It is playing the flute of Krishna. It is also seated in divine meditation like Shankara. The dialectic, at the same time, is accelerating the disintegration of the thoughtforms and entities of the past for whom the hour has struck. There is an increasingly widespread recognition that the old order is nearing its end, and that the Aquarian task of self-regeneration has begun.

> *Lodging the purified inner powers in the Self, the witness, who is pure illumination, gaining steadfastness step by step, let him fix his vision on the fullness of the Eternal.*

SHRI SHANKARACHARYA

Deliverance from Bondage, *The Gupta Vidya* III, 398-400

The Choice

One must clearly delineate the moral lines within the fivefold field of the middle human principles. The only authentic mental standpoint to take is that of total responsibility for oneself, never descending to transfer blame to anything outside oneself. The right discipline for the present and coming age is that of 'the mango principle' enunciated in *The Voice of the Silence*. One must learn to be as soft as that fruit's pulp to the woes and limitations of others, and as hard as its stone to one's own weaknesses and limitations. Only by doing this can one gain the inner firmness and moral strength needed to withdraw consciously from the astral form, and eventually to dissipate that form at will. This in itself is a high stage of development, and it cannot be attained until one has paid one's debts to other human beings. Even where one is still carrying debts to others both mentally and morally, it should still be possible to be profoundly grateful and responsible in relation to one's opportunities as a self-conscious Monad. Nothing less is being aimed at than the fullest possible recovery of the true meaning of the word 'man'. Derived from *manushya*, 'the thinker', it is man alone in Nature who is capable of keeping his head erect, capable of standing firm, capable of having a straight spine and above all capable of consciously directing benevolence towards all beings. But before one can gain full control over, or some comprehension of, the ultimate destination, one must set one's inward course in the right direction. Every human being is intuitively capable of knowing whether one is going in the right direction or not.

The forward march of human evolution has nothing to do with cowardliness or evasion, with pseudo-chelaship or nefarious manipulations. These belong to the murderers of souls, whether they parade themselves in the garb of science or sexology, psychology or religion. Every decent human being will have a natural distaste towards these grotesque mockeries of human life which only serve to weaken human responsibility. But those who consult their own consciences will discover a natural sympathy with that essential tendency in nature which evinces a progressive march towards self-mastery. They will learn to discern a design and compassion in the activity of the apparently blind forces in the vastitude of visible and hidden Nature. They will learn to appreciate the intimate adaptations of natural form to intelligent purpose; through their joyous meditations, they will learn how to assist evolution onwards from within. Rejecting all irrational conceptions of evolution based upon truncated categories, they will begin to cherish the beauty and integrity of the continual process of sifting that is spiritual evolution.

Though sharp in their immediate results and distressing to the inflated personal shadow, the tests of karma are entirely moral. In the long run they can only serve to instruct humanity in the dual law of universal justice and unconditional compassion. Those who willingly submit themselves to these ethical tests and who become freely capable of breathing for the sake of others will earn an entitlement to share in the resplendently noetic civilization of the future. Those who do not will be spewed forth by Nature. Under the ancient though eternally young Avataric impulse of the Aquarian Age, there is challenge, guidance and protection for every human being who aspires to work truly on behalf of the humanity of the future. The choice belongs to each and all.

Purity and Pollution, *The Gupta Vidya* I, 246-247

Spiritual Mountain Climbing

In India, in China and Japan, in Siam and Burma, in Egypt and Greece, in Chaldea and Mesopotamia, later in Rome and in the Arab world and among the Jews, and in the modern age in Europe and the United States of America, also in the last hundred years in the Theosophical Movement, it is the same story of partial understanding leading to misunderstanding, concretization resulting in desecration. That is the karma of the transmission of Divine Wisdom, because the uninitiated will, in the sense in which Jesus spoke of casting pearls before swine, drag down the solar teaching into the murky realm of lunar consciousness polluted by profane sense-perceptions. This is profanation, but at the same time, the immortal soul in those individuals may gain some food for *sushupti* and for *devachan* if they still have some link with the higher Triad. There would also be those who can get their mental luggage ready for another life. One may never really know how the process goes on from the outside, but one can understand why something always had to be kept secret from every person who is self-excluded from the sacred circle of initiates and ascetics. There will always be such a sacred circle, just as there will always be only a few who actually have climbed Himalayan peaks. But there will be very, very many who are fascinated by the enterprise.

Those courageous souls who are truly drawn to spiritual mountain climbing will be struck by the *Stanzas of Dzyan,* the *sutratman* of the *Gupta Vidya,* which forms the basis of the volumes of *The Secret Doctrine.* These *Stanzas* are also included as an appendix to *The Voice of the Silence,* which is derived from the same ancient source. Through their help, it is possible "to reform oneself by meditation and knowledge", but for this to happen, everything depends upon the state of mind and consciousness in which one approaches them. Those who have found them helpful take the *Stanzas* and read them silently again and again. On the whole, reading them aloud would be unwise because one may activate lower psychical forces much faster than one has gained the ability to govern them. This is a hazard with many people because of the ratios of the noetic to psychic in their lives. It is always a good practice to read quietly and absorb ideas with the mind's eye so that one receives the teaching on deeper planes than merely through the astral senses. Because in the Aquarian Age the mind is very crucial, without some understanding no such activity could be truly helpful and it may even degenerate into quasi-religious pseudo-ritual. This one does not want to encourage, and there is a constant danger that people will be pulled back through their *skandhas* into one or another form of ritualistic salvationism.

The Life-Giving Stream, *The Gupta Vidya* II, 33-34

Krishna's Medicinal Method

The Philosophy of Perfection of Krishna, the Religion of Responsibility of the Buddha and the Science of Spirituality of Shankara, constitute the Pythagorean teaching of the Aquarian Age of Universal Enlightenment. There are general and interstitial relationships between the idea of perfectibility, the idea of gaining control over the mind, and the exalted conception of knowledge set forth in the eighteenth chapter of the *Gita*. To begin to apprehend these connections, one must first heed the mantramic injunction from *The Voice of the Silence:* "Strive with thy thoughts unclean before they overpower thee." Astonishingly, there was a moment in the sixties when millions became obsessed with instant enlightenment; fortunately, this is not true at present. Few people now seriously believe that they are going to die as perfected beings in this lifetime. This does not mean that the secret doctrines of the 1975 cycle are irrelevant to the ordinary man who, without false expectations, merely wants to finish his life with a modicum of fulfilment. All such seekers can benefit immensely from calmly meditating upon the *Sthitaprajna*, the Self-Governed Sage, the Buddhas of Perfection. This is the crux of Krishna's medicinal method in the *Gita*. He presents Arjuna with the highest ideal, simultaneously shows his difficulties and offers intensive therapy and compassionate counsel. This therapeutic mode continues until the ninth chapter, where Krishna says, "Unto thee who findeth no fault I will now make known this most mysterious knowledge, coupled with a realization of it, which having known thou shalt be delivered from evil." In the eighteenth chapter he conveys the great incommunicable secret — so-called because even when communicated it resides within the code language of Buddhic consciousness. The authors of all the great spiritual teachings like the *Gita, The Voice of the Silence* and *The Crest Jewel of Wisdom* knew that there is a deep mythic sense in which the golden verses can furnish only as much as a person's state of consciousness is ready to receive.

H.P. Blavatsky dedicated *The Voice of the Silence* to the few, to those who seek to become *lanoos*, true neophytes on the Path. Like Krishna, she gave a shining portrait of the man of meditation, the Teacher of Mankind. In chosen fragments from the *Book of the Golden Precepts*, the merciful warning is sounded at the very beginning: "These instructions are for those ignorant of the dangers of the lower IDDHI." In this age the consequences of misuse of psychic powers over many lives by millions of individuals have produced a holocaust — the harvest of terrible effects. Rigid justice rules the universe. Many human beings have gaping astral wounds and fear that there is only a tenuous connecting thread between their personal consciousness and the light of the higher nature. Human beings have long misused *Kriyashakti*, the power of visualization, and *Itchashakti*, the power of desire. Above all, they have misused the antipodal powers of knowledge, *Jnanashakti*, so that there is an awful abyss between men of so-called knowledge and men of so-called power. What is common to both is that their pretensions have already gone for naught, and therefore many have begun to some extent to sense the sacred orbit of the Brotherhood of Bodhisattvas. On the global plane we also witness today the tragic phenomenon of which *The Voice of the Silence* speaks. Many human beings did not strive with their unclean hobgoblin images of a cold war. The more they feared the hobgoblin, the more they became frozen in their conception of hope. Human beings can collectively engender a gigantic, oppressive elemental, like the idea of a personal God, or the Leviathan of the State, which is kept in motion by reinforcement through fear, becoming a kind of reality and producing a paralysis of the will on the global plane.

Anamnesis, *The Gupta Vidya* II, 256-257

The Fires Of Purification, Purgation and Resolve

The secret mysteries of consciousness which underlie the meta-psychological evolution of mankind will remain unspoken to the vast majority of human beings for ages to come. But every man and woman who wishes to make himself or herself worthy of inclusion in that glorious future is invited to engage in philosophic meditation upon the metaphysical propositions of Gupta Vidya. Therein it is taught that all things in the universe are associated with either spirit or matter, one of these being taken as the permanent element of both. Pure Matter is pure Spirit, and neither can be understood by the finite discursive intellect. All pairs of opposites – light and darkness, heat and cold, fullness and the void – are at once pure Matter and pure Spirit. All are manifestations of Spirit-Matter – Aether-*Akasha*. Aether-*Akasha* is consubstantial with the plane of substance constituting *Buddhi-Manas*, the jewel in every heart and the diamond light in every soul. That light is one with the fiery ground of the entire cosmos. It is the origin of the three and seven invisible fires in nature and the forty-nine fires in human consciousness tapped at will by Adepts. These noumenal fires can be invoked infallibly through concentrated thought that reaches to universal good.

Any human being who hungers for universal good and truly wishes that the earth be a better world, out of the intensity of thought and will, draws closer to the sacred fires in the inmost essence of being. It is only in those Akashic fires that there is true rejuvenation. Though they are known to Adepts by other and secret names, they may be viewed by the neophyte as the fires of purification, purgation and resolve. By the sustained ideation of Mahatmas, they are made accessible to all human beings so that each can emit a powerful vibration in consonance with the global current of Aquarian humanity. Anyone willing to take the Teachings of Gupta Vidya as a true talisman can enter the stream of the great endeavour, which is consubstantial with the electric ocean of Life.

Anyone willing to start afresh, without illusions or expectations, but with a new and growing maturity, can forego the compensations of the shadowy past and rediscover a rightful place in the school of universal human evolution. One of the marks of spiritual maturity is a calm recognition that ethical responsibility is self-compelling. Once the resolve is made to grow up, one will recognize that Krishna is on the side of every Arjuna and against none. Then, like Arjuna, one may stand up and be counted amongst heroic souls worthy of the human heritage. Seeing beyond roles and forms, one may learn to breathe the Sacred Sound and the sacred speech: 'Om Mani Padme Hum, the Jewel in the Lotus, the God in man.' In this spirit the future will draw out and weave together the best, so that all may be on the side of the finest in the human race, allied with the future, under the all-protecting shield of the luminous host of hierophants.

The Fire of Purgation, *The Gupta Vidya* I, 355

Constant Learning

In modern society, there is a constant risk of awareness being reduced to a mechanical series of automatic responses which preclude true thinking and inhibit self-examination. When reflex responses in chaotic cerebration are reinforced through familiar clusters of tawdry images and shallow emotions, perverse thoughts invade one's sphere. This is a pervasive problem in our time of accelerated change and decisive sifting. Consider a person who attempts to become attentive while reading a text but who is not used to it and whose consciousness is shackled to the wandering mind, weak sensory responses and a general lack of attention and order in daily life. Such hapless persons cannot really read exactly what is in the text and cannot focus on it, let alone see around it and probe into profound suggestions buried within and between the lines of the text. To be able to shake the system out of this false familiarity, breeding a banal contempt for the supposedly stable world outside, the greatest teacher is suffering.

In the Aquarian Age in which many see the life-process as the continually enacted and essentially hidden interplay of harmony and disharmony, suffering always comes as a benevolent teacher of wisdom. Pain serves as a shock to one's sense of identity, illusory self-image and acquired or ancestral habits. It challenges one's pride and perversity. It compels one to pause for thought and radically reappraise the meaning of life, obligations, and potentials in oneself and others. When suffering comes, it plumbs below the surface of the psyche, touching depths of untrammeled consciousness. Noumenal and noetic awareness enters into everyday experience, and is saluted by remarkable constellations of poets, singers and seers. Incidents of life once taken for granted suddenly look very different, because one's sensibility has been sharpened. Were this not so, there would be little meaning to the mere succession of events and the mere recurrence of mechanical responses to the sensory stream of consciousness.

There is constant learning, and there is the ever-present possibility of deepening the cognitive basis of awareness, the operative level of self-actualization. This is part of the evolutionary and unending process of etherealization and refinement of life in the cycle of rapid descent and painful ascent. This is an exceedingly slow and subtle process — there is nothing automatic about it — but it is ubiquitous. Such a process of refinement must involve first of all an altered mode of awareness, which for most human beings means the conscious adoption of a radically different perspective on human life and cosmic evolution. But it must also transform the range and reach of one's sense-perceptions, through a better and finer use of the sensory powers of touch, taste, smell, sight and hearing. Further, this process of etherealization and refinement must proceed through a harmonious commingling of centres in the brain-mind and spiritual heart, through inward surrender to the Sovereign Self and the silent invocation of the Light of the Logos.

Self-Transformation, *The Gupta Vidya* II, 288-289

The Gospel of Gratitude

In general, an awareness of individual responsibility is the mark of a *Manasa,* a thinking being and moral agent. Though one cannot put everything right in this life and all the people one has affected are no longer around or alive, still some things can be rectified right now. It is possible to clean up one's copybook significantly without any clues to the complex mathematics of the cosmos. It is a waste of energy to fret and fume over the past, which is already part of our present make-up. Every cell of one's being carries the imprint of every thought, feeling, emotion, word and deed that one emanated in this life. At least, one can be responsible in relation to what one can see. At the present point of history the sense of responsibility has been enormously heightened for the whole of humanity. Never before have there been so many millions of human beings in search of divine wisdom, the science of self-regeneration. *The Voice of the Silence* instructs the disciple: "Look not behind or thou art lost." It is an exercise in futility to look behind because what has receded will recur. Instead of idle regret, it is possible to use the gospel of gratitude to transmute every precipitation of Karma into an avenue for fundamental growth through courageous self-correction.

Gratitude is no longer a threatening term, even in the United States. Many people everywhere respond to the beauty of reverence as it is truly innate to the human soul. Miseducation may foster mental presumption but it cannot extinguish the immortal spark of devotion. In all human beings there are natural feelings and intuitions which can be awakened and quickened. It would indeed be wrong to think that purely by penitence one could wipe out the consequences of past irresponsibility. This is a costly failure to understand the law of ethical causation. If one already has wronged others wilfully or thoughtlessly, feelings of remorse or empathy cannot erase past debts. This untenable doctrine of moral evasion did much harm over two thousand years. It was a travesty of true religion, an arbitrary breach of natural harmony. The irresponsible dogma of vicarious atonement traduced the exalted ethical teaching of Jesus. He taught that the Divine is not mocked: as ye sow, so shall ye reap. This is a central tenet in the teachings of all Initiates, and the erosion of the idea of responsibility is everywhere the consequence of priestcraft and ceremonialism. There are myriad ways in which people run away from the mature acceptance of full responsibility for past misdeeds. The Aquarian sees that true responsibility begins in the realm of thought and must include every thought. Surely one can appreciate the profound integrity of the teaching that every thought connects each human being with every other. The intuitive recognition of universal interdependence and of human solidarity is the basis of an ever-expanding conception of moral responsibility, renewed and refined through successive lives of earthly probation by a galaxy of immortal souls in a vast pilgrimage of self-discovery reaching towards universal self-consciousness.

Knowledge and Negligence, *The Gupta Vidya* III, 125-126

Make Every New Beginning Count

The therapeutic counsel of the great healers of souls is as relevant now as it was in the days of Buddha and Christ. There are those whom the immemorial teaching does not transform, even though they spend a lifetime with it. There are those who are afraid it is going to alter them and therefore never enter the stream. There are those who progressively find it affecting them, and are able by an unspoken trust to use it and be benefitted by it. And then there are those very few who are deeply grateful for the supreme privilege of witnessing the presence of this timeless teaching. They are constantly focussed upon the eternal example nobly re-enacted by Avatars who portray the magnificent capacity to maintain, with beautiful balance and ceaseless rhythm, the awesome heights of cosmic detachment and boundless love. These mighty men of meditation are also illustrious exemplars of the art of living and masterly archers in the arena of action. They cannot be understood in terms of external marks or signs. It is only through their inner light that individuals can come into closer contact with the inner lives of beings so much wiser and nobler than themselves. Those who cherish this truth may find the inner light within their own silent sanctuary through deep meditation, in their incommunicable experience of poignant emotions, in response to soul-stirring music, or in their ethical endeavours through honesty and self-examination.

Human beings willing to take their lives into their own hands can acknowledge when they have used a person as a means to their own end, and see this as unworthy. Highly evolved souls who fall into such abuses will go into a period of penance. They will engage in a chosen discipline of thought and action so as to atone for their past misuse. Penance is not to be understood in terms of externals. True *tapas* touches the core of one's inward integrity. It fosters a calm reliance upon the great law of universal unity and ethical causation. It is rooted in the wisdom that protects right relationships. The tragedy of the human condition is that when we make moral discoveries we cannot readily go back to those we have wronged and rectify matters. Either it would be too painful or the individuals involved are not accessible. But we can correct our relationships at a higher level of integrity. We could prepare ourselves, in a practical way, to come out of the old and smaller circles of loyalty. We could authentically enter into the family of man and become members of that brotherhood of human beings who do their utmost, in the depths of solitude and self-examination as well as in the gamut of their relationships in daily life, to re-enact in simple situations what at an exalted level is effortlessly exemplified by the Brotherhood of Bodhisattvas.

Those who make this heroic effort become pioneers who point to the civilization of the future. They gestate new modes in the realm of pure ideation and bring them down into the region of the visible, laying foundations for a more joyous age in which there will be less defensiveness, fear and strain in the fit between theory and practice. Some want to get there straightaway, but they have never really asked themselves whether they have paid off their debts, or even faced up to the consequences of what they did before. This is a common error, but nonetheless it is insupportable in a cosmos that is a moral order. We cannot erase what went before, though we can make every new beginning count and insert it into a broader context. The great opportunity that the Aquarian Age offers is to gain a sense of proportion in relation to oneself, entering into an invisible brotherhood of comrades who are making similar attempts. Their mutual bonds come alive through their inmost reverence for their teachers, who exemplify in an ideal mode what their disciples strive to make real in their lives through sincere emulation to the best of their knowledge.

Relationship and Solitude, *The Gupta Vidya* III, 324-325

Using Our Skills and Spiritual Resources

How possessive are we about our leisure – limited though it may be? Do we insist that this 'free' time is 'my' time because well earned? We may be quite entitled to what we term our 'private time'. Private time is an elementary human need (although not to the *yogin*, for whom time is a continuous inward state called 'living in the eternal'). But, whilst we are entitled to leisure time, we must, as ethical trustees, be willing to use it well. Furthermore, our chaste or corrupt visualization and use of free time often tells us something about the colour and direction of our spiritual will. If, for example, we use our leisure time constructively, then, in fact, time is a friend and not an enemy – either to us or to others. We work with the critical points within time – called cyclic recurrences – to regenerate ourselves within the spacious transcendental realm of the timeless. If we are wholly unable to use voluntary time well, then we sadly diminish ourselves and rapidly subtract from our opportunities to add to the sum of good. *Adharma* inevitably invites destructive *Karma*, "for whatsoever a man soweth, that shall he also reap."

When we turn to individual skills, we can appreciate the full significance of trusteeship – its subtle power of reconciliation and its ineffable moral beauty. In what sense, we might ask, are our individual skills to be held in sacred trust for others? In what sense can we badly abuse our skills and even use them to exploit others? *The litmus test as to whether or not we are true trustees of our skills lies in our expectations of return for using them.* Our motivation and our expectations are generally interwoven. In the modern West, and increasingly in the modernizing East, skills and specified knowledge are felt to be convertible into personal success and personal status. We might suppose that we are too mature to fall for the 'lure of filthy lucre', the cancer of greed, the canker of soulless competition. However, we are often all too susceptible to self-deception in this regard. We are subject to the satanic temptation that our hard-earned skills should purchase some intangible reward – from spiritual salvation to public praise. If we receive no external acknowledgements, then we are almost certain to be insidiously tempted to retreat into the tortured world of self-pity and self-approbation. This is because the tenuous exercise of borrowed knowledge and routinized skills is inescapably bound up with a fragile and fugitive self-image. Our frail sense of self-regard is disastrously opposed to the Aquarian spirit of effortless renunciation and intelligent sacrifice.

In practice, our daily approximation to distant ideals will depend upon the extent to which a substantial number of individuals balance their timid concern with individual claims to freedom against a calm willingness to consider the moral claims of the larger community of mankind. Can even the most ingenious organization of industry be dynamized by the innate desire to serve, not merely the desire to be served, the readiness to hold in trust and not the urge to appropriate? Psychologically, the spontaneous commitment to serve a community selflessly may be a self-conscious development, but the primary impulse to serve others is as much rooted in the universal desire for self-expression as the familiar instinct of self-preservation. The noble impulse to serve others, first displayed in the family, could progressively develop into the Bodhisattvic vow to serve the community of souls. This rests upon the compelling assumption that as citizens mature into creative individuals, the very process of individuation requires the growing recognition of the just claims of other individuals and of concentric communities, as well as a deepening concern with self-transcendence and the pilgrimage of humanity.

Gandhian Trusteeship, *The Gupta Vidya* III, 347-348

The Heritage of Humanity

Every human being is a receptacle of life-atoms from billions of other beings, immersed in a constant circulation that passes in and out of every astral form. In and through these *shariras* or vestures there is a ceaseless movement in the ocean of life of classes of life-atoms, which themselves belong to the hebdomadic kingdoms and sub-kingdoms of Nature. Each entering and exiting life-atom experiences and retains the impress of the thought and feeling of the human being presiding over the ephemeral vesture. All of these kingdoms and classes of elementals have had an archetypal function in the history of cosmic and human evolution. By combining a firm if rudimentary grasp of the metaphysics of Gupta Vidya concerning the seven creations with a persistent attention to the elementary processes of life, one can acquire through mindfulness a minimal insight into the magical process of breathing, thinking, feeling and willing. Minimally, one can begin to see that crude empirical notions like good luck and bad luck, being accident-prone or fortunate, are inadequate to an understanding of the exactitude and precision of karma. Similarly, one may come to see that neither wishful or dreamy thinking nor mechanistic or reductionist assumptions can be adequate to comprehend or cope with the challenges of life.

The awakening of the divine creative potential within human nature through an apprehension of karma requires a blending of a macro-perspective with a micro-application. Human beings in the Aquarian Age are the cultural inheritors of a vast vision of the physical universe constituted out of billions upon billions of galaxies. Whilst they may have few opportunities to observe the galaxies, they have many opportunities to hear and read about them. The reality of galactic space is much more alive for modern man than it was for the masses of people living before the present century. Through planetariums, through books and through the mass media, millions of people have been able to gain a glimpse of the awesome reality of myriad stars. Through the excitement of mental and physical voyages of discovery, many children of the present century have gained some inkling of the place of the earth amidst the starry heavens. Through this macro-perspective which is the heritage of contemporary humanity, individuals everywhere have gained access to the vast purifying powers of space. At the same time, the capacity to make use of such knowledge in daily life requires a micro-approach, something of that sort of attention stressed with great integrity in the Buddhist tradition. Beginning with Gautama's enigmatic Flower Sermon, there is a subtle emphasis placed upon the mystery of the individual flower, the beauty of the particular petal, the intimations of the individual moment.

Karma and Transmutation, *The Gupta Vidya* III, 366-367

A Deeper Sense of Being

Now, more than ever before, as courageous individuals gain the clarity of philosophic insight *(vijnana)*, rooted in deep meditation *(dhyana)*, they can reconnect themselves with the primordial vibration of the Mysteries, "the eternal thought in the eternal mind", the authentic source of the abundant creative potentials in themselves and in all Humanity. The irreversible tidal wave of the present historical moment will sweep away many of the relics and monuments of moribund traditions and the monstrosities of modern, so-called civilization. Divine Wisdom is immensely vaster and much more ancient than can remotely be sensed within the perspectives of present-day humanity. It is inconceivable that anything can stand in its way, that even the accumulated sins and crimes of fallen sorcerers and their myriad vampirized victims can resist the mighty onrush of the New Cycle, which, working mostly in the realm of *Akasha,* acts as a potent alchemical solvent in the astral light and in the inmost consciousness of hosts of souls, both embodied and awaiting incarnation. It would be a costly illusion for any group of monads, for any religious sect or social coterie, for any nation or continent, to transfer its own sense of doom to the whole of the human family, or to imagine that any power on earth can resist the rising tide of the progressive enlightenment of the humanity of the future.

In a very real sense, all human souls are always exiles in this world, but this is poignantly true of so many in a time of colossal karmic precipitation, widespread sifting between the 'quick' and the 'dead', and the dawning of a new global civilization, rising phoenix-like out of the ashes of the older orders. Porphyry's profound words on self-exile have a peculiar appositeness to our age:

> We resemble those who enter into or depart from a foreign region, not only because we are banished from our intimate associates, but in consequence of dwelling in a foreign land, we are filled with barbaric passions, and manners and legal institutes, and to all these have a great

propensity. Hence, he who wishes to return to his proper kindred and associates should not only with alacrity begin the journey, but, in order that he may be properly received, should meditate upon how he may divest himself of everything of a foreign nature which he has assumed, and should recall to his memory such things as he has forgotten, and without which he cannot be admitted by his kindred and friends. After the same manner, also, it is necessary, if we intend to return to things which are truly our own, that we should divest ourselves of everything of a mortal nature which we have assumed, together with an adhering affection towards it, and which is the cause of our descent; and that we should excite our recollection of that blessed and eternal essence, and should hasten our return to the nature which is without colour and without quality, earnestly endeavouring to accomplish two things: one, that we may cast aside everything material and mortal; but the other, that we may properly return, and be again conversant with our true kindred, ascending to them in a way contrary to that in which we descended hither.

All the outward forms and manifestations that constitute the clutter and outworn furniture of physical existence and psychic fantasy obscure and suppress the spiritual intuitions and intimations in human consciousness. By becoming caught up in the region of ephemera, true inward perception, Buddhic awareness, is blocked. Authentic depth perception is a perception of essences, a laser-like clarity in regard to primary causes, a bringing together of the centripetal, concentrated ideation of *Manas* and the centrifugal, expansive empathy of *Buddhi,* until there emerges a radiation of *Buddhi-Manas-Taijasi* which can flow downward and illumine the brain, the heart and the sensorium. As a human being learns to live progressively and increasingly in the divine egg of *Sat-Chit-Ananda,* a deeper sense of being, of ideation and eros, is awakened in all the vestures; there is a clarification and purification of all perception, and the awakening of an eye for essentials, the eye of transcendental synthesis fusing the standpoints of eternity and time. To light up the promise and possibility of such a radical reorientation of human consciousness in as many souls as possible is the awesome task and the noble prospect of the Aquarian Age, as well as the humanity and civilization of the future.

Kalki Maitreya, *The Gupta Vidya* III, 433-434

Enjoy Fellowship with the Entire Solar System

The term 'Monad' may apply equally to the vastest solar system or to the tiniest atom. The most self-conscious Monads enjoy fellowship with the entire solar system, with all other Monads as well as with the tiniest atoms. When the sage is teaching disciples, he is not addressing them as personalities, but is adjusting their life-atoms and affecting their *sushupti*. He is not talking to the lower mind, but pushing it out, freeing the higher mind in its descent. He is awakening the *Buddhi*. The difference between the Third Root Race and the Fifth is that the former intuitively knew this to be true. In the Aquarian Age, which has entered its second degree, Fifth Race laggards can self-consciously re-enact what was intuitively known by all in the Third Root Race. Self-consciously they could come together and learn from the Teachings of Sages, thereby altering their modes of breathing and becoming a help rather than a hindrance, not only to each other, but also to all living beings on earth.

The Dawning of Wisdom, *The Gupta Vidya* II, p. 60.

APPENDIX IV:

Other Sources

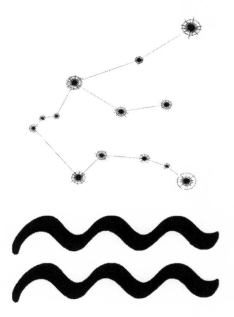

AQUARIAN AXIOMS

(Ancient axioms from a compilation made by H.P. Blavatsky in 1890)

1. Life is built up by the sacrifice of the individual to the whole. Each cell in the living body must sacrifice itself to the perfection of the whole; when it is otherwise, disease and death enforce the lesson.

2. Harmony is the law of life, discord its shadow; whence springs suffering, the teacher, the awakener of consciousness.

3. To obtain the knowledge of Self is a greater achievement than to command the elements or to know the future.

4. Self-knowledge is unattainable by what men usually call 'self-analysis'. It is not reached by reasoning or any brain-powers.

5. Real Self-knowledge is the awakening to consciousness of the divine nature of man.

6. Will creates intelligently; Desire blindly and unconsciously.

7. When desire is for the purely abstract – when it has lost all trace or tinge of 'self' – then it has become pure.

8. Spirituality is not what we understand by the words 'virtue' and 'goodness'. It is the power of perceiving formless, spiritual essences.

9. The discovery and right use of the true essence of Being; this is the whole secret of life.

10. You cannot build a Temple of Truth by hammering dead stones. Its foundations must precipitate themselves like crystals from the solution of Life.

THE THEORY OF CYCLES

It is now some time since this theory, which was first propounded in the oldest religion of the world, Vedaism, then taught by various Greek philosophers, and afterwards defended by the Theosophists of the Middle Ages, but which came to be flatly denied by the *wise men* of the West, like everything else, in this world of negation, has been gradually coming into prominence again. This once, contrary to the rule, it is the men of science themselves who take up. Statistics of events of the most varied nature are fast being collected and collated with the seriousness demanded by important scientific questions. Statistics of wars and of the periods (or cycles) of the appearance of great men – at least those as have been recognised as such by their contemporaries and irrespective of later opinions; statistics of the periods of development and progress at large commercial centres; of the rise and fall of arts and sciences; of cataclysms, such as earthquakes, epidemics periods of extraordinary cold and heat; cycles of revolutions, and of the rise and fall of empires, &c.; all these are subjected turn to the analysis of the minutest mathematical calculations. Finally, even the occult significance of numbers in names of persons and names of cities, in events, and like matters, receives unwonted attention. If, on the one hand, a great portion of the educated public is running into atheism and scepticism, on the other hand, we find an evident current of mysticism forcing its way into science. It is the sign of an irrepressible need in humanity to assure itself that there is a Power Paramount over matter; an occult and mysterious law which governs the world, and which we should rather study and closely watch, trying to adapt ourselves to it, than blindly deny, and break our heads against the rock of destiny. More than one thoughtful mind, while studying the fortunes and verses of nations and great empires, has been deeply struck by one identical feature in their history, namely, the inevitable recurrence of similar historical events reaching in turn every one of them, and after the same lapse of time. This analogy is found between the events to be substantially the same on the whole, though there may be more or less difference as to the outward form of details. Thus, the belief of the ancients in their astrologers, soothsayers and prophets might have been warranted by the verification of many of their most important predictions, without these prognostications of future events implying of necessity anything very miraculous in themselves. The soothsayers and augurs having occupied in days of the old civilizations the very same position now occupied by our historians, astronomers and meteorologists, there was nothing more wonderful in the fact of the former predicting the downfall of an empire or the loss of a battle, than in the latter predicting the return of a comet, a change of temperature, or, perhaps, the final conquest of Afghanistan. The necessity for both these classes being acute, observers apart, there was the study of certain sciences to be pursued *then* as well as they are *now*. The science of today will have become an "ancient" science a thousand years hence. Free and open, scientific study now is to all, whereas it was then confined but to the few. Yet, whether ancient or modern, both may be called exact sciences; for, if the astronomer of today draws his observations from mathematical calculations, the astrologer of old also based his prognostication upon no less acute and mathematically correct observations of the ever-recurring cycles. And, because the secret of this science is now being lost, does that give any warrant to say that it never existed, or that, to believe in it, one must be ready to swallow "magic," "miracles" and the like stuff? "If, in view of the eminence to which modern science has reached, the claim to prophesy future events must be regarded as either a child's play or a deliberate deception," says a writer in the *Novoyé Vremya*, the best daily paper of literature and politics of St. Petersburg, "then we can point at science which, in its turn, has now taken up and placed on record the question, in its relation to past events, whether there is or is not in the constant repetition of events a certain periodicity; in other words, whether these events recur after a fixed and determined period of years with every nation; and if a periodicity there be, whether this periodicity is due to blind chance or depends on the same natural laws, on which are more or less dependent many of the phenomena of human life." Undoubtedly the latter. And the writer has the best mathematical proof of it in the timely appearance of such works as that of Dr. E. Zasse, under review, and of a few others. Several learned works, treating upon this mystical subject, have appeared of late, and of some of these works and calculations we will now treat; the more readily as they are in most cases from the pens of men of eminent learning. Having already in the June number of the THEOSOPHIST noticed an article by Dr. Blohvitz *On the significance of the number Seven*, with every nation and people – a learned paper which appeared lately in the German journal *Die Gegenwart* – we will now summarize the opinions of the press in general, on a more suggestive work by a well-known German scientist, E. Zasse, with certain reflections of our own. It has just appeared in the *Prussian Journal of Statistics*, and powerfully corroborates the ancient theory of Cycles. These periods, which bring around ever-recurring events, begin from the infinitesimal small – say of ten years – rotation and reach to cycles which require 250, 500, 700 and 1000 years, to effect their revolutions around themselves, and within one another. All are contained within the *Máhá-Yug*, the "Great Age" or Cycle of the Manu calculation, which itself revolves between two eternities – the "Pralayas" or *Nights of Brahma*. As, in the objective world of matter, or the system of effects, the minor constellations and planets gravitate each and all around he sun, so in the world of the subjective, or the system of causes, these innumerable cycles all gravitate between that which the finite intellect of the ordinary mortal regards as eternity, and the till finite, but more profound, intuition of the sage and philosopher views as but an eternity within THE ETERNITY. "As above, so it is below," runs the old Hermetic maxim. As an experiment in his direction, Dr. Zasse selected the statistical investigations of all the wars, the occurrence of which has been recorded in history, as a subject which lends itself more easily to scientific verification than any other. To illustrate his subject in the simplest and most easily comprehensible way, Dr. Zasse represents the periods of war and the periods of peace in the shape of small and large rave-lines running over the area of the old world. The idea is not new one, for, the image was used for similar illustrations by ore than one ancient and mediaeval mystic, whether in words or picture – by Henry Kunrath, for example. But it serves well its purpose and gives us the facts we now want. Before he treats, however, of the cycles of wars, the author brings in the record of the rise and fall of the world's great empires, and shows the degree of activity they have played in the Universal History. He points out the fact that if we divide the map of the Old World into five parts – into Eastern, Central, and Western Asia, Eastern and Western Europe, and Egypt – then we will easily perceive that every 250 years, an enormous wave passes over these areas, bringing into each in its turn the events it has brought to the one next preceding. This wave we may call "the historical wave" of the 250 years' cycle. The reader will please follow this mystical number of years.

The first of these waves began in China, 2,000 years B.C. – the "golden age" of this Empire, the age of philosophy, of discoveries and reforms. "In 1750 B.C., the Mongolians of Central Asia establish a powerful empire. In 1500, Egypt rises from its temporary degradation and carries its sway over many parts of Europe and Asia; and about 1250, the historical wave reaches and crosses over to Eastern Europe, filling it with the spirit of the Argonautic expedition, and dies out in 1000 B.C. at the siege of Troy."

A second historical wave appears about that time in Central Asia. "The Scythians leave her steppes, and inundate towards the year 750 B.C. the adjoining countries, directing themselves towards the South and West; about the year 500 in Western Asia begins an epoch of splendour for ancient Persia; and the wave moves on to the east of Europe, where, about 250 B.C., Greece reaches her highest state of culture and civilization – and further on to the West, where, at the birth of Christ, the Roman Empire finds itself at its apogee of power and greatness."

Again, at this period we find the rising of a third historical wave at the far East. After prolonged revolutions, about this time, China forms once more a powerful empire, and its arts, sciences and commerce flourish again. Then 250 years later, we find the Huns appearing from the depths of Central Asia; in the year 500 A.D. a new and powerful Persian kingdom is formed; in 750 – in Eastern Europe – the Byzantine empire; and, in the year 1,000 – on its western side – springs up the second Roman Power, the Empire of the Papacy, which soon reaches an extraordinary development of wealth and brilliancy.

At the same time, the *fourth* wave approaches from the Orient. China is again flourishing; in 1250, the Mongolian wave from Central Asia has overflowed and covered an enormous area of land, including with it Russia. About 1500, in Western Asia, the Ottoman Empire rises in all its might and conquers the Balkan peninsula; but at the same time in Eastern Europe, Russia throws off the Tartar yoke, and about 1750, during the reign of Empress Catherine, rises to an unexpected grandeur and covers itself with glory. The wave ceaselessly moves further on to the West, and, beginning with the middle of the past century, Europe is living over an epoch of revolutions and reforms, and, according to the author, "if it is permissible to prophetize, then, about the year 2,000, Western Europe will have lived one of those periods of culture and progress so rare in history." The Russian press, taking the cue, believes that "towards those days the Eastern Question will be finally settled, the national dissensions of the European peoples will come to an end, and the dawn of the new millennium will witness the abolishment of armies and an alliance between all the European empires." The signs of regeneration are also fast multiplying in Japan and China, as if pointing to the approach of a new historical wave at the extreme East.

If, from the cycle of two-and-a-half century duration, we descend to those which leave their impress every century, and, grouping together the events of ancient history, will mark the development and rise of empires, then we will assure ourselves that, beginning from the year 700 B.C., the centennial wave pushes forward, bringing into prominence the following nations – each in its turn – the Assyrians, the Medes, the Babylonians, the Persians, the Greeks, the Macedonians, the Carthaginians, the Romans and the Germanians.

The striking periodicity of the wars in Europe is also noticed by Dr. E. Zasse. Beginning with 1700 A.D., every ten years have been signalized by either a war or a revolution. The periods of the strengthening and weakening of the warlike excitement of the European nations represent a wave strikingly regular in its periodicity, flowing incessantly, as if propelled onward by some invisible fixed law. This same mysterious law seems at the same time to make these events coincide with astronomical wave or cycle, which, at every new revolution, is accompanied by the very marked appearance of spots in the sun. The periods, when the European powers have shown the most destructive energy, are marked by a cycle of 50 years' duration. It would be too long and tedious to enumerate them from the beginning of History. We may, therefore, limit our study to the cycle beginning with the year 1712, when *all* the European nations were fighting at the same time – the Northern, and the Turkish wars, and the war for the throne of Spain. About 1761, the "Seven Years' War"; in 1810 the wars of Napoleon I. Towards 1861, the wave has a little deflected from its regular course, but, as if to compensate for it, or, propelled, perhaps, with unusual forces, the years directly preceding, as well as those which followed it, left in history the records of the most fierce and bloody war – the Crimean war – in the former period, and the American Rebellion in the latter one. The periodicity in the wars between Russia and Turkey appears peculiarly striking and represents a very characteristic wave. At first the intervals between the cycles, returning upon themselves, are of thirty years' duration – 1710, 1740, 1770; then these intervals diminish, and we have a cycle of twenty years – 1790, 1810, 1829-30; then the intervals widen again – 1853 and 1878. But, if we take note of the whole duration of the in-flowing tide of the warlike cycle, then we will have at the centre of it – from 1768 to 1812 – three wars of seven years' duration each, and, at both ends, wars of two years.

Finally, the author comes to the conclusion that, in view of facts, it becomes thoroughly impossible to deny the presence of a regular periodicity in the excitement of both mental and physical forces in the nations of the world. He proves that in the history of all the peoples and empires of the Old World, the cycles marking the millenniums, the centennials as well as the minor ones of 50 and 10 years' duration, are the most important, inasmuch as neither of them has ever yet failed to bring in its rear some more or less marked event in the history of the nation swept over by these historical waves.

The history of India is one which, of all histories, is the most vague and least satisfactory. Yet, were its consecutive great events noted down, and its annals well searched, the law of cycles would be found to have asserted itself here as plainly as in every other country in respect of its wars, famines, political exigencies and other matters.

In France, a meteorologist of Paris went to the trouble of compiling the statistics of the coldest seasons, and discovered, at the same time, that those years, which had the figure 9 in them, had been marked by the severest winters. His figures run thus: In 859 A.D., the northern part of the Adriatic sea was frozen and was covered for three months with ice. In 1179, in the most moderate zones, the earth was covered with several feet of snow. In 1209, in France, the depth of snow and the bitter cold caused such a scarcity of fodder that most of the cattle perished in that country In 1249, the Baltic Sea, between Russia, Norway and Sweden remained frozen for many months and communication was held by sleighs. In 1339, there was such a terrific winter in England, that vast numbers of people died of starvation and exposure. In 1409, the river Danube was frozen from its sources to its mouth in the Black Sea. In 1469 all the vineyards and orchards perished in consequence of the frost. In 1609, in France, Switzerland and Upper Italy, people had to thaw their bread and provisions before they could use them. In 1639, the harbour of Marseilles was covered with ice to a great distance. In 1659 all the rivers in Italy were frozen. In 1699 the winter in France and Italy proved the severest and longest of all. The prices for articles of food were so much raised that half of the population died of starvation. In 1709 the winter was no less terrible. The ground was frozen in France, Italy and Switzerland, to the depth of several feet, and the sea, south as well as north, was covered with one compact and thick crust of ice, many feet deep, and for a considerable space of miles, in the usually open sea. Masses of wild beasts, driven out by the cold from their dens in the forests, sought refuge in villages and even cities; and the birds fell dead to the ground by hundreds. In 1729, 1749 and 1769 (cycles of 20 years' duration) all the rivers and streams were ice-bound all over France for many weeks, and all the fruit trees perished. In 1789, France was again visited by a very severe winter. In Paris, the thermometer stood at 19 degrees of frost. But the severest of all winters proved that of 1829. For fifty-four consecutive days, all the roads in France were covered with snow several feet deep, and all the rivers were frozen. Famine and misery reached their climax in the country in that year. In 1839 there was again in France a most terrific and trying cold season. And now the winter of 1879 has asserted its statistical rights and proved true to the fatal influence of the figure 9. The meteorologists of other countries are invited to follow suit and make their investigations likewise, for the subject is certainly one of the most fascinating as well as instructive kind.

Enough has been shown, however, to prove that neither the ideas of Pythagoras on the mysterious influence of numbers, nor the theories of ancient world-religions and philosophies are as shallow and meaningless as some too forward free-thinkers would have had the world to believe.

H. P. Blavatsky
Theosophist, July, 1880

THE CHRONOLOGY OF THE BRAHMINS

Evolution proceeds on the laws of analogy in Kosmos as in the formation of the smallest globe. Thus the above, applying to the *modus operandi* at the time when the Universe was appearing, applies also in the case of our Earth's formation.

This Stanza opens by speaking of thirty crores, 30,000,000, of years. We may be asked — What could the ancients know of the duration of geological periods, when no modern scientist or mathematician is able to calculate their duration with anything like approximate accuracy? Whether they had or had not better means (and it is maintained that they had them in their Zodiacs), still the chronology of the ancient Brahmins shall now be given as faithfully as possible.

No greater riddle exists in science, no problem is more hopelessly insoluble, than the question: How old — even approximately — are the Sun and Moon, the Earth and Man? What does modern science know of the duration of the ages of the World, or even of the length of geological periods?

Nothing; *absolutely nothing.*

If one turns to science for chronological information, one is told by those who are straightforward and truthful, as for instance Mr. Pengelly, the eminent geologist, "We do not know."[1] One will learn that, so far, no trustworthy numerical estimate of the ages of the world and man could be made, and that both geology and anthropology are at sea. Yet when a student of esoteric philosophy presumes to bring forward the teachings of Occult Science, he is at once sat upon. Why should this be so, since, when reduced to their own physical methods, the greatest scientists have failed to arrive even at an approximate agreement?

It is true that science can hardly be blamed for it. Indeed, in the Cimmerian darkness of the prehistoric ages, the explorers are lost in

---

[1] For a similar admission see Prof. Lefevre's *Philosophy*, p. 481.

a labyrinth, whose great corridors are doorless, allowing no visible exit into the Archaic past. Lost in the maze of their own conflicting speculations, rejecting, as they have always done, the evidence of Eastern tradition, without any clue, or one single certain milestone to guide them, what can geologists or anthropologists do but pick up the slender thread of Ariadne where they first perceive it, and then proceed at perfect random? Therefore we are first told that the farthest date to which documentary record extends is now generally regarded by Anthropology as but "the earliest distinctly visible point of the pre-historic period." (*Encyclopædia Britannica.*)

At the same time it is confessed that "beyond that period stretches back a vast indefinite series of prehistoric ages." (*Ibid.*)

It is with those specified "Ages" that we shall begin. They are "prehistoric" to the naked eye of matter only. To the spiritual eagle eye of the seer and the prophet of every race, Ariadne's thread stretches beyond that "historic period" without break or flaw, surely and steadily, into the very night of time; and the hand which holds it is too mighty to drop it, or even let it break. Records exist, although they may be rejected as fanciful by the profane; though many of them are tacitly accepted by philosophers and men of great learning, and meet with an unvarying refusal only from the official and collective body of *orthodox* science. And since the latter refuses to give us even an approximate idea of the duration of the geological ages — save in a few conflicting and contradictory hypotheses — let us see what Aryan philosophy can teach us.

Such computations as are given in Manu and the Purânas — save trifling and most evidently *intentional* exaggerations — are, as already stated, almost identical with those taught in esoteric philosophy. This may be seen by comparing the two in any Hindu calendar of recognised orthodoxy.

The best and most complete of all such calendars, at present, as vouched for by the learned Brahmins of Southern India, is the already mentioned Tamil calendar called the "Tirukkanda

Panchanga," compiled, as we are told, from, and in full accordance with, secret fragments of Asuramaya's data. As Asuramaya is said to have been the greatest astronomer, so he is whispered to have also been the most powerful "Sorcerer" of the "WHITE ISLAND, which had become BLACK with sin," *i.e.,* of the islands of Atlantis.

The "White Island" is a symbolical name. Asuramaya is said to have lived (see the tradition of Jhana-bhaskara) in Romaka-pura in the West: because the name is an allusion to the land and cradle of the "Sweat-born" of the Third Race. That land or continent had disappeared ages before Asuramaya lived, since he was an Atlantean; but he was a direct descendant of the Wise Race, the Race that never dies. Many are the legends concerning this hero, the pupil of Surya (the Sun-God) himself, as the Indian accounts allege. It matters little whether he lived on one or another island, but the question is to prove that he was no myth, as Dr. Weber and others would make him. The fact of "Romaka-pura in the West" being named as the birth-place of this hero of the archaic ages, is the more interesting because it is so very suggestive of the esoteric teaching about the "Sweat-born" Races, the men born from the pores of their parents. "ROMAKUPAS" means "hair-pores" in Sanskrit. In Mahâbhârata XII. 10,308, a people named Raumyas are said to have been created from the pores of Virabhadara, the terrible giant, who destroyed Daksha's sacrifice. Other tribes and people are also represented as born in this way. All these are references to the later Second and the earlier Third Root Races.

The following figures are from the calendar just referred to; a footnote marks the points of disagreement with the figures of the Arya Samaj school:

I. From the beginning of cosmic evolution,[2] up

---

[2] The esoteric doctrine says that this "cosmic evolution" refers only to our solar system; while exoteric Hinduism makes the figures refer, if we do not mistake, to the whole Universal System.

to the Hindu year *Tarana* (or 1887) ....1,955,884,687 years.

II. The (astral) mineral, vegetable and animal kingdoms up to Man, have taken to evolve[3] ....300,000,000 years.

III. Time, from the first appearance of "Humanity" (on planetary chain) .... 1,664,500,987 years.[4]

---

[3] Another point of disagreement. Occultism says: "The astral prototypes of the mineral, vegetable and animal kingdoms up to man have taken that time (300 million years) to evolve, re-forming out of the cast-off materials of the preceding Round, which, though very dense and physical in their own cycle, are relatively ethereal as compared with the materiality of our present middle Round. At the expiration of these 300 million years, Nature, on the way to the physical and material, down the arc of descent, begins with mankind and works downwards, hardening or materialising forms as it proceeds. Thus the fossils found in strata, to which an antiquity, not of eighteen, but of many hundreds of millions of years, must be ascribed, belong in reality to forms of the preceding Round, which, while living, were far more ethereal than physical, as *we know the physical*. That we perceive and disinter them as tangible forms, is due to the process of materialization or crystallization referred to, which took place subsequently, at the beginning of the Fourth Round, and reached its maximum after the appearance of man, proceeding parallel with his physical evolution. This alone illustrates the fact that the degree of materiality of the Earth changes *pari passu* with that of its inhabitants. And thus man now finds, as tangible fossils, what were once the (to his present senses) ethereal forms of the lower kingdoms. The above Brahmanical figures refer to evolution beginning on Globe A, and in the First Round. In this Volume we speak only of this, the Fourth Round."

[4] This difference and the change of cyphers in the last three triplets of figures, the writer cannot undertake to account for. According to every calculation, once the three hundred millions are subtracted, the figures ought to stand, 1,655,884,687. But they are given as stated in the Tamil calendar above-named and as they were translated. The school of the late Pandit Dayanand Saraswati, founder of the Arya Samaj, gives a date of 1,960,852,987. See the "Arya Magazine" of Lahore, the cover of which bears the words: "Aryan era 1,960,852,987."

IV. The number that elapsed since the *"Vaivasvata Manvantara"*[5] —
or the *human* period — up to the year 1887,
is just ....18,618,728 years.

V. The full period of one *Manvantara* is .... 308,448,000 years.

VI. 14 "Manvantaras" *plus* the period of one
Sâtya Yuga make ONE DAY OF BRAHMÂ,
or a complete Manvantara and make ....4,320,000,000 years.

Therefore a *Maha-Yuga* consists of ....4,320,000 years.[6]

The year 1887 is from the commencement
of Kali-Yuga ....4,989 years.

---

[5] VAIVASVATA Manu is the one human being — some versions add to him the seven Rishis — who in the *Matsya* Avatar allegory is saved from the Deluge in a boat, like Noah in the Ark. Therefore, this *Vaivasvata Manvantara* would be the "post-Diluvian" period. This, however, does not refer to the later "Atlantean" or Noah's deluge, nor to the Cosmic *Deluge* or *Pralaya* of obscuration, which preceded our Round, but to the appearance of mankind in the latter Round. There is a great difference made, however, between the *"Naimitika,"* occasional or incidental, *"Prakritika,"* elemental, *"Atyantika,"* the absolute, and *"Nitya,"* the perpetual Pralaya; the latter being described as "Brahmâ's contingent recoalescence of the Universe at the end of Brahmâ's DAY." The question was raised by a learned Brahmin Theosophist: "Whether there is such a thing as *Cosmic* Pralaya; because, otherwise, the *Logos* (Krishna) would have to be reborn, and he is *Aja* (unborn)." We cannot see why. The *Logos* is said to be born only metaphorically, as the Sun is born daily, or rather a beam of that Sun is born in the morning and is said to die when it disappears, whereas it is simply reabsorbed into the parent essence. Cosmic *Pralaya* is for things visible, not for the *Arupa*, formless, world. The Cosmic or Universal *Pralaya* comes only at the end of one hundred years of Brahmâ; when the Universal dissolution is said to take place. Then the *Avyaya*, say the exoteric scriptures, the eternal life symbolized by Vishnu, assuming the character of Rudra, the *Destroyer*, enters into the *Seven* Rays of the Sun and drinks up all the waters of the Universe. "Thus fed, the seven solar Rays dilate to *seven Suns* and set fire to the whole Cosmos. . . ."
[6] Since a Maha-Yuga is the 1,000th part of a day of Brahmâ.

To make this still clearer in its details, the following computations by Rao Bahadur P. Sreenivas Row, are given from the *"Theosophist"* of November, 1885.

	Mortal years.
360 days of mortals make a year	1
Krita Yuga contains	1,728,000
Treta Yuga contains	1,296,000
Dwapara Yuga contains	864,000
Kali Yuga contains	432,000

The total of the said four Yugas constitute a Maha Yuga	4,320,000
Seventy-one of such Maha-Yugas form the period of the reign of one Manu	306,720,000
The reign of 14 Manus embraces the duration of 994 Maha-Yugas, which is equal to	4,294,080,000
Add *Sandhis, i.e.,* intervals between the reign of each Manu, which amount to six Maha-Yugas, equal to	25,920,000
The total of these reigns and interregnums of 14 Manus, is 1,000 Maha-Yugas, which constitute a Kalpa, *i.e.*, one day of Brahmâ	4,320,000,000
As Brahmâ's Night is of equal duration, one Day And Night of Brahmâ would contain	8,640,000,000
360 of such days and nights make one year of Brahmâ make	3,110,400,000,000
100 such years constitute the whole period of Brahmâ's age, *i.e.*, Maha-Kalpa	311,040,000,000,000

These are the exoteric figures accepted throughout India, and they dovetail pretty nearly with those of the Secret works. The latter, moreover, amplify them by a division into a number of esoteric cycles, never mentioned in Brahmanical popular writings — one of which, the division of the Yugas into racial cycles, is given elsewhere as an instance. The rest, in their details, have of course never been made public. They are, nevertheless, known to every *"Twice-born"* (Dwija, or Initiated) Brahmin, and the Purânas contain references to some of them in veiled terms, which no matter-of-fact Orientalist has yet endeavoured to make out, nor could he if he would.

These sacred astronomical cycles are of immense antiquity, and most of them pertain, as stated, to the calculations of Narada and Asuramaya. The latter has the reputation of a giant and a sorcerer. But the antediluvian giants (the Gibborim of the Bible) were not all bad or Sorcerers, as Christian Theology, which sees in every Occultist a servant of the Evil one, would have it; nor were they worse than many of "the faithful sons of the Church." A Torquemada and a Catherine de Medicis certainly did more harm in their day and in the name of their Master than any Atlantean giant or demigod of antiquity ever did; whether his name was Cyclops, or Medusa, or yet the Orphic Titan, the *anguipedal* monster known as Ephialtes. There were *good* "giants" in days of old just as there are *bad* "pigmies" now; and the Rakshasas and Yakshas of Lanka are no worse than our modern dynamiters, and certain Christian and civilised generals during modern wars. Nor are they myths. "He who would laugh at Briareus and Orion ought to abstain from going to, or even talking of, Karnac or Stonehenge," remarks somewhere a modern writer.

As the Brahmanical figures given above are approximately the basic calculations of our esoteric system, the reader is requested to carefully keep them in mind.

In the *"Encyclopædia Britannica"* one finds, as the last word of science, that the antiquity of man is allowed to stretch *only over* "tens of thousands of years."[7] It becomes evident that as these figures may be made to fluctuate between 10,000 and 100,000, therefore they mean very little if anything, and only render still denser the darkness

---

[7] *See* article *"Geology,"* in *"Encyclopædia Britannica."*

surrounding the question. Moreover, what matters it that science places the birth of man in the "pre- or post-glacial drift," if we are told at the same time that the so-called "ice age" is simply a long succession of ages which "shaded without abrupt change of any kind into what is termed the human or Recent period . . . the overlapping of geological periods having been the rule from the beginning of time." The latter "rule" only results in the still more puzzling, even if strictly *scientific* and correct, information, that "even to-day man is contemporary with the ice-age in the Alpine valleys and in the Finmark."[8]

Thus, had it not been for the lessons taught by the *Secret Doctrine,* and even by exoteric Hinduism and its traditions, we should be left to this day to float in perplexed uncertainty between the indefinite ages of one school of science, the "tens of thousands" of years of the other, and the 6,000 years of the Bible interpreters. This is one of the several reasons why, with all the respect due to the conclusions of the men of learning of our modern day, we are forced to ignore them in all such questions of pre-historic antiquity.

Modern Geology and Anthropology must, of course, disagree with our views. But Occultism will find as many weapons against these two sciences as it has against astronomical and physical theories, in spite of Mr. Laing's assurances that[9] "in (chronological) calculations of this sort, concerning older and later formations, there is no *theory,* and they are based on positive *facts,* limited only by a certain possible (?) amount of error either way," occultism will prove, scientific confessions in hand, that geology is very much in error, and very often even more so than Astronomy. In this very passage by Mr. Laing, which gives to Geology pre-eminence for correctness over Astronomy, we find a passage in flagrant contradiction to the admissions of the best Geologists themselves. Says the author —

---

[8] This allows a chance even to the Biblical "Adam Chronology" of 6,000 years. (*Ibid.*)
[9] See his "*Modern Science and Modern Thought.*"

> "In short, the conclusions of Geology, at any rate up to
> the Silurian period,[10] when the present order of things was
> fairly inaugurated, are approximate (truly so) *facts* and not
> *theories*, while the astronomical conclusions are *theories*
> based on *data so uncertain*, that while in some cases they
> give results incredibly short . . . in others they give results
> almost incredibly long."

After which, the reader is advised that the safest course "seems to
be to *assume* that Geology really proves the *duration of the present order
of things* to have been somewhere over 100 millions of years," as
"Astronomy gives an enormous though unknown time in the past,
and to come in the future, for the birth, growth, maturity, decline,
and death of the Solar System, of which our Earth is a small planet
now passing through the habitable phase." (p. 49.)

Judging from past experience, we do not entertain the slightest
doubt that, once called upon to answer "the absurd unscientific and
preposterous claims of exoteric (and esoteric) Aryan chronology,"
the scientist of "the results incredibly short," *i.e.*, only 15,000,000
years, and the scientist, who "would require 600,000,000 years,"
together with those who accept Mr. Huxley's figures of 1,000,000,000
"since sedimentation began in Europe" (*World Life*), would all be as
dogmatic one as the other. Nor would they fail to remind the
Occultist and the Brahmin, that it is the modern men of science alone
who represent exact science, whose duty it is to fight *inaccuracy* and
superstition.

The earth is passing through the "habitable phase" only for the
present order of things, and as far as our present mankind is concerned
with its actual "coats of skin" and phosphorus for bones and brain.

We are ready to concede the 100 millions of years offered by
Geology, since we are taught that our present physical mankind —
or the *Vaivasvata* humanity — began only 18 millions of years ago.

---

[10] To the Silurian period as regards Molluscs and Animal life — granted;
but what do they know of man?

But Geology has no facts to give us for the duration of geological periods, as we have shown, no more indeed than has Astronomy. The authentic letter from Mr. W. Pengelly, F.R.S., quoted elsewhere, says that: "It is at present, and perhaps always will be, impossible to reduce, even approximately, geological time into years or even into millenniums." And having never, hitherto, excavated a fossil man of any other than the *present form* —what does Geology know of him? It has traced zones or strata and, with these, primordial zoological life, down to the Silurian. When it has, in the same way, traced man down to his primordial protoplasmic form, then we will admit that it may know something of primordial man. If it is not very material "to the bearings of modern scientific discovery on modern thought," whether "man has existed in state of constant though slow progression for the last 50,000 years of period of 15 millions, or for the last 500,000 years of a period of 150 millions" ("Modern Science, etc." p. 49), as Mr. S. Laing tells his readers, it is very much so for the claims of the Occultists. Unless the latter show that it is a *possibility*, if not a perfect certainty, that man lived 18 millions of years ago, the Secret Doctrine might as well have remained unwritten. An attempt must, therefore, be made in this direction, and it is our modern geologists and men of science generally who will be brought to testify to this fact in the third part of this volume. Meanwhile, and notwithstanding the fact that Hindu Chronology is constantly represented by the Orientalists as a fiction based on no "*actual* computation,"[11] but simply a "childish boasting," it is never-the-less often twisted out of recognition to make it yield to, and fit in with, Western theories. No figures have ever been more meddled with and tortured than the famous 4, 3, 2, followed by cyphers of the Yugas and Maha-Yugas.

As the whole cycle of prehistoric events, such as the evolution and transformation of Races and the extreme antiquity of man, hangs upon the said Chronology, it becomes extremely important to check

---

[11] Wilson's "*Translation of Vishnu Purâna,*" Vol. I., pp. 50, 51.

it by other existing calculations. If the Eastern Chronology is rejected, we shall at least have the consolation of proving that no other — whether the figures of Science or of the Churches — is one whit more reliable. As Professor Max Muller expresses it, it is often as useful to prove what a thing is not as to show what it may be. And once we succeed in pointing out the fallacies of both Christian and scientific computations — by allowing them a fair chance of comparison with our Chronology — neither of the two will have a reasonable ground to stand upon, in pronouncing the esoteric figures less reliable than its own.

We may here refer the reader to our earlier work "*Isis Unveiled,*" Vol. I., p. 32, for some remarks concerning the figures which were cited a few pages back.

To-day a few more facts may be added to the information there given, which is already known to every Orientalist. The sacredness of the cycle of 4320, with additional cyphers, lies in the fact that the figures which compose it, taken separately or joined in various combinations, are each and all symbolical of the greatest mysteries in Nature. Indeed, whether one takes the 4 separately, or the 3 by itself, or the two together making 7, or again the three added together and yielding 9, all these numbers have their application in the most sacred and occult things, and record the workings of Nature in her eternally periodical phenomena. They are never erring, perpetually recurring numbers, unveiling, to him who studies the secrets of Nature, a truly divine System, an *intelligent* plan in Cosmogony, which results in natural cosmic divisions of times, seasons, invisible influences, astronomical phenomena, with their action and reaction on terrestrial and even moral nature; on birth, death, and growth, on health and disease. All these natural events are based and depend upon cyclical processes in the Kosmos itself, producing periodic agencies which, acting from without, affect the Earth and all that lives and breathes on it, from one end to the other of any Manvantara. Causes and effects are esoteric, exoteric, and *endexoteric,* so to say.

In *Isis Unveiled* we wrote that which we now repeat: "*We are at the bottom of a cycle and evidently in a transitory state.* Plato divides the intellectual progress of the universe during every cycle into fertile and barren periods. In the sublunary regions, the spheres of the various elements remain eternally in perfect harmony with the divine nature, he says; 'but their parts,' owing to a too close proximity to earth, and their commingling with the *earthly* (which is matter, and therefore the realm of evil), 'are sometimes according, and sometimes contrary to (divine) nature.' When those circulations — which Eliphas Levi calls ' currents of the astral light' — in the universal ether which contains in itself every element, take place in harmony with the divine spirit, our earth and everything pertaining to it enjoys a fertile period. The occult powers of plants, animals, and minerals magically sympathize with the 'superior natures,' and the divine soul of man is in perfect intelligence with these 'inferior' ones. But during the barren periods, the latter lose their magic sympathy, and the spiritual sight of the majority of mankind is so blinded as to lose every notion of the superior powers of its own divine spirit. We are in a barren period: the eighteenth century, during which the malignant fever of scepticism broke out so irrepressibly, has entailed unbelief as an hereditary disease upon the nineteenth. The divine intellect is veiled in man; his animal brain alone *philosophizes*." And philosophizing alone, how can it understand the "SOUL DOCTRINE"?

H.P. Blavatsky
The Secret Doctrine, ii 66-74

CYCLES

A PAPER READ BY WILLIAM Q. JUDGE
before the Aryan T. S., October 22, 1889

In advancing these few observations upon the doctrine of cycles, no claim to an exhaustive study of the matter is made. This paper is merely by way of suggestion.

The subject was brought before my mind by our discussion some evenings ago, when the question of the descent upon earth, or ascent from it, of celestial beings or progressed souls engaged our attention. It seemed certain that such ascent and descent were governed by cyclic laws, and therefore proceeded in regular periods. Some sentences from the *Wisdom of the Egyptians* by Synesius in matter furnished me by Bro. Chas. Johnston, now of India, read:

> After Osiris, therefore, was initiated by his father into the royal mysteries, the gods informed him . . . that a strong tribe of envious and malignant damons were present with Typhos as his patrons, to whom he was allied and by whom he was hurled forth into light, in order that they might employ him as an instrument of the evil which they inflict on mankind. For the calamities of nations are the banquets of the evil damons.

Yet you must not think that the gods are without employment, or that their descent to this earth is perpetual. For they *descend according to orderly periods of time,* for the purpose of imparting a beneficent impulse in the republics of mankind. But this happens when they harmonize a kingdom and send to this earth for that purpose souls who are allied to themselves. For this providence is divine and most ample, which frequently through one man pays attention to and affects countless multitudes of men.

For there is indeed in the terrestrial abode the sacred tribe of heroes who pay attention to mankind, and who are able to give them assistance even in the smallest concerns. . . . This heroic tribe is, as it were, a colony from the gods established here in order that this terrene abode may not be left destitute of a better nature. But when matter excites her own proper blossoms to war against the soul, the resistance made by these heroic tribes is small when the gods are absent; for everything is strong only in its appropriate place and time. . . . But when the harmony adapted in the beginning by the gods to all terrene things becomes old, they descend again to earth that they may call the harmony forth, energize and resuscitate it when it is as it were expiring. . . . When, however, the whole order of mundane things, greatest and least, is corrupted, then it is necessary that the gods should descend for the purpose of imparting another orderly distribution of things.

And in the *Bhagavad Gita* it is said by Krishna:

> When Righteousness
> Declines, O Bharata! when Wickedness
> Is strong, I rise, from age to age, and take
> Visible shape, and move a *man with men,*
> Succoring the good and thrusting the evil back,
> And setting Virtue on her seat again,

And

> At the approach of Brahma's day, which ends after a thousand ages, all manifested objects come forth from the non-developed principle. At the approach of Brahma's night they are absorbed in the original principle. This collective mass of existing things, thus coming forth out of the absolute again and again, is dissolved at the approach of that night; and at the approach of a new day it emanates again spontaneously.

In the foregoing quotations two great aspects of cyclic law are stated.

The latter has reference to the great cycle which includes all cycles of every kind. All the minor cycles run their course within it. When it begins a new creation is ushered in, and when it ends the great day of dissolution has arrived. In Arnold's translation of the *Bhagavad Gita* the beginning of this great cycle is beautifully called by him *"this vast Dawn,"* and of the close he reads:

> When that deep night doth darken, all which is
> Fades back again to Him who sent it forth.

The real figures expressing the mortal years included in this period are not given. Each Manwantara, according to the Hindus, is divided into the four Yugas or Ages, with a certain number of years allotted to each. Speaking on this subject in the *Key to Theosophy* (page 83), H. P. Blavatsky gives us a clue thus:

> Take as a first comparison and a help towards a more correct conception, the solar year; and as a second, the two halves of that year, producing each a day and a night of six months duration at the North Pole. Now imagine, if you can, instead of a solar year of *365* days, *ETERNITY*. Let the sun represent the universe, and the polar days and nights of six months *each-days and nights lasting each 182 trillions and quadrillions of years* instead of 182 days each. As the sun rises every morning on our *objective* horizon out of its (to us) *subjective* and antipodal space, so does the Universe emerge periodically on the plane of objectivity, issuing from that of subjectivity - the antipodes of the former. This is the "Cycle of Life." And as the sun disappears from our horizon, so does the Universe disappear at regular periods when the "Universal Night" sets in....

This is about the best idea we can get of it. It is impossible for the human mind to conceive these periods. No brain can grasp 182 trillions of years, much less if quadrillions are added. Few if any persons can mentally traverse the full extent of even *a million.* But we can make an approximation to the idea by using her suggestion of dividing the year and calling six months a day and six months a night, and then extending each into what is equivalent to infinity with us, since it is impossible to seize such immense periods of time.

And carrying out the correspondence suggested by her, we have at once a figure of the inclusion of all the minor cycles, by calling each day when we rise and night when we sleep as the beginning and ending of minor cycles. Those days and nights go to make up our years and our life. We know each day and can calculate it, and fairly well throw the mind forward to see a year or perhaps a life.

A quotation from Vol. I, at 31 of *Isis Unveiled* will give us the Indian figures. She says:

> The Maha-Kalpa embraces an untold number of periods far back in the antediluvian ages. Their system comprises a Kalpa or grand period of 4,320,000,000 years which they divide into four lesser yugas running as follows:

Satya yug	=	1,728,000 years
Treta yug	=	1,296,000 years
Dwapara yug	=	864,000 years
Kali yug	=	432,000 years
		4,320,000 years

> which make one divine age or Maha yuga; seventy-one Maha Yugas make 306,720,000 years, to which is added a sandhi, or twilight, equal to a Satya yuga or 1,728,000 years, to make a manwantara of 308,448,000 years. Fourteen manwantaras make 4,318,272,000 years, to which must be added a sandhyamsa or dawn, 1,728,000, making the Kalpa or grand period of 4,320,000,000. As we are now (1878) only in the Kali Yuga of the 28th age of the 7th manwantara of 308,448,000 years, we have yet sufficient time before us to wait before we reach even half of the time allotted to the world.

Further H. P. Blavatsky clearly states that the other cycles are carried out within this greater one, as at 34, Vol. I.

As our planet revolves once every year around the sun and at the same time once in every 24 hours upon its own axis, thus traversing minor cycles within a larger one, so is the work of the smaller cyclic periods accomplished and recommenced within the Great Saros.

Leaving the region of mathematics, we find this great period represents the extension of pigmy man into the vast proportions of the great man, whose death at the close of the allotted period means the resolving of all things back into the absolute. Each of the years of this Being embraces of our years so many that we cannot comprehend them. Each day of his years brings on a minor cataclysm among men; for at the close of each one of his days, metaphorically he sleeps. And we, as it were, imitating this Being, fall asleep at night or after our diurnal period of activity.

We are as minor cells in the great body of this Being, and must act obediently to the impulses and movements of the body in which we are enclosed and take part.

This greater man has a period of childhood, of youth, of manhood, of old age; and as the hour arrives for the close of each period, cataclysms take place over all the earth. And just as our own future is concealed from our view, so the duration of the secret cycle which shows the length of life of this Being is hidden from the sight of mortals.

We must not, however, fall into the error of supposing that there is but one of such great Beings. There are many, each being evolved at the beginning of a new creation. But here we touch upon a portion of the ancient philosophy which is fully explained only to those who are able to understand it by virtue of many initiations.

The Sandhya and Sandhyamsa referred to in the quotation taken from *Isis Unveiled* are respectively the twilight and the dawn, each being said to be of the same length and containing the same number of years as the first or golden age -*i.e.*, 1,728,000. It is in strict correspondence with our own solar day which has its twilight and dawn between day and night.

In going over the figures of the four ages, a peculiarity is noticed to which I refer at present as merely a curiosity. It is this:

The digits of Satya Yug 1. 7. 2. 8. added together make 18; those of Treta Yug 1. 2. 9. 6 make 18; those of Dwapara Yug 8. 6. 4 make 18;

while those of Kali Yug 4. 3. 2 sum up only 9; but if those of the grand total of 4,320,000 be added together they make 9, and that with Kali give 18 again. 18 is a number peculiar to Krishna in the *Bhagavad Gita*, and the poem has 18 chapters in it. If the three 18's and one 9 found as above be added together, the result will be 63, and 3x6 = 18, and if added make 9, and 18 added gives nine. If we multiply the three 18's and 9 produced from the different ages, we get 5. 8. 3. 2. which, if treated as before, give 18 again. And in the process of thus multiplying we discover a recurrence of the three eighteens and one 9, only inverted, as: The first 18 multiplied by the second one gives 3. 2. 4, which added results in 9; 324 multiplied by the third 18 gives 5. 8. 3. 2, which being added gives 18; and the product of the multiplication of 5,832 by 9, which is the result of adding the figures of Kali Yuga, is 5. 8. 4. 1, which on being added gives 18 again.[1] Now, as the last of these apparently fanciful operations, let us add together the results gained by multiplying the figures which were obtained during the various steps we have gone through and then adding the results.

The first figures are 1 x 8	=	8	
The second 3 x 2 x 4	=	24	
The third 5 x 8 x 3 x 2	=	240	
The fourth 5 x 8 x 4 x 1	=	160	
These added together give	...	4.3.2	
which are the digits of Kali Yuga			

Now turning to *Isis Unveiled* at p. 32 of Vol. 1, we find this remarkable paragraph:

> Higgins justly believed that the cycle of the Indian system, of 432,000, is the true key of the secret cycle.

[1] Readers may not be able to perform the calculations exactly as stated in the article above, as some of the original steps were not included.

But in the following paragraph she declares it cannot be revealed. However, we may get some clues, for we see in the figures of Kali Yuga, 432,000, and in the great total (leaving out the Sandhis), 4,320,000. What this secret cycle is, I, however, am not competent to say. I only desire to throw out the hints.

Having thus glanced over the doctrine of the great cycle which includes all others, let us now devote a little consideration to the cycle referred to in the passages from the Egyptian Wisdom first quoted.

This cycle may be called for the present purpose The Cycle of Descending Celestial Influences. By "descending" I mean descending upon us.

Osiris here signifies most probably the good side of nature, and his brother Typhos the evil. Both must appear together. Typhos is sometimes called in the Egyptian books the opposer, and later with us, is known as the Devil. This appearance of Typhos at the same time with Osiris is paralleled in the history of the Indian Krishna who was a white Adept, for at the same time there also reigned a powerful Black magician named Kansa, who sought to destroy Krishna in the same way as Typhos conspired against the life of Osiris. And Rama also, in Hindu lore the great Adept or ruling god, was opposed by Ravana, the powerful Black magician king.

In instructing Osiris after the initiation, the gods foresaw two questions that might arise within him and which will also come before us. The first is the idea that if the gods are alive and do not mingle with men to the advantage of the latter and for the purpose of guiding them, then they must necessarily be without any employment. Such a charge has been made against the Beings who are said to live in the Himalayas, possessed of infinite knowledge and power. If, say the public, they know so much, why do not they come among us; and as they do not so come, then they must be without employment, perpetually brooding over nothing.

The instructor answered this in advance by showing how these Beings – called gods – governed mankind through efficient causes proceeding downward by various degrees; the gods being perpetually concerned in their proper sphere with those things relating to them, and which in their turn moved other causes that produced appropriate effects upon the earth, and themselves only coming directly into earthly relations when that became necessary at certain "orderly periods of time," upon the complete disappearance of harmony which would soon be followed by destruction if not restored. Then the gods themselves descend. This is after the revolution of many smaller cycles. The same is said in *Bhagavad-Gita.*

But frequently during the minor cycles it is necessary, as the *Egyptian Wisdom* says, "to impart a beneficent impulse in the republics of mankind." This can be done by using less power than would be dissipated were a celestial Being to descend upon earth, and here the doctrine of the influence among us of Nirmanakayas[2] or Gnanis is supported in the Egyptian scheme in these words:

> For there is indeed in the terrestrial abode the sacred
> tribe of heroes, who pay attention to mankind, and who are
> able to give them assistance even in the smallest concerns.

This heroic tribe is, as it were, a colony from the gods established here in order that this terrene abode may not be left destitute of a better nature.

These "heroes" are none other than Nirmanakayas, Adepts of this or previous Manwantaras who remain here in various states or conditions. Some are not using bodies at all, but keep spirituality alive among men in all parts of the world; and others are actually using bodies in the world. Who the latter are it would of course be impossible for me to know, and if I had the information, to give it out would be improper.

---

[2] For more on *Nirmanakayas*, please see *"The Voice of the Silence".*

And among this "sacred tribe of heroes" must be classed other souls. They are those who, although now inhabiting bodies and moving among men, have passed through many occult initiations in previous lives, but are now condemned, as it were, to the penance of living in circumstances and in bodies that hem them in, as well as for a time make them forget the glorious past. But their influence is always felt, even if they themselves are not aware of it. For their higher nature being in fact more developed than that of other men, it influences other natures at night or in hours of the day when all is favorable. The fact that these *obscured adepts* are not aware now of what they really are, only has to do with their memory of the past; it does not follow, because a man cannot remember his initiations, that he has had none. But there are some cases in which we can judge with a degree of certainty that such adepts were incarnated and what they were named. Take Thomas Vaughan, Raymond Lully, Sir Thomas More, Jacob Boehme, Paracelsus, and others like them, including also some of the Roman Catholic saints. These souls were as witnesses to the truth, leaving through the centuries, in their own nations, evidences for those who followed, and suggestions for keeping spirituality bright seed-thoughts, as it were, ready for the new mental soil. And as well as these historical characters, there are countless numbers of men and women now living who have passed through certain initiations during their past lives upon earth, and who produce effects in many directions quite unknown to themselves now. They are, in fact, old friends of "the sacred tribe of heroes," and can therefore be more easily used for the spreading of influences and the carrying out of effects necessary for the preservation of spirituality in this age of darkness. We find in our present experience a parallel to this forgetting of previous initiations. There is hardly one of us who has not passed through circumstances in early life, all of which we have forgotten, but which ever since sensibly affect our thoughts and life. Hence the only point about which any question can be raised is that of reincarnation. If we believe in that doctrine, there is no great difficulty in admitting that many of us may have been initiated to some extent and forgotten it for the time. In connection with this we find in the 2d volume of the *Secret Doctrine,* at page 302, some suggestive words. The author says:

> Now that which the students of Occultism ought to know is that the "third eye" is indissolubly connected with Karma.

> In the case of the Atlanteans, it was precisely the Spiritual being which sinned, the Spirit element being still the "Master" principle in man, in those days. *Thus it is in those days that the heaviest Karma* of the Fifth Race was generated *by our Monads.*

Hence the assertion that many of us are now working off the effects of the evil Karmic causes *produced by us in Atlantean bodies.*

In another place she puts the date of the last Atlantean destruction as far back as 11,000 years ago, and describes them as a people of immense knowledge and power. If we allow about 1,000 years for our period in Devachan, we will have only passed through some eleven incarnations since then; and supposing that many more have been our lot – as is my opinion, then we have to place ourselves among those wonderful though wicked people at the height of their power. Granting that we were guilty of the sinful practices of the days in which we then lived, and knowing the effect of Karma, it must follow that since then we have passed through many very disagreeable and painful lives, resembling by analogy dreadful situations in the years between youth and maturity. No wonder, then, if for the time we have forgotten outwardly what we then learned.

But all these historical personages to whom I have referred were living in a dark cycle that affected Europe only. These cycles do not cover the whole of the human race, fortunately for it, but run among the nations influenced for the allotted period, while other peoples remain untouched. Thus while Europe was in darkness, all India was full of men, kings and commoners alike, who possessed the true philosophy; for a different cycle was running there.

And such is the law as formulated by the best authorities. It is held that these cycles do not include the whole of mankind at any one time. In this paper I do not purpose to go into figures, for that requires a very careful examination of the deeds and works of numerous historical personages in universal history, so as to arrive by analysis at correct periods.

It is thought by many that the present is a time when preparation is being made by the most advanced of the "sacred tribe of heroes" for a new cycle in which the assistance of a greater number of progressed souls from other spheres may be gained for mankind. Indeed, in *Isis Unveiled* this is plainly stated.

Writing in 1878, Madame Blavatsky says in Vol. I of *Isis:*

> Unless we mistake the signs, the day is approaching when the world will receive the proofs that only ancient religions were in harmony with nature, and ancient science embraced all that can be known. Secrets long-kept may be revealed; books long-forgotten and arts long-time-lost may be brought out to light again; papyri and parchments of inestimable importance will turn up in the hands of men who pretend to have unrolled them from mummies or stumbled upon them in buried crypts; tablets and pillars, whose sculptured revelations will stagger theologians and confound scientists, may yet be excavated and interpreted. Who knows the possibilities of the future? *An era of disenchantment and rebuilding will soon begin-nay, has already begun. The cycle has almost run its course; a new one is about to begin,* and the future pages of history may contain full proof that –
>
>> If ancestry can be in aught believed,
>> Descending spirits have conversed with man
>> And told him secrets of the world unknown.

Now the way to get at the coming on of the period or close of a larger cycle without wandering in the mazes of figures, is to regard the history and present state of mankind as known.

Thus in the darker age of Europe we find India almost unknown and America wholly so. That was a period when cycles were operating apart from each other, for men were separated from and ignorant of each other. In these continents there were great and powerful nations ruling in both North and South America, but they were not in communication with Europe or India.

Now, however, China knows of and communicates with England and America, and even dark Africa has constant visitors from all civilized nations, and to some extent is affected by us. Doubtless in the greater number of towns in Africa the white man and his doings are more or less like fables, but we with larger knowledge know that those fables rest upon the *fact* of our explorations there.

Judging, then, from the appearances in the affairs of men, we can conclude that now some great cycle is either ending or beginning, and that a number of minor circles are approaching each other.

At the same time with these social or material cycles, there are corresponding ones on a higher plane. One is quite easy to trace. It is the influence of Eastern metaphysics upon the Western mind. This higher cycle had been revolving for many years among the Orientals before we came within its power. Our falling under it is due to a physical cycle as a means. That one which is represented in the progress of trade, of science, of means for transportation. In this way the philosophical system of India and Tibet has begun to affect us, and no man can calculate its course.

Taking into account the spiritual cycles all so intimately connected with Karma and reincarnation, one would be compelled to conclude that this cycle will not be slow or weak. For, if we in Europe and America are the reincarnations of the ancients who formulated this philosophy, we must certainly be powerfully affected upon having it presented to our notice in this life. And as the very air is getting filled with theosophical ideas, and children are growing up every day, the conclusion is irresistible that as the new generation grows up it will be more familiar with theosophical terms and propositions than we were in our youths. For in every direction now, children are likely to hear Karma, Reincarnation, Buddhism, Theosophy, and all these ideas mentioned or discussed. In the course of twenty-five years, then, we shall find here in the United States a large and intelligent body of people believing once more in the very doctrines which they, perhaps ages ago, helped to define and promulgate.

Why not, then, call one of our present cycles the cycle of the Theosophical Society? It began in 1875, and, aided by other cycles then beginning to run, it has attained some force. Whether it will revolve for any greater length of time depends upon its earnest members. Members who enter it for the purpose of acquiring ideas merely for their own use will not assist. Mere numbers do not do the work, but sincere, earnest, active, unselfish members will keep this cycle always revolving. The wisdom of those who set it in motion becomes apparent when we begin to grasp somewhat the meaning of cyclic law. The Society could have remained a mere idea and might have been kept entirely away from outward expression in organization. Then, indeed, ideas similar to those prevalent in our Society might have been heard of. But how? Garbled, and presented only here and there, so that perhaps not for half a century later would they be concretely presented. A wise man, however, knows how to prepare for a tide of spiritual influence. But how could an every-day Russian or American know that 1875 was just the proper year in which to begin so as to be ready for the oncoming rush now fairly set in? To my mind the mere fact that we were organized with a definite platform in that year is strong evidence that the "heroic tribe of heroes" had a hand in our formation. Let us, then, not resist the cycle, nor, complaining of the task, sit down to rest. There is no time for rest. The weak, the despairing, and the doubting may have to wait, but men and women of action cannot stand still in the face of such an opportunity.

> Arise, then, O Atlanteans, and repair the mischief
> done so long ago!
> Roll on, O Wheel, roll on and conquer;
> Roll on forevermore!

William Q. Judge
Path, December, 1889

CYCLES AND CYCLIC LAW

Final address by W.Q. Judge at Parliament of Religions, 1893.

Ladies and gentlemen: This is our last meeting; it is the last impulse of the Cycle which we began when we opened our sessions at this Parliament. All the other bodies which have met in this building have been also starting cycles just as we have been. Now, a great many people know what the word "cycle" means, and a great many do not. There are no doubt in Chicago many men who think that a cycle is a machine to be ridden; but the word that I am dealing with is not that. I am dealing with a word which means a return, a ring. It is a very old term, used in the far past. In our civilization it is applied to a doctrine which is not very well understood, but which is accepted by a great many scientific men, a great many religious men, and by a great many thinking men. The theory is, as held by the ancient Egyptians, that there is a cycle, a law of cycles which governs humanity, governs the earth, governs all that is in the universe. You may have heard Brother Chakravarti say the Hindus are still teaching that there is a great cycle which begins when the Unknown breathes forth the whole universe, and ends when it is turned in again into itself. That is the great cycle.

In the Egyptian monuments, papyri, and other records the cycles are spoken of. They held, and the ancient Chinese also held, that a great cycle governs the earth, called the sidereal cycle because it related to the stars. The work was so large that it had to be measured by the stars, and that cycle is 25,800 and odd years long. They claim to have measured this enormous cycle. The Egyptians gave evidence they had measured it also and had measured many others, so that in these ancient records, looking at the question of cycles, we have a hint that man has been living on the earth, has been civilized and uncivilized for more years than we have been taught to believe. The ancient Theosophists have always held that civilization with humanity went around the earth in cycles, in rings, returning again and again upon itself, but that at each turn of the cycle, on the point of return it was higher than before. This law of cycles is held in Theosophical doctrine to be the most important of all, because it is at the bottom of all. It is a part of the law of that unknown being who is the universe, that there shall be a periodical coming from and a periodical returning again upon itself.

Now, that the law of cycles does prevail in the world must be very evident if you will reflect for a few moments. The first cycle I would draw your attention to is the daily cycle, when the sun rises in the morning and sets at night, returning again next morning, you following the sun, rising in the morning and at night going to sleep again, at night almost appearing dead, but the next morning awaking to life once more. That is the first cycle. You can see at once that there are therefore in a man's life just as many cycles of that kind as there are days in his life. The next is the monthly cycle, when the moon, changing every 28 days, marks the month. We have months running to more days, but that is only for convenience, to avoid change in the year. The moon gives the month and marks the monthly cycle.

The next is the yearly cycle. The great luminary, the great mover of all, returns again to a point from whence he started. The next great cycle to which I would draw your attention, now we have come to the sun – it is held by science and is provable I think by other arguments the next cycle is that the sun, while stationary to us, is in fact moving through space in an enormous orbit which we can not measure. As he moves he draws the earth and the planets as they wheel about him. We may say, then, this is another great cycle. It appears reasonable that, as the sun is moving through that great cycle, he must draw the earth into spaces and places and points in space where the earth has never been before, and that it must happen that the earth shall come now and then into some place where the conditions are different and that it may be changed in a moment, as it were, for to the eye of the soul a thousand years are but a moment, when everything will be different. That is one aspect of cyclic doctrine, that the sun is drawing the earth in a great orbit of his own and is causing the earth to be changed in its nature by reason of the new atomic spaces into which it is taken.

We also hold that the earth is governed by cyclic law throughout the century as in a moment. The beings upon it are never in the same state. So nations, races, civilizations, communities are all governed in the same way and moved by the same law. This law of cycles is the law of reincarnation that we were speaking of today: that is, that a man comes into the world and lives a day, his life is as a day; he dies out of it and goes to sleep, elsewhere waking; then he sleeps there to wake again the next great day; after a period of rest, he again enters life; that is his cycle. We hold in Theosophical philosophy it has been proven by the Adepts by experiment that men in general awake from this period of rest after 1,500 years. So we point in history to an historical cycle of 1,500 years, after which old ideas return. And if you will go back in the history of the world you will find civilization repeating itself every 1,500 years, more or less like what it was before. That is to say, go back 1,500 years from now and you will find coming out here now the Theosophists, the philosophers, the various thinkers, the inventors of 1,500 years ago. And going further back still, we hold that those ancient Egyptians who made such enormous pyramids and who had a civilization we cannot understand, at that dim period when they burst on the horizon of humanity to fall again, have had their cycle of rest and are reincarnating again even in America. So we think, some of us, that the American people of the new generation are a reincarnation of the ancient Egyptians, who are coming back and bringing forth in this civilization all the wonderful ideas which the Egyptians held. And that is one reason why this country is destined to be a great one, because the ancients are coming back, they are here, and you are very foolish if you refuse to consider yourselves so great. We are willing you should consider yourselves so great, and not think you are born mean, miserable creatures.

The next cycle I would draw your attention to is that of civilizations. We know that civilizations have been here, and they are gone. There is no bridge between many of these. If heredity, as some people claim, explains everything, how is it not explained why the Egyptians left no string to connect them with the present? There is nothing left of them but the Copts, who are poor miserable slaves. The Egyptians, as a material race, are wiped out, and it is so because it is according to the law of cycles and according to the law of nature that the physical embodiment of the Egyptians had to be wiped out. But their souls could not go out of existence, and so we find their civilization and other civilizations disappearing, civilizations such as the ancient civilization of Babylon, and all those old civilizations in that part of the East which were just as strange and wonderful as any other. And this civilization of ours has come up instead of going down, but it is simply repeating the experience of the past on a higher level. It is better in potentiality than that which has been before. Under the cyclic law it will rise higher and higher, and when its time comes it will die out like the rest.

Also religions have had their cycles. The Christian religion has had its cycle. It began in the first year of the Christian era and was a very different thing then from what it is now. If you examine the records of Christianity itself you will see that the early fathers and teachers taught differently in the beginning from that which the priests of today are teaching now. Similarly you will find that Brahminism has had its cycle. Every religion rises and falls with the progress of human thought, because cyclic law governs every man, and thus every religion which man has.

So it is also with diseases. Is it not true that fevers are governed by a law of recurrence in time; some have three days, some four days, nine days, fifteen days, three years and so on? No physician can say why it is so; they only know that it is a fact. So in every direction the law of cycles is found to govern. It is all according to the great inherent law of the periodical ebb and flow, the Great Day and Night of Nature. The tides in Ocean rise and fall; similarly in the great Ocean of Nature there is a constant ebb and flow, a mightier tide which carries all with it. The only thing that remains unshaken, immovable, never turning is the Spirit itself. That, as St. James said –

and he doubtless was himself a wise Theosophist – is without variableness and hath no shadow of turning.

Now, this great law of periodical return pertains also to every individual man in his daily life and thought. Every idea that you have, every thought, affects your brain and mind by its impression. That begins the cycle. It may seem to leave your mind, apparently it goes out, but it returns again under the same cyclic law in some form either better or worse, and wakes up once more the old impression. Even the very feelings that you have of sorrow or gladness will return in time, more or less according to your disposition, but inevitably in their cycle. This is a law it would do good for every one to remember, especially those who have variations of joy and sorrow, of exaltation and depression. If when depressed you would recollect the law and act upon it by voluntarily creating another cycle of exaltation, on its returning again with the companion cycle of lower feeling it would in no long time destroy the depressing cycle and raise you to higher places of happiness and peace. It applies again in matters of study where we use the intellectual organs only. When a person begins the study of a difficult subject or one more grave than usual, there is a difficulty in keeping the mind upon it; the mind wanders; it is disturbed by other and older ideas and impressions. But by persistency a new cycle is established, which, being kept rolling, at last obtains the mastery.

We hold further – and I can only go over this briefly – that in evolution itself, considered as a vast inclusive whole, there are cycles, and that unless there were these turnings and returnings no evolution would be possible, for evolution is but another word for cyclic law. Reincarnation, or re-embodiment over and over again, is an expression of this great law and a necessary part of evolution.

Evolution means a coming forth from something. From out of what does the evolving universe come? It comes out from what we call the unknown, and we call it "unknown" simply because we do not know what it is. The unknown does not mean the non-existent; it simply means that which we do not perceive in its essence or fulness. It goes forth again and again, always higher and better; but while it is rolling around at its lower arc it seems to those down there that it is lower than ever; but it is bound to come up again. And that is the answer we give to those who ask, What of all those civilizations that have disappeared, what of all the years that I have forgotten? What have I been in other lives, I have forgotten them? We simply say, you are going through your cycle. Some day all these years and experiences will return to your recollection as so much gained. And all the nations of the earth should know this law, remember it and act upon it, knowing that they will come back and that others also will come back. Thus they should leave behind something that will raise the cycle higher and higher, thus they should ever work toward the perfection which mankind as a whole is striving in fact to procure for itself.

W.Q. Judge, World's Parliament of Religions, 1893

The present period is one of those watersheds in human evolution that represent the end of a complex series of events in recorded history. It involves the end of the old monastic orders, including the Hindu, Tibetan, Chaldean, Egyptian, Jewish and Christian. All of these will disappear in their older forms. If one is attached to these forms, this will seem to be a great loss, a sort of spiritual discontinuity in human affairs. If, on the other hand, one is detached and therefore able to penetrate to the core of the cycle, one will understand the continuity of the transition and sense that which will tap the quintessence of these old orders and yet transcend them. At the end of every long epoch of human evolution, at the dawning of a new epoch, there is inevitably a night of disintegration. Even if one is able to overcome one's doubts, fears and anxieties in the face of the necessary dissolution of forms, it is still difficult to envisage in advance which of the inexhaustible possibilities of Divine Wisdom will be realized in a subsequent period of development. The wisest of beings are truly agnostic about the future. All neophytes would be wise in their turn not to attempt to extrapolate on the basis of what they think they know about recorded history and the tragedies of the twentieth century. Most human beings are so self-absorbed in their petty personal concerns that they know almost nothing even of the little story called recorded history over three thousand years, much less the broader global developments that have taken place in the first five thousand years of the Kali Yuga.

Raghavan Iyer
The Gupta Vidya II, Dhyana Marga

GLOSSARY

abhyasa	Constant practice; exertion
Adhiyajna	Primordial sacrifice; region of sacrifice
Aditi	Vedic name for *Mulaprakriti;* the abstract aspect of *Parabrahman,* though both manifested and unknowable
ahankara	Egoism; the sense of 'I', self-identity
Akasha	Space, universal solvent, spiritual substance, the *upadhi* of Divine Thought
ananda	Bliss, joy
antaskarana	The bridge between the lower mind (head) and the higher mind (heart), between the divine Ego and the personal soul of man
Anupadaka	Parent-less, self-existing
Ashwatha	Sacred tree used to kindle the sacrificial fire: the Bo tree; the Tree of Knowledge, *ficus religiosa*
asuras	Class of celestial beings born from the breath — *Asu* — of Brahmā-Prajapati; the spiritual and divine ancestors of Manasic humanity
Atma	The Universal Spirit, the divine Monad, the seventh Principle in the septenary constitution of man; the Supreme Soul
Atman	SELF; divine breath; the universal Self
Barhishad Pitris	*Also* Lunar Pitris. Lunar Gods, those who evolved astral prototypes of the human form; called in India the Fathers, "Pitris" or the lunar ancestors, and subdivided into seven classes or hierarchies
bhakti	Devotion
bodhichitta	*Lit.* 'seed of enlightenment'; embryo of spiritual man
Bodhisattva	*Lit.* 'he whose essence *(sattva)* has become Wisdom *(Bodhi)';* enlightened being who remains in *samsara* to serve and help humanity

Book of Dzyan, The	*Also 'The Stanzas of Dzyan'.* An ancient, esoteric text written in an unknown language upon which *The Secret Doctrine* and *The Voice of the Silence* are based; *see* Dzyan
Brahmā	The creative Logos; the creator of the manifest universe in the Indian pantheon, the first of the Trimurti (three forms) of Brahmā, Vishnu and Shiva (creator, sustainer and destroyer/ regenerator) existing periodically in manifestation then returning to *pralaya* (dissolving into non-manifestation) at the end of this cycle
Brahma	*Also Brahman.* The impersonal, supreme and incognizable principle of the universe; the Ultimate Reality; the attributeless Absolute
Brahma Vach	Divine wisdom; divine speech
Buddhi	Intellection, intuitive discernment, direct perception, resolute conviction, wisdom; the Universal Soul; the spiritual soul in man (the sixth principle), vehicle of *Atman;* divine discernment; Universal Intelligence
chela	Disciple, especially the initiated disciple
daimon	Inner voice of conscience and intuition; an aspect of the human soul
Daiviprakriti	Divine Nature; primordial, homogeneous light; the Light of the Logos
devachan	A post-mortem state of heavenly bliss wherein the Ego assimilates and enjoys the fruition of the good karma and harvest of the universal thought and intuition of the last life
dharma	Duty, moral law; social and personal morality; natural law, natural obligation; teaching, essence
Dhyan Chohan	*Lit.* 'Lord of Light'; one of the highest gods; *pl.* the primordial divine intelligences and agents of divine law through which *Mahat* manifests and guides the Kosmos

dhyana	Contemplation, meditation; state of abstraction; the fifth *paramita*
Dhyani	Divine embodiment of ideation; man of meditation
Dzyan	*Lit.* 'to reform one's self by meditation and knowledge'; *see The Book of Dzyan*
Eros	The third personage of the Hellenic primordial trinity of Ouranos, Gaea and Eros; the abstract and universally beneficent creative force in nature, degraded by later attributions; *see also kama*
Fohat	The active (male) potency of the *Sakti* (female power) in nature; Higher Eros or *Kamadeva,* the essence of cosmic force or electricity; *Daiviprakriti;* the link between spirit and matter
Great Breath	Symbolizing eternal ceaseless Motion; the One Life, eternal yet periodic in its regular manifestations; Absolute, omni-present Consciousness
guna	Propensity; quality; constituent
Gupta Vidya	Secret Wisdom, highest knowledge
guru	Venerable teacher; religious preceptor; spiritual teacher
Guruparampara	Sacred lineage of teachers
Hatha yoga	The practice of the lower form of Yoga, in which physical means for purposes of spiritual development are used; the opposite of Raja Yoga
Hermes-Thot	(Often written Hermes-Thoth) The archetype of Initiators; God of Wisdom with the Ancients, who, according to Plato, whether as Egyptian god Thot or Greek god Hermes, 'discovered number, geometry, astronomy and letters'
Hermes Trismegistus	A lineage of Initiators in ancient Egypt, ultimately trace-able to Shiva as Dakshinamurti, Initiator of Initiates; Initiates who transferred from latent to active potency a precise and comprehensive knowledge of the complex laws governing the seven kingdoms of Nature, constituting a divine gnosis

Hiranyagarbha	The radiant or golden egg or womb; esoterically, the luminous 'fire mist' or ethereal stuff from which the universe was formed
Ishtaguru	One's chosen teacher
Ishwara	The sovereign Lord; the omnipresent Spirit; the controller of maya
Itchashakti	The divine power of the will; one of the seven powers in nature and the human being
jnana	Wisdom; knowledge
Kali Yuga	The dark age; the fourth age; the iron age that began in 3102 B.C.
kalpa	Cosmic cycle, day of Brahmā
kama	Desire, attraction, passion; cleaving to existence; creative impetus and longing; *see also* Eros
kama manas	The desire mind, the lower *Manas* or human animal soul, the reflection of the higher *Manas*
karana	Instrument of action; basis of causation
karana sharira	The causal body; the inmost sheath
karma	Act, action; the law of ethical equilibrium
Krishna	The eighth Avatar of Vishnu
Kriyashakti	Creative imagination; a cosmic and human power
Kwan Yin	The female logos, the "Mother of Mercy"
lanoo	A disciple; *see also* chela
laya	Absorption, dissolution, repose; resting place; motionless point, still center; zero point
linga sharira	Astral body, aerial vesture, prototypal, vital body; *eidolon; doppelgänger*
Logos	The 'Verbum'; the 'Word'; the manifested Deity, the outward expression of the ever-concealed Cause
Lunar Pitris	*See* Barhishad Pitris
mahamanvantara	The manifestation of cosmos from *mahapralaya;* out-breathing of the Great Breath

Mahat	The first principle of universal intelligence and consciousness; the primal basis of individuation; cosmic ideation; the cosmic Mind behind manifested Nature and the great hebdomadal Heart of all humanity
Mahatma	Great soul; exalted exemplar of self-mastery and human perfection
Manas	Mind; the faculty of cognition, choice and self-awareness
Manasa	"The efflux of the divine mind"; the divine sons of Brahmā-Viraj, identical with the Kumara, the Manasaputra, and are identified with the human "Egos"
Manasaputras	The sons of (universal) Mind; human "Egos"; spiritual individuality of each human being
manvantara	Cosmic cycle of manifestation
maya	Illusion, appearance; the cosmic power behind phenomenal existence
moksha	Deliverance, emancipation
Monad	The Unity, the One; the unified triad *(Atma-Buddhi-Manas),* or the duad *(Atma-Buddhi);* the immortal part of man
Mulaprakriti	Root Nature; undifferentiated primordial substance; unmanifested matrix of all forms
nous	A Platonic term for the Higher *Manas* or Soul; Spirit as distinct from animal soul or psyche; divine consciousness or mind in man
OM	The mystic monosyllable; the soundless sound; the Word
para	*Lit.* 'beyond' or 'above'
Pitris	The ancestors or creators of mankind, of seven classes, three incorporeal *(arupa),* and four corporeal; *see* Solar Pitris and Lunar Pitris
prakriti	Nature in general; spiritual nature, as distinct from *purusha,* Spirit; together the two primeval aspects of the One Unknown Deity

pralaya	A period of obscuration or repose — planetary, cosmic or universal — the opposite of *manvantara*
prana	Life-Principle; the breath of life
Pranava	The sacred Word, OM
Purusha	Spirit; the primeval man; the supreme being; the animating principle in all beings
Raja Yoga	System of developing spiritual powers through union with the Supreme Spirit; regulation and concentration of thought
rajas	One of the three *gunas* which constitute the qualities or divisions of matter; activity and change
Rg Veda, Rig Veda	The first and most important of the four Vedas; recorded in Occultism as having been delivered by great sages on Lake Manasarovar beyond the Himalayas
Root Race	The human Race has been compared to a tree — the mainstem may be compared to the Root-Race, its larger limbs to seven Sub-Races
Rta, rita	Cosmic order, divine law; righteousness
samsara	Conditionality, as contrasted with *nirvana;* realm of becoming, in contrast to Being; birth and death; conditioned existence; illusion
samskâra	In Hindu philosophy the term is used to denote the impressions left upon the mind by individual actions or external circumstances, and capable of being developed on any future favorable occasion- even in a future birth. The samskâra denotes, therefore, the germs of propensities and impulses from previous births to be developed in this, or the coming reincarnations. The true meaning is as given above and as such is connected with karma and its working
Sangha, the	Order of monks; assembly; community; preservers, transmitters and teachers of the dharma
Sat-Chit-Ananda	Abstract reality, consciousness and bliss
sattva	One of the three *gunas* which constitute the qualities or divisions of matter; the quality of goodness or purity; *see gunas*

satya	Supreme truth
Shankaracharya	The great religious teacher and legendary reformer of India, the founder of Advaita Vedanta philosophy; *also* Shankara
sharira	Body
Shiva	Third god of the Hindu *Trimurti* Brahma-Vishnu-Shiva; in his character of Destroyer, he destroys only to regenerate on a higher plane
Sophrosyne	Ancient Greek concept of self-control, restraint, soundness of mind, prudence and temperance
sunyata	'Void' or 'nothingness', but not a mere negation: the ineffable non-dual Reality that transcends all limitations and dualities, including *nirvana* and *samsara*
sushupti	Deep sleep consciousness
sutratman	Thread soul; reincarnating individuality
svasamvedana	*Lit.* the 'reflection which analyses itself'; *see paramartha*
swaraj	Freedom; self-rule, disciplined rule from within; political independence
tamas	The lowest of the three *gunas* which constitute the qualities or divisions of matter; the quality of darkness, foulness, inertia, and ignorance
tapas	Moral fervor; self-suffering; specific austerities and pro-longed contemplation; that which burns up impurities
TAT	*Lit.* 'That'; *Brahman;* beyond the three worlds; the pre-existent
Theosophia	"Divine Wisdom", the substratum of truth and knowledge which underlies the universe, from which of all the great world-religions and philosophies were derived; pure divine ethics. While *Theosophia* cannot be put entirely in words, Theosophy is what can be expressed at this time
Theosophy	The maximal expression of *Theosophia* at this time in history; *See Theosophia*

Thot-Hermes	*See* Hermes-Thot
Tsong-Kha-Pa	1357-1419 A.D. The 'model of virtue': Tibetan Buddhist founder of a new reformed order, the Gelugpa, to which all Dalai Lamas belong; stated by H.P. Blavatsky to have initiated a Seven Century Plan to infuse the Wisdom current into Western consciousness through various agents of the Society of Sages
turiya	Spiritual wakefulness; the fourth or highest state of the soul
Upanishads	Esoteric doctrines; interpretations of the Vedas by the methods of Vedanta
Vedas	The most ancient and sacred Sanskrit works: the *Rig, Atharva, Sama, Yajur Vedas*; from the root *vid* 'to know' or 'divine knowledge'
Verbum	The Word; the manifested Deity, the outward expression of the ever-concealed Cause; *see* Logos
Word, the	*See* Verbum
Yang	The masculine active principle in nature that in Chinese cosmology is exhibited in light, heat, or dryness
Yin	The feminine passive principle in nature that in Chinese cosmology is exhibited in darkness, cold, or wetness
yoga	Unswerving concentration; fusion, integration; union with the divine; skill in action
yogin	Practitioner of yoga; proficient in yoga

INDEX

1

18 is a number peculiar to Krishna in the *Bhagavad Gita* 201
1975 Cycle 16, 27, 35, 36
1975 cycle, During the, there is no more need to make any concessions to
    the weak in the West that were unknown in the East 109
1975 Cycle, keynote of the, can only be understood in terms of the relation
    of the Logos, of Avalokitesvara, to the descent of Atman in the human
    race in its entirety 113

2

2,000, about the year, Western Europe will have lived one of those periods
    of culture and progress so rare in history 180

4

4320, sacredness of the cycle of, with additional cyphers 194

9

9, those years, which had the figure in them, had been marked by the
    severest winters 182

A

abhyasa, practice, the lower line of the Aquarian glyph............................... 52
Absolute Freedom of Human Thought, the keynote and the keystone of
    every century 13
Aether-*Akasha* 156

Aether-*Akasha* is consubstantial with the plane of substance constituting *Buddh-Manas*, the jewel in every heart and the diamond light in every soul 156

Agni, cosmic fire of, is correlated with the luminous waters of space called *Akasha* 101

Akasha 24, 38, 39, 40, 43, 64, 65, 94, 98, 99, 168

Akasha-Vach is mystic Nature pervading the entire cosmos 38

Akashic energy and ideation, internal reservoirs of, potentially available to the aspiring human soul are virtually infinite 34

alienation of the mind is very real 47

Alkahest, a universal divine flame which, in its boundless, colourless, intangible, soundless and inexhaustible energy, may be used only for the sake of all 99

America usually moves about thirty years behind Europe in acknowledging significant shifts in thought 12

American people of the new generation are a reincarnation of the ancient Egyptians, who are coming back and bringing forth in this civilization all the wonderful ideas which the Egyptians held 211

Anahata, the indestructible centre, the constant pulsation of the spiritual heart known in Sanskrit as the 44

analogy and correspondence 127

ancient science embraced all that can be known 206

Aniyamsam Aniyasam 56

Antaskarana, in the, there are authentic longings for the higher nature ... 122

anu is also the absolute Motion or eternal vibration of the Great Breath differentiated in the primordial manifested ATOM, equivalent to Brahmā 60

anu is not subject to multiplication or division in either the pregenetic or primogenetic states 60

anu is the *Aniyamsam Aniyasam,* the smallest of the small 60

Aquarian Age 4, 11, 13, 18, 29, 34, 52, 55, 58, 62, 63, 65, 70, 73, 77, 78, 79, 80, 85, 90, 94, 98, 108, 110, 117, 121, 124, 129, 145, 153, 158, 166, 170

Aquarian Age is typified by the concept of vertical ascent, whereas during the nineteenth century and before, the idea of horizontal movement was far more prevalent 78

Aquarian Age offers, The great opportunity that the, is to gain a sense of proportion in relation to oneself, entering into an invisible brotherhood of comrades 163

Aquarian Age will bring about a lot of psychological disturbances arising in the vestures because of the unwillingness to let go of what is dead or dying 130

Aquarian Age, each good and true human soul may discern the spiritual possibilities of the 14

Aquarian Age, forerunners of the 104

Aquarian Age, H.P. Blavatsky powerfully spelt out the choices open to the West thirteen years before the beginning of the 4

Aquarian Age, has entered its second degree 171

Aquarian Age, has entered its second degree, the threshold of the epoch of Universal Enlightenment, and moves steadily towards its millennial culmination 55

Aquarian Age, In the, the mental fire of devotion and sacrifice means purgation, and no substitute will serve 41

Aquarian age, in the, spiritual life is in the mind 115

Aquarian Age, Pythagorean teaching of the, of Universal Enlightenment 154

Aquarian Age, restoration of the dual sense of individual dignity and human solidarity is a primary object of the 92

Aquarian Age, self-consciously engaged in the transformation of the energy-field of the entire earth, that grand project which is the task of the 34

Aquarian Age, take-offs and landings, the vertical ascent and descent in consciousness, are critical to the 132

Aquarian Age, the regenerative tendencies of the 58

Aquarian Age, where there is more freedom from competitiveness and more openness to universal truths, could lead to a new kind of soul-etiquette 29

Aquarian civilization of the future 127

Aquarian civilization, transformation from Piscean to, poses an extraordinary challenge 34

Aquarian cycle, the pristine avataric descent of the, has been accompanied by a tremendous acceleration in the programme of evolution 113

Aquarian diffusion of the true ideal of spiritual science and lifelong learning 28

Aquarian spirit of effortless renunciation and intelligent sacrifice 165

Aquarian task of self-regeneration has begun 149

Aquarian therapeutics, the living germs of 43

Aquarius as a serpent coiled in a spiral around a jar containing liquid fire, ancient Egyptians depicted 42

Aquarius, awakening mind of the age of 100

Arnold Toynbee xvii
astral body 72, 81, 83
astral vesture 121, 123
astronomical, sacred, cycles are of immense antiquity.............................. 190
Asuramaya, said to have been the greatest astronomer............................ 186
asuras.. 84
asuras are the spiritual and the divine ancestors of Manasic humanity 84
Atlantean obsession with the will to dominate completely inverts the
    principles of proportion, degree and design that govern the evolution of
    the organic vestures which human beings presently inhabit.................. 68
Atma Vidya 57
Atma-Buddhi... 7, 25, 76
Atma-Buddhi is the Guru and it speaks to the soul as the inner voice of the
    daimon, the voice of the Master.. 45
Atma-Buddhi-Manas of the atom... 25
Atma-Buddhi-Manasic or noumenal aspects of invisible atoms, what is
    seemingly void is extremely full of... 60
Atman..7, 23, 25, 45, 61, 64, 73, 132
atom as applied to the first three creations refer to spiritual and formless
    realities.. 60
atom, Greek root of, literally means 'uncuttable', 'indivisible' or 'individual'
    and corresponds to the Sanskrit term *anu*.................................. 60
atomic energies derive from the indivisible unity of the One Life, whilst
    molecular actions stem from the interplay of vital though secondary
    emanations 61

B

babies are not in Kali Yuga, but rather experience something like a Satya
    Yuga, albeit briefly 106
Bacon's vital insight that "Knowledge is power" echoed the ancient Eastern
    view that knowledge can liberate men... 66
benevolence, To increase, one must locate oneself correctly through
    meditation, heightening awareness from a central point of harmony ... 32
Bhagavad Gita 32, 57, 89, 147
Bodhi, the hidden flame in the heart... 44
Bodhisattva 109
Bodhisattvas 122, 139
Bodhisattvic ethics... 119

Brahma Vach 90

Brahma Vach has supplanted *Brahma Vidya* as a synonym for *Theosophia*... 36

Brahma Vidya was often used as an equivalent to *Theosophia* 35

Brahmanical figures are approximately the basic calculations of the
esoteric system 190

Brotherhood of Bodhisattvas........... xviii, 8, 17, 57, 90, 108, 127, 129, 155, 163

Buddha 16, 31, 93, 104, 113, 147, 148, 149, 162

Buddha-nature 148

Buddhi 117, 121, 122, 171

Buddhi, the light of the *Atman*, is both indiscrete in relation to the eternal
motion of the Great Breath and discrete in relation to the mayavic field
of vibratory Monadic emanations 64

Buddhi-Manas 25, 37, 61, 110

Buddhi-Manasic, the emotional and mental nature 121

Buddhi-Manas-Taijasi 110, 169

Buddhi-Taijasi 146

C

capacity to discern the patterns of Nature is the prerequisite for enlisting
the forces of Nature on behalf of human designs 68

certitude 103, 104

Chitkala 118

Christ 104, 113

City of Man 146

City of Man, the Aquarian design of *Civitas Humanum* 71

civilization of the future.................................... 16, 34, 57, 70, 108, 135, 163, 170

civilization, ancient Theosophists have always held that, with humanity
went around the earth in cycles, in rings, returning again and again
upon itself 210

collapse of the acquisitive and parochial civilizations of the past two
millennia is approaching completion 135

Compassionate sacrifice and intelligent suffering are the necessary means
to an understanding of harmony 30

contemplation.. 118

continuity of consciousness...................................... 45, 74, 80, 82, 129

continuity of consciousness which one seeks is, in fact, a mode of
mirroring the metaphysical integrity of cosmic unity 129

cosmic divisions of times, seasons, invisible influences, astronomical phenomena, with their action and reaction on terrestrial and even moral nature; on birth, death, and growth, on health and disease 194

cosmic harmony and human solidarity, The idea of, is as old as the Vedas and is vital to every authentic spiritual tradition 31

cosmos, entire, is intensely alive and there is intelligence in every point of space... 82

crisis, every individual and collective, is a crisis of self-concept, self-reference and identity 3

cultures grow infatuated with telling their inflated history only after they have begun to decay 21

Cycle of Descending Celestial Influences 202

cycle of the Theosophical Society 208

cycle, a law of cycles which governs humanity, governs the earth, governs all that is in the universe 209

cycle, a word which means a return, a ring 209

cycle, sidereal, so named, because it related to the stars 209

cycle, there is a great, which begins when the Unknown breathes forth the whole universe, and ends when it is turned in again into itself. 209

cycles marking the millenniums, the centennials as well as the minor ones of 50 and 10 years' duration, are the most important........................... 182

cycles of revolutions 176

cycles, in addition to these social or material, there are corresponding ones on a higher plane 207

cycles, law of, is held in Theosophical doctrine to be the most important of all, because it is at the bottom of all 210

cycles, these, do not include the whole of mankind at any one time 205

cyclic law, evolution is but another word for 213

cyclic law, the meaning of 208

D

Daiviprakriti 37, 64, 110

Daiviprakriti is Vach in its *madhyama* form 36

Dakshinamurti, the Initiator of Initiates 16, 28, 74, 113

Declaration of Interdependence xix

devas and devatas 82

devotion to the invisible prototype that is the Guru is signified by the higher line in the symbol of Aquarius 46

devotion, from *de votum,* 'to dedicate by a vow' 49

dharma 57, 85

dharma, that which upholds a human being, linking him or her to the
entire fabric of human life 33

dhyana 168

Dhyanis 23

Diamond Soul, the true Self of all, Every person has within him or her the
possibility of coming closer to the 94

dianoia 51, 52, 58

dichotomy between science and religion is delusive 57

divine discipline 85

Divine Instructors, it was no longer possible for, to come openly into the
world in the Age of Zeus 27

Divine Prototype, voice of the, may appear to come from outside oneself 104

draw the larger circle xx

Dwapara Yuga contains 864,000 years 189

Dzyan 18, 35

Dzyan means self-reform through meditation 36

E

early modern science is one of the minor contributions of the Brotherhood
of Bodhisattvas 17

education, To think clearly, logically and incisively must be the true
purpose of 117

Egyptian teachers of Sais, the great, next to whom the Greeks were as little
children 20

elemental, Human beings can collectively engender a gigantic, oppressive,
like the idea of a personal God, or the Leviathan of the State 155

Elohim 81

emotion, Every, registers an appropriate record in the astral vesture 123

energy, every point in space is the intersection of myriad vibrating fields
of 59

enlightenment 10, 40, 54, 147, 168

eternal duration 117

Eternity and Time, exalted paradigm of the union of, is *Adhiyajna,* seated
near the circle of infinite eternal light and radiating compassionate
guidance to all beings who toil in the coils of Time 95

ethical self-awareness 124

Every human being has the same evolutionary task as every other human

being who ever lived, lives now or will live in the future 126
Evolution proceeds on the laws of analogy 184

F

faults which bedevil them lie in themselves and not in the stars 58
fear of God is not the beginning of wisdom... 24
fifth hierarchy, task of, to inform the empty and ethereal animal form,
    creating out of it the rational man.. 92
Fifth Root Race, Sixth and Seventh Sub-Races of the................................. 131
Fifth Root Race, we are in, going from the Fifth Sub-Race to the Sixth Sub-
    Race, this process is giving birth to a profound spiritual sensitization of
    intelligence through the elevation of life-atoms..................................... 110
First Root Race, human beings began in the, as extremely ethereal and
    spiritual beings 110
First Sub-Race of the Third Root Race, restoration of the primordial
    spirituality of, by the end of the present Fifth Root Race 106
Fohat.. 65, 97
Fourth Race.. 119
Fourth Race, the Lemurian and Atlantean periods..................................... 16
Fourth Round 130
fusion of *Buddhi* and *Manas* at the highest level is inseparable from the
    path of adeptship.. 121

G

Gandhi's soul-force is equivalent to the atomic noetic force of *Buddhi* 70
Gethsemane, Garden of 139, 140
gnosis, divine, a precise and comprehensive knowledge of the complex
    laws governing the seven kingdoms of Nature 16
gods, the, descend according to orderly periods of time 196
Golden Age.. 44, 143, 145
golden age is eternally associated with Shiva-Saturn and the hosts of the
    Kumaras.. 26
Golden Age, in the, humans showed spontaneous reverence to Magus-
    Teachers 17
Golden Rule.. 145
Great Saros.. 199

Gupta Vidya affirms that it is possible for human beings to cooperate with the invisible world self-consciously and to find meaning and dignity through obedience to the Law of Karma 70

Gupta Vidya, in, there is no cleavage between the aim of Self-knowledge (Atma Vidya) and the practical ideal of helping Nature and working on with her (Ahimsa Yagna) 57

Gupta Vidya, methodology of, is linked to the process of self-regeneration . 126

Guruparampara chain 28, 115

H

H.P. Blavatsky 2

harmonious and gentle action in the sphere of daily duties are the *ABCs* of *Theosophia,* 39

Harmony is the law of life, discord its shadow 175

Heraclitus designated the eyes and ears as false witnesses to the soul 93

Hermes .... xix, 15, 16, 18, 22

Hermes is a generic name, associated with potent thought, and linked to Mercury-Buddha, a Dhyani 16

Hermes is the paradigm of the oldest sacred tradition, going back a million years ago to India *(Bharata Dwipa)* 18

Hermes taught all sciences to the nascent Mediterranean civilization 16

Hermes, the journal xix

Hermes-Thot 28

HermesThot, a god, the pristine archetype of Initiators in ancient Egypt . 16

Hermetic method, Descending from the universal to the particular is essential to the 23

Hermetic work of the 1975 Cycle 22

Herodotus, *Euterpe* 20

hierarchies, all, from the Dhyanis through the *danavas* and *daityas*, to the *devas* or gods, the *devatas* and elementals, are represented within the individual human being 23

hierarchies, conception of the cosmic, in Nature and in Man which unites the spiritual with the physical, and both of these with the moral and the political 22

higher Triad 152

Hiranyagarbha 23, 95

How old are the Sun and Moon, the Earth and Man? 184

Human beings are continually concerned with the boundaries between

themselves as individuals 33
Human beings in the First Race were gods or *devas*, and in the Second Race they were demi-gods 15
human form is almost entirely empty space devoid of anything that might be considered matter... 59
human judgement and natural law alike stand upon a common ground, a single transcendental source of Being 56
human souls at the present time of metamorphosis, there is a growing recognition and widespread acknowledgement of a fresh opportunity for... 79
humanity follows the cyclic path of transformation wherein each element of human nature is transmuted into a self-conscious aspect of Divine Wisdom.. 11
humanity of the future 151
humanity, In a sense, is presently engaged in this adolescent phase 121
humanity, only purpose for being in a human form is to be a true servant to 148

I

immortal soul 7, 48, 75, 76
immortal soul, there is an indestructible element in every, which enables a human being again and again to make a fresh start............................ 76
inertia... 93
inevitable recurrence of similar historical events 176
initiation..21, 28, 31, 45, 73, 83, 84
initiation is to be understood as individuation through the universalization of consciousness 74
intimate relationship between temporal identity and cyclic existence is symbolized in the identification of the lifetime of Brahmā with the existence of the universe 95
invisible Sun, Human beings should understand the analogy between terrestrial dawn-light and the noumenal and causal light of the 37
inward ascent towards self-awakening consciousness is inconceivable apart from the acquisition of freedom of movement in and through the vestures.. 81
Ishtaguru.. 90
Isis Unveiled 2
Itchashakti, the power of desire.. 155

J

Jacob's Ladder of ideation, by constructing and using a, an individual can insert himself or herself into the evolutionary programme..................... 80

jagrat, swapna and *sushupti,* the three states of consciousness.................... 82

Jesus taught that the Divine is not mocked: as ye sow, so shall ye reap, a central tenet in the teachings of all Initiates.. 161

Jewel in the Lotus..xvii, 157

Jivanmukta, the Sage or perfected Yogin 118

Jnanashakti... 155

K

Kalachakra, Time's circle 57

Kali Yuga affords a great opportunity for those capable of taking and adhering to vows 107

Kali Yuga contains 432,000 years.. 189

Kali Yuga, in, karmic causes may be rapidly exhausted, and illusions rapidly destroyed 107

Kalpa or grand period of 4,320,000,000 years 199

kama.. 122

kama manas 105, 122, 146

kama manas is in essence sacred. It is lent to human beings to show them how to connect and how to discriminate 23

kama-manas... 49

karana sharira.. 9, 18, 24

karana sharira is that it is the ground of the latent knowledge called to active potency by Hermes 18

karana sharira, permanent vesture of the monad... 18

karana sharira, the vast human inheritance of spiritual wisdom and scientific magic was assimilated into the 18

Karma is generous to each and every human soul in need of help 103

karma of the transmission of Divine Wisdom 152

karma will be kind in the next birth if the basics have been learnt in this lifetime 39

karma, tests of, are entirely moral 151

Kingdom of God is within you 139

Krishna 104, 113, 155, 157

Krishna's medicinal method in the *Gita* 154
Krita Yuga contains 1,728,000 years 189
Kriyashakti... 84
Kriyashakti, the power of visualization 155
Kumaras 26, 95

L

lanoos, true neophytes on the Path.. 155
law of cycles, in every direction the, is found to govern. It is all according
    to the great inherent law of the periodical ebb and flow, the Great Day
    and Night of Nature... 212
Law of Karma actually ordains that every single person has a divine
    destiny which he or she alone can and must fulfill 104
law of periodical return pertains also to every individual man in his daily
    life and thought 213
Light of the Logos 37, 159
line of life's meditation.. 45
linga sharira 9, 123
linga sharira, the astral form... 83
Lodge of Mahatmas..xviii
Lodge of Mahatmas has sustained a cyclic effort to ameliorate this
    anguished condition since the fourteenth century 4
Logos 30, 31, 36, 64, 70, 95, 110, 143, 146, 147, 148
Lokasangraha 69

M

Magic is an exact and definite knowledge of the noumenal laws of
    invisible Nature 17
Mahabuddhi, the latent power of self-consciousness 82
Mahat... 114
Mahatattwa creation 60
Mahatmas and Adepts, One need only open the door to the free
    movement of, to solve myriads of persisting problems among myriads
    of responsive human beings 27
Mahatmas, sustained ideation of... 156
man, it is a possibility that, lived 18 millions of years ago......................... 193

man, nothing less is being aimed at than the fullest possible recovery of the true meaning of the word 150

Manas 121, 122, 130, 131

Manas, the power of abstract ideation.. 131

Manasa Dhyanis, one can help others to recover the lost link with the ... 122

Manasa, an awareness of individual responsibility is the mark of a, a thinking being and moral agent 160

Manasaputras.. 15

Manas-Taijasi, refined mentality.. 110

mango principle enunciated in *The Voice of the Silence,* right discipline for the present and coming age 150

Manu calculation, Cycle of the, revolves between two eternities – the "Pralayas" or *Nights of Brahma*.. 178

Manwantara, is divided into the four Yugas or Ages............................... 198

materialism, the flame of modern, artificial and cold, will be extinguished for lack of fuel 6

meditation..90, 113, 118, 121, 122, 152, 155

meditation and contemplation are neither episodic nor dependent upon any technique.. 80

meditation and contemplation, anyone who genuinely begins to participate in a life of, becomes in an anticipatory mode a partaker of *soma*.. 81

mental asceticism 117, 125

mental asceticism is the reverse of psychic passivity and self-indulgent fatalism.. 125

mental luggage, get your, ready for another life 152

mental posture.. 44

meta-geometry 17, 134

methodology of Gupta Vidya is, in fact, evolution made self-conscious. 126

millennium, dawn of the new, will witness the abolishment of armies and an alliance between all the European empires 180

mind goes awry, When imagination is polluted, the.................................... 49

mind, an invisible organ corresponding to the tongue, to the divine prerogative of speech, and to the power of conceptualization 49

mind, when the, is misused and mutilated, the whole of one's being cannot cooperate with that treacherous mind.. 46

misuse of the mind is very old and goes back many lives, to the time when the mind was enormously powerful and was employed on behalf of personal status and power 50

modern science is significantly based upon the scattered and leaked
   secrets of medieval and ancient classical knowledge...............................21
moment of choice, must come finally in the Fifth Round, far in the future....130
Monad, may apply equally to the vastest solar system or to the tiniest
   atom...171
Monads... 19, 73, 171
Moral and Political Thought of Mahatma Gandhi......................................xvii
most perceptive peoples of the globe soon understood that their smug
   American benefactor was so self-deluded as to be incapable of offering
   timely help..136
mukhya, or fourth creation, sometimes called the *primary creation* because it
   is the first of a series of four creations connected with material form ... 60
mutilation of the higher faculties by dogmatic religion and materialistic
   science 126
Mysteries in the Fifth Root Race, the patron of the, is Shiva, the mighty
   Yogin, the paragon of all the Adepts and the foremost ruler of the
   divine dynasties..85
Mysteries, restoration of the, and an elimination of the worldly worship of
   secondary and tertiary emanations through religious systems and
   mindless rituals..35
Mystery Schools 18

N

nation's, a, spiritual decline accompanies its material ascent.......................19
Nature actually affords individuals innumerable occasions for the
   clarification and purification of perception and intention.......................56
Nature cannot negate despair without human assistance 4
nature, essential tendency in, which evinces a progressive march towards
   self-mastery 151
Never before have there been so many millions of human beings in search
   of divine wisdom, the science of self-regeneration.................................160
New Cycle, working mostly in the realm of *Akasha*, acts as a potent
   alchemical solvent in the astral light and in the inmost consciousness of
   hosts of souls...168
nirodha, a condition of balance 50
noetic and psychic action, difference between, is the difference between
   seeing from within without and seeing only from outside 61

noetic magic, a summoning from latency to active potency of arcane knowledge that was originally impressed in the imperishable soul-memory of all humanity 17

nous 51

Nous 114

nous as the matter-moving mind, Platonic idea of 76

number and of mathematics, immanent influence of the power of, within all cyclic phenomena 96

O

occult and mysterious law which governs the world 176

occult significance of numbers 176

old age, in, those beset by a sense of failure, a fear of death and a feeling of audience deprivation seek refuge in reminiscence 21

Om Mani Padme Hum 157

P

Para Vach is beyond both manifestation and nonmanifestation 36

Para Vach is linked to Vaikhari Vach by Akasha 38

Para Vach, the latent sound and light in *Parabrahm* 36

Parabrahm 36, 60, 73

paradox of human self-consciousness that Nature will always negate vanity 4

Paramatman 85

Parapolitics—Toward the City of Man xvii

particle physics 18, 59

Pashyanti Vach, coexistent with the Logos and inseparable from its own highest self-awareness 36

Passover 139

Patanjali 50

Path 31, 69, 83

peak experiences 7

perfectibility 146

periodicity of the wars in Europe 181

periodicity, whether there is or is not in the constant repetition of events a certain 177

personal self-importance 103

Pharisees 139

philosophic fusion of science and religion, of vidya and dharma, is
    essential to the structure of the Aquarian civilization of the future 57

Philosophy of Perfection of Krishna 154

physical form, Every point in the, each life-atom, is shot through and
    through with reflected Mahabuddhi, the latent power of self-
    consciousness 82

physics and chemistry have partially revealed the complex matrix of
    differentiations of the ATOM, as they apply to the lowest planes 62

Piscean to Aquarian civilization, transformation from, poses an
    extraordinary challenge 34

Plato 15, 19, 20, 26, 27, 33

Plato - no pleasure can ever have any meaning to the heart if the mind and
    imagination are not involved 51

Plato, in *The Statesman,* speaks of the Golden Age as a time of universal
    well-being wherein all basic needs were fulfilled 26

Plato, the hubris of Thrasymachus in *The Republic* 68

Platonic-Upanishadic method, born with the human race 29

post-Newtonian conception of space, a post-Euclidian geometry, and a
    post-Cartesian algebra founded upon matrices and groups 134

powers will be needed and pretensions will go for naught, the time will
    come when 41

Prayag, the meeting-place of rivers, corresponds to a spiritual centre in
    every human being 90

prostration 44

Protagoras, "Man is the measure of all things." 3

psuche, a self-moving agent 76

psyche 158

psychic force 70

Pymander 114

Pythagoras 31, 124

Pythagoras required all his diligent pupils to study arithmetic, geometry,
    astronomy and music 31

Pythagoras taught his disciples to be extremely humble about That which
    is No Number 34

Pythagoras taught spiritual courage arises out of the conviction that the
    race of men is immortal 11

Pythagorean teaching of the Aquarian Age of Universal Enlightenment 154

Pythagoreans asserted that the doctrine of Numbers, the chief of all in
     Esotericism, had been revealed to man by the celestial deities.............. 31

Q

quadrivium 22
quantum mechanics.. 18

R

Raghavan N. Iyer xv
Rama, The time of, a million years ago, was the last great Golden Age 26
Stanzas of Dzyan, read them silently 153
regeneration of global civilization through such a tapping of the inward
     spiritual resources of humanity.. 28
reincarnation.. 123
religion of renunciation of the personal self and the science of Buddhic
     correlation.. 58
Religion of Responsibility of the Buddha... 154
religion rises and falls with the progress of human thought, because cyclic
     law governs every man, and thus every religion which man has 212
revolutions 96
Robert Crosbie... 2

S

sacred places of pilgrimage correspond to secret centres in the human
     constitution.. 90
sacred tribe of heroes.. 196, 203, 206
Sadducees.. 139
Sandhya, the creative vibratory light at the dawn of differentiation 36
Sat-Chit-Ananda, ... 169
sattva, rajas and tamas, the three gunas 82
science and true religion, creative individuals must learn to cultivate
     moral courage and cool magnanimity so that they may plumb the
     depths of pure, within themselves 58
science of spirituality and the religion of responsibility are rooted in the
     metaphysics of the universe, and therefore have the complete support of
     cosmic will and design.. 70

Science of Spirituality of Shankara 154
science of today will have become an "ancient" science a thousand years
    hence 177
science, Fortunately, this adolescent state of, is coming to an end 25
science, the best, forces a rethinking of one's view of human nature,
    human potential, and the place of man in the cosmos 12
sciences, entire face of the, has been transformed in the first decades of the
    Aquarian Age 63
Secret Doctrine 2
Secret Doctrine is the essence of all these religious traditions 89
Self against self, he or she who does not know what it is to live in the
    world, and yet not be of the world, is incapable of guarding 84
self becomes the enemy of the Self because it is afraid of facing the facts 124
Self-alienation is caused by the wearing of the false mask, the loathsome
    mask of the personal self 52
self-alienation, the only way to overcome, is by attunement to the
    Universal Mind through the contemplation of universal ideas 48
Self-knowledge is unattainable by what men usually call 'self-analysis'. 175
selfless action xx
self-purgation, ceaseless, is a prelude to total self-transformation and can
    be lit from small beginnings 45
self-purification 140
self-regenerating modes of thought and patterns of living 131
self-reliance 69
self-reliance, the challenge of true 14
self-respect, it is only through noetic self-command that there can be
    genuine 70
serve others, primary impulse to, is as much rooted in the universal desire
    for self-expression as the familiar instinct of self-preservation 165
seven sciences, the *trivium* and *quadrivium* 22
Seven, on the significance of the number 178
sevenfold human constitution were likened to a miniature solar system, If
    the, the centre of consciousness would reside on one of the planets of
    that system 132
Shabdabrahman, the Divine Sound surrounded by the supernal light of the
    Gayatri 102
Shakespeare recognized the old Pythagorean and Hermetic conception of
    man as a microcosm of the macrocosm 66
Shankara 149

Shiva 104
Shiva is the spur to the spiritual regeneration of humanity 95
Sixth Century Impulsion in the septenary series initiated by Tsong-Kha-Pa...35
sixth or seventh hierarchy, neither was capable of completing self-
    conscious intelligent man 92
slay the lunar form at will - *The Voice of the Silence* 83
solitary contemplation 118
Soma 73, 81, 84, 85
Soma is the maker of seers, the generator of hymns, the protector of prayer
    and the soul of sacrifice 85
Soma, is also the name of the sacred beverage drunk by the Brahmins and
    the Initiates during their mysteries and sacrificial rites 72
sophrosyne 124, 125
sophrosyne, the self-government of the soul by its superior element coupled
    with the consent of the inferior element 69
soul, reasonable part of the 117
soul-force 69
soul-force, As Gandhi taught, the peril of our time arises from the abuse,
    misuse and neglect of 70
spiritual alchemy 42
spiritual attention, only through developing the natural powers of
    concentration and, can they enrich their collective future 14
spiritual cycles all so intimately connected with Karma and reincarnation ...207
Spiritual life is the paradigm of learning. Its reflections are all the other
    forms of learning, but these reflections no longer reflect 54
spiritual progress for oneself, concern for, must be rooted out and
    dispelled as a pernicious form of spiritual materialism 7
Spiritual Sun 97
spiritual Teachers, solar line of, can be traced back to Shiva as
    Dakshinamurti 16
spiritual will 30, 33, 43, 71, 103, 137, 164
Spiritual will has to do with true self-esteem, moral firmness and
    continuity of consciousness 43
Spirituality is not what we understand by the words 'virtue' and
    'goodness' 175
spirituality of advanced science 12
Sthitaprajna, the Self-Governed Sage, the Buddhas of Perfection 154
Sub-Races, Fifth, Sixth and Seventh 131
Suddhasattva, the substance of the gods 37
sushupti 152, 171

sutratman, the repository of the fragrant aroma of past learning 76
sutratmic continuity and present learning, relationship between, is likely
    to remain obscure unless one is ready to probe deeply into the simplest
    things of life 76
sutratmic thread 75
sutratmic thread, It is the continuity of this, that enables individuals to
    learn and recollect in any lifetime 75
svasamvedana, reflective self-conscious thought, the greatest gift of the
    human being 51
swapna 82
swaraj 69
swaraj or self-rule based upon *swadeshi* or self-reliance 69
symbolism of a sacred pilgrimage conveys clues to the inner meaning of
    the teaching 90

T

Tamil calendar, the "Tirukkanda Panchanga" 186
tapas 54, 129
tapas, True, touches the core of one's inward integrity. It fosters a calm
    reliance upon the great law of universal unity and ethical causation .. 162
temper 124
temper, In the ancient schools one would not be allowed to begin serious
    study of yoga until one had mastered one's 124
The Crest Jewel of Wisdom 154
The Secret Doctrine is replete with instruction concerning meditation and
    self-study 127
The Theory of Cycles - H.P. Blavatsky 96
Theosophia xvii
theosophical ideas, the very air is getting filled with 207
Theosophical Movement .... xviii, xix, 152
theurgy 16, 18, 84
Third Eye 19, 84
Third Race, The seven divine dynasties were thereafter to be found in the 16
Third Race, with the lighting-up of *Manas* and the incarnation of the
    Manasaputras 15
Third Root Race 171
Thot-Hermes was the secretary of King Saturn presiding over the pre-
    dynastic Golden Age 26

Treta Yuga contains 1,296,000 years... 189
Triad in every human being, the inmost invisible, and the source of all
    thought, will and feeling has an invisible central point in Akasha 42
trivium... 22
Troilus and Cressida portrays the Pythagorean conception of cosmic
    hierarchies and their continual relevance to human society 66
trustees of our skills, The litmus test as to whether or not we are true, lies
    in our expectations of return for using them 164
trusteeship... 164
turiya state of spiritual freedom from captivity to the three *gunas* 82

U

unborn who are always far more numerous than those who are presently
    incarnated 54
uninitiated will drag down the solar teaching into the murky realm of
    lunar consciousness polluted by profane sense-perceptions................. 152
United Lodge of Theosophists xviii
Universal Man.. xx
Universal Mind 48
universe is a virtual image of the eternal motion or vibration of the
    unmanifest Word, scintillating around a set of points of nodal resonance
    within that Word itself... 95
universe is an extremely intelligent universe, People have now become far
    more aware that the invisible... 65
Upanishads 30

V

Vach xix
Vach is Sarasvati, the goddess of wisdom and beauty 37
Vaikhari Vach, the objective manifested universe...................................... 37
Verbum... 114
vidya 57
vidya, or Science - in its essence is concerned with primary causes and is
    rooted in a mature apprehension of noetic consciousness 16
void, the immense, would reveal itself as alive at every point with the
    vibration of the Great Breath in its complex rhythmic differentiations . 59

W

Wailing Wall 140
West, for nearly two millennia the, has suffered spiritual deprivation
    through its self-imposed idolatry of psychic materialism 4
western world adopted instead the self-mutilating worship of the cross of
    matter rather than heed the call of the Christos 4
what is real in oneself and can be realized in practice is the only element
    that truly counts 9
Whenever an individual makes a new beginning, such a commencement
    could signify the start of a new phase of learning 76
Wisdom is attainable only through love of the gods and recognition of
    their immanence within the human temple 24
wisdom, recognition of the correspondences between the celestial and
    terrestrial is the beginning of 24
Wise Race, the Race that never dies 186

X

xenoglossy 75

Y

yoga 123, 124
yugas, four, may be understood in terms of a descent from the most golden
    age to the most decadent, followed by a reascent to a golden age 106

Z

zodiacal ages indicate the alchemical transmutation of the meta-
    psychological elements underlying formative change 73
zodiacal transition from the Piscean to the Aquarian Age, the formative
    forces of the emerging cosmopolis may be glimpsed through
    contemplating the 73

Made in the USA
Middletown, DE
30 May 2022

66401747R00165